The 30 Day MBA

For many of the topics in the book there are direct links to the **free** teaching resources of the world's best business schools.

There are also links to hundreds of hours of **free** video lectures given by other distinguished Business School professors, from top schools including Cranfield, Wharton, Chicago, Harvard and CEIBS (China Europe International Business School).

You can download Duke University's top ranking Fuqua School of Business's lecture material on forecasting; a vital aid to anyone preparing sales projections.

Link into Cranfield's School of Management's Research Paper Series and see the latest insights in global supply chain logistics, or watch Harvard's Professor Michael Porter – a leading world proponent of international business strategy methodology – outline his ideas.

You can find a list of all these online resources and more at **http://www.koganpage.com/editions/the-30-day-mba/9780749463311** and interspersed within the chapters.

SECOND EDITION

The 30 Day MBA

Colin Barrow

KoganPage

LONDON PHILADELPHIA NEW DELHI

Publisher's note

Every possible effort has been made to ensure that the information contained in this book is accurate at the time of going to press, and the publishers and author cannot accept responsibility for any errors or omissions, however caused. No responsibility for loss or damage occasioned to any person acting, or refraining from action, as a result of the material in this publication can be accepted by the editor, the publisher or the author.

First published in Great Britain and the United States in 2009 by Kogan Page Limited
Second edition 2011. Reprinted 2011

Apart from any fair dealing for the purposes of research or private study, or criticism or review, as permitted under the Copyright, Designs and Patents Act 1988, this publication may only be reproduced, stored or transmitted, in any form or by any means, with the prior permission in writing of the publishers, or in the case of reprographic reproduction in accordance with the terms and licences issued by the CLA. Enquiries concerning reproduction outside these terms should be sent to the publishers at the undermentioned addresses:

120 Pentonville Road	1518 Walnut Street, Suite 1100	4737/23 Ansari Road
London N1 9JN	Philadelphia PA 19102	Daryaganj
United Kingdom	USA	New Delhi 110002
www.koganpage.com		India

© Colin Barrow, 2009, 2011

The right of Colin Barrow to be identified as the author of this work has been asserted by him in accordance with the Copyright, Designs and Patents Act 1988.

ISBN   978 0 7494 6331 1
E-ISBN   978 0 7494 6332 8

British Library Cataloguing-in-Publication Data

A CIP record for this book is available from the British Library.

Library of Congress Cataloging-in-Publication Data

Barrow, Colin.
   The 30 day MBA : your fast track guide to business success / Colin Barrow. – 2nd ed.
      p. cm.
   Includes index.
   ISBN 978-0-7494-6331-1 – ISBN 978-0-7494-6332-8   1. Industrial management.
2. Management–Study and teaching.   3. Master of business administration degree.
I. Title.   II. Title: Thirty-day MBA.
   HD31.B36895 2011
   650–dc22

                                                                    2011009256

Typeset by Graphicraft Ltd, Hong Kong
Printed and bound in Great Britain by CPI books
Manufacturing managed by Jellyfish Solutions Ltd

CONTENTS

LIST OF FIGURES

LIST OF TABLES

Introduction

- The real value of an MBA
- What an MBA knows
- Why YOU need that knowledge too
- Where to get MBA knowledge – from the best schools (not just from one)
- How to use this book

The value of MBA knowledge, along with everything else in the business world, is being put to the test as never before in the credit crunch era that swept across the developed world in 2007. In September 2008, when Lehman Brothers – a bank that had withstood the carnage of the great depression of 1929 – collapsed, the queues of employees exiting their offices worldwide included alumni of almost every premier business school. Yet by the autumn of 2010 the wheel had spun yet again. A round-up of news from the business schools showed MBA recruitment had rebounded sharply. In the summer of 2010 Abby Scott, Executive Director of Career Services at Berkeley's Haas School of Business reported the fastest growth in MBA recruitment since she joined the school a decade earlier. Admittedly the school has something of an advantage with four giant technology companies – Apple, Google, IBM and Microsoft – all in the neighbourhood. These firms are all in the top tier of the world's most valuable global brands, a sector that showed its resilience over this turbulent period, so much so, that branding as a subject has moved up the MBA subject ladder (as reflected in its new found prominence in Chapter 3).

Regina Resnick, managing director of Columbia Business School Career Management Center, reports demand for MBAs firmly on an upward trend with consulting firms back in the market. In 2010 McKinsey & Co and other consulting firms such as Bain & Co and the Boston Consulting Group, are reputed to have hired MBAs in near industrial quantities from Harvard and other top schools including Wharton, Columbia, Northwestern, Chicago,

London and Michigan. In 2010 Duke's Fuqua School of Business placed MBAs across nearly every business sector – Deloitte (consulting), Johnson & Johnson (pharmaceuticals), Pepsi (food and drink) and Apple, where they'll be working in operations and supply chain to help extend the iPad's near-dominance of the tablet market.

Business Schools are assimilating the lessons from the credit crunch. For example, in October 2010 Columbia Business School in New York, recognizing that the dynamics of business post-credit crunch required a greater degree of interdisciplinary cooperation, offered their faculty the chance to earn an extra US $30,000–US $40,000 (€21,600 / €28,900: £19,000 / £25, 400) a year. To get this bonus they had to instigate research with professors from other departments within the school. Glen Hubbard, the school's Dean, claims one of the things that quickly became apparent in the 2007–08 financial crisis was 'how business people failed to connect the dots'. The shifting balance of economic power from West to East has led business schools to forge partnerships with schools on other continents, and to review their teaching strategies. Wharton, for example, will soon unveil a new MBA curriculum, the result of a year's worth of study and work by the faculty and to be implemented in time for the Class of 2013.

This new edition will keep you up to speed with the very latest thinking and teaching from the world's top business schools.

A personal experience

I left the family business, in my case the Army, after a few short years. I hadn't given much thought to a career before I 'joined up' and I followed a similar approach when I left. I found a job in sales and within a year or so was in a very junior management position. The company I worked for was in the vanguard of some new communications technology that was in great demand. One of my clients, a major newspaper publisher, was keen that we should adapt our product more closely to their needs. The changes looked relatively minor, just some alterations to casing, a tweak or two in program-ming, and the prospects of some big future orders and commission cheques looked distinctly possible.

I made the case to my boss, the area sales manager, detailing the likely level of demand my client would have for the product, the price we could achieve and when they would need deliveries. He in turn promised to push it hard with his boss, the sales and marketing director. A month went by and my boss reported back that the directors had considered the proposal and decided not to proceed. I thought either my boss had made a poor presentation of my facts or the board had failed to grasp the nature of the opportunity. Either way, I'd lost the chance of an order and big payout.

A few months later, during an evening around the bar at a company sales conference with the chairman's son, who was wisely to pursue a career as a distinguished playwright, I discovered the truth of what happened to my irresistible opportunity. Though profitable, in a modest way, the company

I worked for was strapped for cash. In fact the chairman had recently had to sell his Rolls and buy a Bentley on hire purchase, using the balance to help pay the wages for a month. The 'modest' tweaks I was proposing called for new moulds from a supplier to which the company already owed a small fortune. I was shortly to discover that the technology on which our products were based was already about to be overtaken by an international competitor with a global reach and that the economy was about to go into one of the UK's then all-too-frequent economic troughs.

It was at this point that I realized that, in common with millions of others in business, I had little knowledge outside my own narrow discipline. My cash-starved employer had no real incentive to train me, or any of his employees, in any subject that didn't have a reasonably immediate payback. I had spent two years at Sandhurst being trained thoroughly. I had a rudimentary grasp of what engineers, infantry and artillery could do, as well as the abilities and role of the navy and air force in any task in which I was likely to be involved. But now in business, outside of sales, in which I had been given just two days of instruction, I was totally ignorant. Accounts, production, supply, global competitors, substitute products and the economic climate were all a closed book. I wasn't even aware that the client whom I thought was so large and powerful was about to be swept away in a maelstrom of technological change. I left the company, took an MBA, and went on to line and staff positions around the world and then to running businesses, small at first and eventually quite large. A spell in consulting was followed by a return to the business school world, this time to teach and research in some great schools in the UK, mainland Europe, the United States and Asia.

Anyone who wants to play a more rounded role in shaping and implementing the direction of the organization they work in, but are inhibited by their lack of fundamental business knowledge, needs MBA knowledge. Reading this book will equip them to take part in strategic decision making on an equal footing with MBA graduates, while feeling at ease in the process. It places MBA skills within reach of all professionals in large and small organizations in both the public and private sectors, providing them with a competitive edge over less knowledgeable colleagues.

What is MBA knowledge?

Business schools have tended to complicate and intellectualize the subject of business but it basically boils down to a dozen disciplinary areas, each with a number of components. The disciplines contain the tools with which you can analyse a business situation effectively, drawing on both internal information relevant to the business and external information on its markets, competitors and general business environment as a prelude to deciding what to do.

The emphasis here in the contents of this book is on the terms 'concepts' and 'tools'. The business world is full of conflicting theories and ideas on how organizations could or should work, or how they could be made to work better. They come in and out of fashion, get embellished or replaced over time. Even concepts that appear to be new are often little more than old ideas revisited. Quantitative Easing (QE), for example, a term that took the economics world by storm in 2010, was in fact first coined in September 1995 by the economist Dr Richard Werner, Professor of International Banking at the School of Management, University of Southampton (UK). The idea of QE is itself over 200 years old having first been used in 1797 by the government of a British Prime Minister, William Pitt the younger, in response to a request by two Bank of England directors. (**www.cps.org.uk/ cps_catalog/Quantitative%20Easing.pdf**).

In business, for example, there is no such thing as a universal optimal capital structure, or the right number of new products to bring to market, or whether or not going for an acquisition is a winning strategy. What's best in terms of, say, a debt to equity ratio varies with the type of organization and the prevailing conditions in the money market. That ratio will be different for the same organization at different times and when it is pursuing different strategies. Layering an inherently risky marketing strategy, say diversifying, with a risky financing strategy, using borrowed rather than shareholders' money, creates a potentially more risky situation than any one of those actions in isolation. But whichever choices a business makes, the tools used to assess financial and marketing strengths and weaknesses are much the same. It is the concepts and tools to be used in those disciplines that this book explains, and it shows you how to use both of these individually and to assess a business situation comprehensively.

The MBA disciplines

These are a dozen or so core disciplines that comprise the subject matter of an MBA programme. Many business schools eschew some vital elements within these disciplines as they are considered either too practical, unsexy from a research/career prospective or more skill or art oriented than academic. A prime example is the field of selling, which fits naturally into the marketing domain but, much to the surprise of MBA students, often fails to appear on the syllabus. There are thousands of professors of marketing, distribution and logistics, market research, advertising, industrial marketing, strategic communications and every subsection of marketing, but there are no professors of selling. Yet most employers, and students for that matter, feel that their MBA's value would be enhanced by a sound grounding in selling and sales management.

Some business schools miss out personal development, social responsibility and ethics, entrepreneurship, business planning or even quantitative methods.

Almost all of them miss out business history – a core subject at Harvard – and business law – essential at all top schools. You will find all of these disciplinary areas covered in this book.

Accounting

This covers the basic assembly and interpretation of raw financial data, from double-entry bookkeeping through to the construction of the key accounting reports – profit and loss, cash flow and balance sheet. It continues through to the accounting concepts and ground rules and the auditing process and the tools required to access a business's financial health and performance.

Business history

This is a brief review of the processes that led to the creation of the types of business enterprise we have today, showing how they came about, their significance and development. The main area covered is the development of modern industry from 1800, but the trading laws and business structures created in Babylon and the activities of mediaeval merchants are also relevant to an understanding of the pedigree of today's business environment. The watchword here is: 'Those who cannot remember the past are condemned to repeat it.'

Business law

From intellectual property, employment and legal structures, through to the laws governing contracts and corporate governance, organizations are constrained in their actions by local and international laws.

Economics

In the 1990s there was a prevailing view that globalization and technology would check inflation and keep prices so low that consumers would keep consuming. The death of the economic cycle was announced alongside the birth of the 'long boom'. Today, those same forces are credited with creating a more volatile world with more violent economic swings. For the manager, a grasp of elements of macro and microeconomics is essential to making sense of the business environment.

Entrepreneurship

Until the late 1980s entrepreneurship was a paragraph or two in an economics textbook. The discovery by David Birch, a researcher in the United

States, that small and new businesses accounted for over 80 per cent of new jobs propelled entrepreneurship from a footnote to a core discipline important equally to potential participants and government policy makers.

Research into entrepreneurship published in 2010 has brought a biological dimension into play. Research at Case Western Reserve University in Ohio and NUS (National University of Singapore) Business School, shows how genes interact with different types of environment to create conditions either more or less favourable to producing entrepreneurs and leaders.

Ethics and social responsibility

One of the primary goals of business is to make the world a better place. Until recently this was something that business moguls did after a lifetime of being responsible for oil spills, deforestation and generally polluting the planet. Sure, Exxon can't solve the world's energy problems and Wal-Mart and Nike can't solve the poverty experienced by the 250 million child workers and their families. But increasingly businesses are being required to work within accepted guidelines and to take part in the debate about morals and responsibilities. Monsanto alone can't decide whether genetically modified crops are safe or desirable and stem cells and cloning are not subjects where it can be left to industry alone to set boundaries. But those working in an industry have a wider constituency than their shareholders and their own careers.

Finance

Finance covers the vital areas of where a business gets its money from and the risks and responsibilities associated with each of those sources. Debt, equity, bonds, debentures, IPOs, private equity and business angels are part of this area's vocabulary, as is appraising capital investment decisions.

Marketing

The outward face of a business is addressed to its customers and its success or failure is the measure of how well it performs in the marketplace. Markets have to be identified, product attributes accessed, competitors understood and advertising messages developed to reach chosen markets. Marketing is perhaps the discipline with the largest number of misunderstood and misapplied business tools of all.

Operations

This discipline is concerned with how products and services are got ready for market (production), delivered or executed, and the management information system designed to track performance.

Organizational behaviour

Organizing, inspiring, motivating, rewarding and managing both individuals and teams is the enduring challenge in organizations as they grow and develop. Often people are the defining advantage that one organization has and can sustain over its competitors.

Personal development (and lifetime learning)

Techniques for improving career prospects are an increasingly important aspect of MBA curricula. This is hardly surprising, as the success of acquiring MBA skills is measured, in part at least, by increases in salary and improved job prospects and satisfaction. Business schools offer some of these topics during the programme but many form part of their repeat business portfolio. This area is one that should be constantly revisited and in this book it appears as an appendix.

Quantitative and qualitative analysis

This is where it all began. Frederick Winslow Taylor, author of *The Principles of Scientific Management* (1911), set out to 'measure each and every task and establish a system of work'. The first person to have on his business card the title 'Consultant to Business', he was the pioneer of the school of 'getting at the facts'. This is also where many business schools started out. Cranfield School of Management was born out of the Work Study Department, itself part of the School of Production.

Strategy

This is the unifying discipline, often called business strategy. It deals with the core purpose of an enterprise and how it should respond to the challenges of a fast-changing environment. It centres not just on how strategy is shaped, for example using Porter's Five Forces, but on the recognition that no organization can be truly great in the absence of shared goals, values and a sense of purpose – a shared picture of the future of the enterprise.

Where can you get MBA skills and knowledge?

The most obvious answer to this question is – at a business school. There you will find talented teachers (some!), eager, self-motivated, likeminded students and a wealth of teaching resources, including books, journals, case studies and library facilities. Whilst it is true that much of the useful knowledge, theory and practice of business is generated and disseminated from business schools, you don't actually have to go there yourself. You can get all that expertise on tap, mostly for free – and even hear the best professors from the very best business schools deliver their keynote lectures and research. This book shows you how.

A brief history of business schools

The claim to being the world's first business school is, like everything else in business, hotly disputed. The honour is usually said to rest with Wharton, founded in 1881 by Joseph Wharton, a self-taught businessman. A miner, he made his fortune through the American Nickel Company and the Bethlehem Steel Corporation, later to become the subject of the earliest business case studies. The school is based in an urban campus at Philadelphia's University of Pennsylvania.

It wasn't until 1900 that Tuck School of Business, part of Dartmouth College, began conferring advanced degrees in management sciences. In 1908 the Harvard Business School opened, with a faculty of 15 and some 80 students, and two years later it was offering a Management Masters programme. By 1922 Harvard was running a doctoral programme pioneering research into business methods.

Today, over a thousand business schools around the globe offer MBA programmes, minting some 100,000 new graduates each year. It wasn't until the late 1950s that the first business schools in the UK opened their doors – with LBS (London Business School), Cranfield and the Manchester Business School in the vanguard. In mainland Europe it took a further two decades for business schools to establish a niche in the market. The harmonization of university education in Europe, under the Bologna Accord in 2010, has already created some 300 new management master's degrees. It is unlikely that the quality of education delivered will keep pace with the rise in quantity.

But despite these impressive numbers, they represent barely a drop in the management ocean. For every manager or executive with an MBA there are over 200 with no formal business qualification. That an MBA from one of the top business schools delivers value to most of those who take it and to the organizations for which they work is beyond reasonable doubt. One of the measures any self-respecting business school boasts is the salary rise its alumni achieve in the three years after graduation; typically between 50 and 70 per cent.

However, Shanghai Jiao Tong University's Antai College of Economics & Management (ACEM), where the average MBA could expect a salary hike of 177 per cent over three years, is a whole lot different from those coming out of Vlerick Leuven Gent who netted just 50 per cent. Outside of the top 100 business schools, many graduates will see no hike in pay and even perhaps find it hard to get a job.

So should you go to business school?

So could and should everyone put up the £100,000 (US $158,000/€114,000) or so required in fees and salary forgone, muster the appropriate GMAT score and take an MBA at a top school? It takes a brave person to give up a job and become a student, perhaps only a few years into their career, with unpaid loans and mortgages looming large.

Then there is the agonizing choice of which school to pick, assuming money is no option. Well, according to Della Bradshaw, Business Education Editor of the *Financial Times* in London and for the past ten years overseer of the newspaper's business school ranking system, perhaps North American business schools are no longer top of the pile. When the *FT* began ranking MBA programmes in 1999, 20 of the top 25 schools were from the United States, with the remaining five from Europe; however, in 2010 there were just 11 US schools in the top 25, a further 11 were in Europe and three in Asia. In the top five two are from Europe and three from the United States. A recognized weakness of the North American business schools is their inability to penetrate the hold that European and Asian schools have on international students and faculty – vital ingredients in an increasingly global business environment.

Next there is the problem of deciding how good a school really is. Whilst the *FT* puts the London Business School top, the *Economist* gives the crown to IESE in Spain, the *Wall Street Journal* plumps for Dartmouth's Tuck School, *Business Week* goes for the University of Chicago (Booth) and *Forbes* has Stanford as number one.

Luckily you don't have to make that decision – you can have your cake and eat it. You certainly need MBA knowledge if you are dissatisfied with your progress, but you don't need to go to a business school to get it.

In the following chapters you will get a flavour of how all the top business schools teach, in the areas in which they excel. Download their teaching notes, read up on their latest research and see their faculty teach. A better strategy than just attending one business school – however great.

Using this book and your own resources

Very few people study at a business school and even fewer study at a top school. The growth in MBA numbers comes almost exclusively from those taking an online MBA; part-time executive MBAs, and MBA 'lite' programmes such as those run at Kellogg School of Management – the best of an MBA, taking 20 days spread out over nine months, with perhaps another ten days of preparation. Ergo – *The 30 Day MBA*.

If you decide, as do most students of business, that business school is not the only way to acquire an MBA skill set, or perhaps it is not right for you now for reasons of cost, time or convenience, or if you can't get into a top school for any other reason, then you can fall back on your own resources.

Each chapter in the book covers the essential elements of one of the core disciplines in a top MBA programme. There are links to external readings and resources, online library and information sources, case examples and links to online self-assessment tests so you can keep track of your learning achievements.

For many of the topics there are direct links to the *free* teaching resources of the world's best business schools. You can watch and listen as Professor Porter explains how his Five Forces strategy model works, exactly as he might have taught it in his Harvard lecture theatre. There are also links in the book to hundreds of hours of *free* video lectures given by other distinguished business school professors, from top schools including LBS (London Business School), Imperial, Oxford and Aston. You can download Duke University's top-ranking Fuqua School of Business's lecture material on forecasting, or link into Cranfield School of Management's Research Paper Series and see the latest insights into business and the management of organizations.

You certainly don't need to spend a fortune in time or money to gain MBA knowledge and skill. There is no aspect of business school teaching and virtually no world-class professor that you can't listen to for free to complement the content of this book. But you do need willpower! But if you do decide that business school is right for you, the appendix will help you choose the right one for you, and the book will be a sound preparation for the programme and a worthwhile resource when you start revising for the exams.

How this book is organized and how to use it

All business disciplines claim, some with more justification than others, that theirs is the overarching subject or starting point. The marketers claim the customer as king; human resources specialists persist in believing that nothing happens without people; strategists insist that competitive advantage is fundamental to enduring success; entrepreneurs say that they are in at the birth of all ventures; accountants see the only truth being in numbers; even quantitative analysis has history on its side as being a founding subject in management theory.

To sidestep the argument, in part at least, this book is organized alphabetically, in three groupings. Accounting, finance, marketing and organizational behaviour are together at the start of the book. These contain the basic tools that an MBA will use or need to refer to more or less every working day. Strategy comes at the end of the book as the coordinating discipline. It could just as easily come at the beginning, but to understand strategy you need a reasonable grasp of the four first disciplines. The five bookend disciplines are in something of a chicken and egg situation. You can't have any one of these without the other, but where it all begins is more academic than useful as a point for debate.

The remaining disciplines are covered, also in alphabetical order, in the middle of the book. Ideally you should read the first four chapters first; these will take about half of your 30 days. If you are an accountant, have taken a business or economics degree, or have a marketing or human resources professional qualification, that time will be scaled back. Then if you have an immediate strategic issue at work, perhaps concerned with an acquisition, divestment, entering a new market or changing direction, go straight to the chapter on strategy. While reading that, you will almost certainly need to refresh yourself on some aspects of the first four chapters. This chapter will probably need a further three or four days to assimilate. The middle chapters you can read in order of personal preference, or alphabetically as set out. That should take up the remaining 10 days or so of your schedule. By way of a bonus you will find that a number of the tools and concepts straddle disciplines. For example, while Maslow's hierarchy of needs is covered in the marketing chapter, it is equally applicable in dealing with employees or negotiating with suppliers. Break-even analysis is equally applicable in accounting, marketing and economics.

This weighting corresponds closely to the emphasis you will find put on these subjects at top business schools. Also, as at school, you should tackle the subjects in bursts of an hour or so and certainly not in whole days and weeks. You need to take time to assimilate the subject and try the concepts out in live situations. So, for example, you could spend a couple of hours reading the section on balance sheets, then get your own company's balance sheet and check out your understanding of it. If you need any further clarification you could talk in an informed way with your company's accountant.

You should draw up a timetable spread over the time period allocated for your 30-day MBA, say 12, 24 or 36 weeks. Then mark out the hours allocated for each subject, not forgetting to leave an hour or so to review each area. You will also need to build in a couple of days for revision before you take your final exam.

The subject areas within each chapter correspond to what you would find in the syllabus at major business schools in terms of theoretical under-pinning and the practical application of that theory that you would pick up from fellow students.

You can find an appendix online (details below). You should visit this on a regular basis to ensure you have all the advantages that an MBA would hope for in terms of career progression. Here you will find out how to update your skills and knowledge by taking short courses at top business schools around the globe. The cost of these ranges from a few hundred pounds to several thousand and, by attending, you may well get onto the school's alumni list, plugging into a valuable business network in the process.

Tracking your progress

You will find a dozen short tests on the Kogan Page website (**www.koganpage. com/resources/books**, password: TT8005). Use these to check your understanding of each subject. If there is anything you are not clear on, go back over the relevant chapters.

As a rough guide you should be aiming to get six out of every ten questions right. MBAs, unlike undergraduate degrees, don't come with grades. You either pass or fail. Also the 'pass' mark can vary with the quality of those taking the exams. Read up on the normal distribution curve to see how this works.

Accounting

01

- Accounting conventions and principles
- The bookkeeping process
- Cash-flow forecasts and statements
- Calculating profit
- Balancing the books
- Finding financial facts
- Business ratios

By the autumn of 2010 evidence was mounting that a key aspect of the catastrophic implosion of Lehman Brothers had, in part at least, been brought about by an accounting trick known in the trade as Repo 105. With the approval of their auditors, Ernst and Young (E&Y), Lehman managed to make US $50 billion (£32bn/€66bn) of debt invisible and in effect disappear from its balance sheet. This creative use of accounting is more or less the opposite of how the whole subject of accounting came into being.

Sometime before 3000 BC the people of Uruk and other sister-cities of Mesopotamia began to use pictographic tablets of clay to record economic transactions. The script for the tablets evolved from symbols and provides evidence of an ancient financial system that was growing to accommodate the needs of the Uruk economy. There is detailed evidence that almost every country had some form of record keeping, from China to ancient Rome, where the heads of families maintained daily entry of household receipts and payments in an *adversaria* or daybook, and monthly postings were made to a cashbook known as a *codex accepti et expensi*. Accounting is the process of recording and analysing transactions that involve events that can be assigned a monetary value. By definition, financial information can be only a partial picture of the performance of an enterprise. People, arguably a business's most valuable asset, don't appear anywhere in the accounts, except for football clubs and the like where people are the subject of a transaction.

Although accounting has become more complex, involving ever more regulations, and has moved from visible records written in books to key strokes in a software program, the purpose is the same:

- to establish what a business owns by way of assets;
- to establish what a business owes by way of liabilities;
- to establish the profitability, or otherwise, at certain time intervals, and how that profit was achieved.

Pacioli, about whom we will hear more in the bookkeeping section below, claimed wisely that 'frequent accounting makes for long friendship'. But accounts must not only be timely, but should be reliable too, and no matter where accounting is studied you can be certain that the general principles will be universally applied.

An MBA is unlikely to be required to perform the recording side of the accounting process. But it is only by knowing how accounts are prepared and the rules governing the categorizing of assets and liabilities that you can gain a good understanding of what the figures really mean. For example, it is not obvious to the uninitiated that a company's shares are classed as a liability and that there is not the remotest possibility that the assets as recorded will realize anything like the figures shown in the accounts.

The rules of the game

Accounting is certainly not an exact science. Even the most enthusiastic member of the profession would not make that claim. There is considerable scope for interpretation and educated guesswork as all the facts are rarely available when the accounts are drawn up. For example, we may not know for certain that a particular customer will actually pay up, yet unless we have firm evidence that they won't, for example if the business is failing, then the value of the money owed will appear in the accounts.

Obviously, if accountants and managers had complete freedom to interpret events as they wished, no one inside or outside the business would place any reliance on the figures, so certain ground rules have been laid down by the profession to help get a level of consistency into accounting information.

Fundamental conventions

These are the enduring principles that govern the way in which the accounting profession assembles and presents financial information.

Money measurement

In accounting, a record is kept only of the facts that can be expressed in money terms. For example, the state of the managing director's health and the news that your main competitor is opening up right opposite in a more attractive outlet are important business facts. No accounting record of them is made, however, and they do not show up on the balance sheet, simply because no objective monetary value can be assigned to these facts.

Expressing business facts in money terms has the great advantage of providing a common denominator. Just imagine trying to add computer equipment and vehicles, together with a 4,000 sq m office, and then arriving at a total. You need a common term to be able to carry out the basic arithmetical functions, and to compare one set of accounts with another.

Business entity

The accounts are kept for the business itself, rather than for the owner(s), bankers, or anyone else associated with the firm. The concept states that assets and liabilities are always defined from the business's viewpoint. So, for example, were a business owner to lend his business money it would appear in the accounts as a liability, though in effect he might see it as his own money. Anything done with that money, say buying equipment, would appear in the accounts as an asset of the business. The owner's stake is accounted for only by the increase or decrease in net worth of the enterprise as a whole.

Cost concept

Assets are usually entered into the accounts as the cost at date of purchase. For a variety of reasons, the real 'worth' of an asset will probably change over time. The worth, or value, of an asset is a subjective estimate on which no two people are likely to agree. This is made even more complex, and artificial, because the assets themselves are usually not for sale.

So in the search for objectivity, the accountants have settled for cost as the figure to record. It does mean that a balance sheet does not show the current worth or value of a business. That is not its intention. Nor does it mean that the 'cost' figure remains unchanged forever. For example, a motor vehicle costing US $/£/€6,000 may end up looking like Table 1.1 after two years.

The depreciation is how we show the asset being 'consumed' over its working life. It is simply a bookkeeping record to allow us to allocate some of the cost of an asset to the appropriate time period.

The time period will be determined by factors such as the working life of the asset. The tax authorities do not allow depreciation as a business expense, so this figure can't be manipulated to reduce tax liability, for example. A tax

TABLE 1.1   Example of the changing 'worth' of an asset

	Year 1	Year 2
Fixed assets	$/£/€	$/£/€
Vehicle	6,000	6,000
Less cumulative depreciation	1,500	3,000
Net asset	4,500	3,000

relief on the capital expenditure, known as 'writing down', is allowed, using a formula set by government that varies from time to time dependent on current economic goals, for example to stimulate capital expenditure.

Other assets, such as freehold land and buildings, will be revalued from time to time, and stock will be entered at cost, or market value, whichever is the lower, in line with the principle of conservatism (see later in this chapter).

Other methods for recording assets

While cost at date of purchase is the norm for accounting for assets in conventional enterprises, there are certain types of businesses and certain situations when other methods of recording a monetary figure are used:

- Market value: This is usually used when an asset is actually to be sold and there is an established market for that particular type of asset. This could arise when a business or part of a business is to be closed down.

- Fair value: This is described as the estimated price at which an asset could be exchanged between knowledgeable but unrelated willing parties who have not, and may not, actually exchange. This basis is often used in the due diligence process, where, because of particular synergies, a price higher than market value (resulting in goodwill) could reasonably be set.

- Market to market: This is where market value is calculated on a daily basis, usually by financial institutions such as banks and stockbrokers. This can result in dramatic changes in value in turbulent market conditions, requiring additional assets, including cash, to be found to cover a fall in market price. This approach is blamed for helping to create liquidity 'black holes' by forcing banks to sell assets to meet liquidity targets, which in turn forces prices lower, requiring yet more assets to be sold.

Going concern

Accounting reports always assume that a business will continue trading indefinitely into the future – unless there is good evidence to the contrary. This means that the assets of the business are looked at simply as profit generators and not as being available for sale. Look again at the motor vehicle example above. In year 2, the net asset figure in the accounts, prepared on a 'going concern' basis, is US $/£/€3,000. If we knew that the business was to close down in a few weeks, then we would be more interested in the car's resale value than its 'book' value: the car might fetch only £2,000, which is quite a different figure.

Once a business stops trading, we cannot realistically look at the assets in the same way. They are no longer being used in the business to help generate sales and profits. The most objective figure is what they might realize in the marketplace.

Dual aspect

To keep a complete record of any business transaction we need to know both where money came from and what has been done with it. It is not enough simply to say, for example, that a bank has lent a business £1m; we have to show how that money has been used, for example to buy a property, increase stock levels, or in some other way. You can think of it as the accounting equivalent of Newton's third law: 'For every force there is an equal and opposite reaction.' Dual aspect is the basis of double-entry bookkeeping (see below).

The realization concept

A particularly prudent sales manager once said that an order was not an order until the customer's cheque had cleared, he or she had consumed the product, had not died as a result, and, finally, had shown every indication of wanting to buy again. Most of us know quite different salespeople who can 'anticipate' the most unlikely volume of sales. In accounting, income is usually recognized as having been earned when the goods (or services) are dispatched and the invoice sent out. This has nothing to do with when an order is received, how firm an order is or how likely a customer is to pay up promptly. It is also possible that some of the products dispatched may be returned at some later date – perhaps for quality reasons. This means that income, and consequently profit, can be brought into the business in one period and has to be removed later on.

Obviously, if these returns can be estimated accurately, then an adjustment can be made to income at the time. So the 'sales income' figure that is seen at the top of a profit and loss account is the value of the goods dispatched and invoiced to customers in the period in question.

TABLE 1.2 Example of a badly matched profit and loss account

Profit and loss account for January, year 20XX	
	$/£/€
Sales income for January	4,000
Less telephone bill (last quarter)	800
Profit before other expenses	3,200

The accrual concept

The profit and loss account sets out to 'match' income and expenditure to the appropriate time period. It is only in this way that the profit for the period can be realistically calculated. Suppose, for example, that you are calculating one month's profits when the quarterly telephone bill comes in. The picture might look like Table 1.2.

This is clearly wrong. In the first place, three months' telephone charges have been 'matched' against one month's sales. Equally wrong is charging anything other than January's telephone bill against January's income. Unfortunately, bills such as this are rarely to hand when you want the accounts, so in practice the telephone bill is 'accrued' for. The figure (which may even be absolutely correct if you have a meter) is put in as a provision to meet this liability when it becomes due.

Accounting conventions

These concepts provide a useful set of ground rules, but they are open to a range of possible interpretations. Over time, a generally accepted approach to how the concepts are applied has been arrived at. This approach hinges on the use of three conventions: conservatism, materiality and consistency.

Conservatism

Accountants are often viewed as merchants of gloom, always prone to take a pessimistic point of view. The fact that a point of view has to be taken at all is the root of the problem. The convention of conservatism means that, given a choice, the accountant takes the figure that will result in a lower end profit. This might mean, for example, taking the higher of two possible expense figures. Few people are upset if the profit figure at the end of the day is higher than earlier estimates. The converse is never true.

Materiality

A strict interpretation of depreciation (see above) could lead to all sorts of trivial paperwork. For example, pencil sharpeners, staplers and paperclips, all theoretically items of fixed assets, should be depreciated over their working lives. This is obviously a useless exercise and in practice these items are written-off when they are bought.

Clearly, the level of 'materiality' is not the same for all businesses. A multinational might not keep meticulous records of every item of machinery under £1,000. For a small business this may represent all the machinery it has.

Consistency

Even with the help of those concepts and conventions, there is a fair degree of latitude in how you can record and interpret financial information. You should choose the methods that give the fairest picture of how the firm is performing and stick with them. It is very difficult to keep track of events in a business that is always changing its accounting methods. This does not mean that you are stuck with one method forever. Any change, however, is an important step.

The rule makers

The accounting professional bodies, with a little prodding from governments, are responsible for ensuring that accounting reports conform to what are known as Generally Accepted Accounting Practices (GAAP). A new entrant, International Accounting Standards, is challenging that term as GAAP rules have been interpreted differently on different continents and indeed largely ignored on others.

The rule book has to be adapted to accommodate changes in the way business is done. For example, international business across frontiers is now the norm, so rules on handling currency and reporting taxable profits in different countries have to be accommodated within a company's accounts in a consistent manner.

Although an MBA isn't usually expected to know all the rules, you should be able to get up to date before any meetings where the subject is likely to come up. You can keep track of changes in company reporting rules on the websites of the American Institute of CPAs (**www.aicpa.org** > publications > financial management & reporting), the Institute of Chartered Accountants (**www.icaew.com** > Accounting and corporate reporting > UK GAAP) and the International Financial Reporting Standards (**www.ifrs.org** > stay informed).

Protecting investors

When confidence in US businesses was rocked badly with a series of high-profile financial frauds, Enron and Worldcom for example, the US government introduced the Sarbanes–Oxley Act, known less commonly but better understood as 'The Public Company Accounting Reforms and Investor Protection Act – 2002'. The Act's purpose is to close the loopholes opened up by creative accountants, who are always devising ways to overstate profits and understate liabilities, and so make it easier for shareholders to see how profitable a business really is. The act doesn't just apply to US companies; any businesses with shares listed on a US stock market that does business in the United States is swept into the net. Check out **www.sarbanes-oxley.com** for the low-down on that Act.

The UK version is The Companies (Audit, Investigations and Community Enterprise) Act. You can read up on the UK rules at the Office of the Public Sector Information (**www.opsi.gov.uk** > Legislation > UK > Acts > Public Acts 2004 > Companies (Audit, Investigations and Community Enterprise) Act 2004).

Auditors – the gatekeepers

All public companies, that is, those listed on a stock exchange, are required to have an annual audit by a qualified accountant appointed by the directors and approved of by the shareholders. Any company with outside shareholders and indeed all but the smallest private companies are required by law to be audited. The auditors' job is to examine the accounts, ensure that they conform with the prevailing accounting rules and give an opinion about the financial statements. Though the auditors' report may be 50 pages long, with a score or more footnotes, the findings are summarized in a single sentence: 'The financial statements give a true and fair view of the state of affairs of the company at (a certain date) and the financial statements have been properly prepared in accordance with the Companies Act 2006.'

The Companies Act 2006, the longest Act ever introduced, has brought in some tough rules on how auditors, among others, should report on company accounts. MBAs, unless they are also accountants, don't get involved in doing audits. But they are expected to know who's who in the auditing world. *Accountancy Age* (**www.accountancyage.com/resource/top50**) will keep you informed as to who's who in the auditing world.

Bookkeeping – the way transactions are recorded

Until Luca Pacioli wrote what was in essence the world's first accounting book, over 500 years ago, accounting records were maintained in single-entry

TABLE 1.3 An example of a double-entry ledger

General Journal of Andrew's Bookshop			
Date	Description of entry	Debit $/£/€	Credit $/£/€
10 July	Rent expense	250	
	Cash		250

format; one event merited one record. This meant that errors could be prevented only by a major duplication of effort, for example by having different people making and counting up parallel records. Pacioli, a mathematician who worked for the Doge of Venice, came up with a system of double-entry bookkeeping that required two entries for each transaction and so provides built-in checks and balances to ensure accuracy. Each transaction requires an entry as a debit and as a credit.

To give an example, selling goods in a double-entry system might result in two separate journal entries – a debit reducing the stock by $/£/€250 and a corresponding credit of $/£/€250 of new cash in – a double entry (see Table 1.3). The debits in a double-entry system must always equal the credits. If they don't, you know there is an error somewhere. So, double entry allows you to balance your books, which you can't do with the single-entry method.

Pacioli's genius lay in seeing that the ultimate balancing number in a company's accounts was the profit or loss for the owners of that enterprise. In fact he required at least two entries or as many as are required to balance the books. Let us take the above example to its logical conclusion. On the not unreasonable assumption that the business plans to make a profit from selling goods, the figures will look rather different. To keep the numbers simple, let's suppose the goods they sold cost them $/£/€125 (a 50 per cent margin); then the entries would be as follows. Goods in stock go down by $/£/€125, while cash goes up by $/£/€250. That net change of $/£/€125 is balanced by an increase in profits of $/£/€125, so the assets and liabilities are kept in balance.

In this example, had the goods sold for less than was paid there would have been a loss, which would have reduced the value of the owner's stake in the business by a corresponding amount.

This is all an MBA student needs to know about bookkeeping; the main part of the knowledge they require is how to interpret the figures once recorded.

Cash flow

There is a saying in business that profit is vanity and cash flow is sanity. Both are necessary, but in the short term, and often that is all that matters in a business as it struggles to get a foothold in the shifting sands of trading, cash flow is life or death. The rules on what constitutes cash are very simple – it has to be just that, or negotiable securities designated as being as good as cash. Cash flow is looked at in two distinct and important ways: as a projection of future expected cash flows; and as an analysis of where cash came from and went to in an accounting period and the resultant increase or decrease in cash available.

Cash-flow forecasts

The future is impossible to predict with great accuracy but it is possible to anticipate likely outcomes and be prepared to deal with events by building in a margin of safety. The starting point for making a projection is to make some assumptions about what you want to achieve and test those for reasonableness.

Take the situation of High Note, a business being established to sell sheet music, small instruments and CDs to schools and colleges, which will expect trade credit, and members of the public who will pay cash. The owner plans to invest $/£/€10,000 and to borrow $/£/€10,000 from a bank on a long-term basis. The business will require $/£/€11,500 for fixtures and fittings. A further $/£/€1,000 will be needed for a computer, software and a printer. That should leave around $/£/€7,500 to meet immediate trading expenses such as buying in stock and spending $/£/€1,500 on initial advertising. Hopefully customers' payments will start to come in quickly to cover other expenses, such as some wages for bookkeeping, administration and fulfilling orders. Sales in the first six months are expected to be $/£/€60,000 based on negotiations already in hand, plus some cash sales that always seem to turn up. The rule of thumb in the industry seems to be that stock is marked up by 100 per cent, so $/£/€30,000 of bought-in goods sell on for $/£/€60,000.

On the basis of the above assumptions it is possible to make the cash-flow forecast set out in Table 1.4. It has been simplified and some elements such as VAT and tax have been omitted for ease of understanding.

The maths in the table is straightforward; the cash receipts from various sources are totalled, as are the payments. Taking one from the other leaves a cash surplus or deficit for the month in question. The bottom row shows the cumulative position. So, for example, while the business had $/£/€2,450 cash left at the end of April, taking the cash deficit of $/£/€1,500 in May into account, by the end of May only $/£/€950 ($/£/€2,450 – $/£/€1,500) cash remains.

TABLE 1.4 High Note six-month cash-flow forecast (£/$/€)

Month	April	May	June	July	Aug	Sept	Total
Receipts							
Sales	4,000	5,000	5,000	7,000	12,000	15,000	48,000
Owners' cash	10,000						
Bank loan	10,000						
Total cash in	24,000	5,000	5,000	7,000	12,000	15,000	48,000
Payments							
Purchases	5,500	2,950	4,220	7,416	9,332	9,690	39,108
Rates, electricity, heat, telephone, internet etc	1,000	1,000	1,000	1,000	1,000	1,000	
Wages	1,000	1,000	1,000	1,000	1,000	1,000	
Advertising	1,550	1,550	1,550	1,550	1,550	1,550	
Fixtures/fittings	11,500						
Computer etc	1,000						
Total cash out	21,550	6,500	7,770	10,966	12,882	13,240	
Monthly cash							
Surplus/deficit(–)	2,450	(1,500)	(2,770)	(3,966)	(882)	1,760	
Cumulative cash balance	2,450	950	(1,820)	(5,786)	(6,668)	(4,908)	

Overtrading

In the example above, the business looks like having insufficient cash, based on the assumptions made. An outsider, a banker perhaps, would look at the figures in August and see that the faster sales grew the greater the cash-flow deficit became. We know, using our crystal ball, the position will improve from September and that if we can only hang on in there for a few more months we should eliminate our cash deficit and perhaps even have a surplus. Had we made the cash-flow projection at the outset and raised more money, perhaps by way of an overdraft, spent less on fixtures and fittings, or set a more modest sales goal, hence needing less stock and advertising, we would have had a sound business. The figures indicate a business that is trading beyond its financial resources, a condition known as overtrading, anathema to bankers the world over.

Cash-flow spreadsheet

You can do a number of 'what if' projections to fine-tune cash-flow projections using a spreadsheet: Business Link (**www.businesslink.gov.uk/ Finance_files/Cash_Flow_Projection_Worksheet.xls**) has a cash-flow spreadsheet that you can copy and paste into an Excel file on your computer.

Statement of cash flows for the year

A cash-flow statement summarizes exactly where cash came from and how it was spent during the year. At first glance it seems to draw on a mixture of transactions included in the profit and loss account and balance sheet for the same period end, but this is not the whole story. Because there is a time lag on many cash transactions, for example tax and dividend payments, the statement is a mixture of some previous year and some current year transactions; the remaining current year transactions go into the following year's cash-flow statement, during which the cash actually changes hands. Similarly, the realization and accrual conventions relating to sales and purchases respectively result in cash transactions having a different timing to when they were entered in the profit and loss account.

Example

A company had sales of $/£/€5 million this year and $/£/€4 million last year and these figures appeared in the profit and loss accounts of those years. Debtors at the end of this year were $/£/€1 million and at the end of the previous year were $/£/€0.8 million. The cash inflow arising from sales this year is $/£/€4.8 million ($/£/€0.8 million + $/£/€5 million – $/£/€1 million) whereas the sales figure in the profit and loss account is $/£/€5 million.

For these reasons it is not possible to look at just this year's profit and loss account and balance sheet to find all the cash flows; you need the previous year's accounts too. The balance sheet will show the cash balance at the period end but will not easily disclose all the ways in which it was achieved. Compiling a cash-flow statement is quite a technical job and some training plus inside information is needed to complete the task. Nevertheless, the bulk of the items can be identified from an examination of the other two accounting statements for both the current and previous years.

From an MBA perspective it is understanding the requirement for a cash-flow statement as well as the other two accounts that is important, as well as being able to interpret the significance of the cash movements themselves.

XYZ plc

The un-audited condensed cash-flow statement for XYZ plc, established as a supplier of container solutions for source-separated waste, is shown in Table 1.5. Initially one man and a desk, the company grew to become a leading supplier of kerbside recycling boxes as well as a key supplier of other types of waste and recycling container solutions. Turnover by 2010 was running at over £30/$47/€34 million a year, with operating profit in excess of £1/$1.6/€1.13 million.

The three columns represent the cash activities for two equivalent six-month periods and for the whole of the preceding year. The cash of £2,126 ($3,336/€2,395) thousand generated to 31 December 2010 (bottom of the right-hand column) is carried over to the start of the June 2011 six-month period (second figure from bottom of left-hand column). By adding the net increase (or decrease) in cash generated in this period we arrive at the closing cash position.

The cash-flow statement then gives us a complete picture of how cash movements came about: from normal sales activities; the purchase or disposal of assets; or from financing activities. This is an expansion of the sparse single figure in the company's closing balance sheet stating that cash in current assets is £3,751 ($5,886/€4,226) thousand.

The profit and loss account (income statement)

If you look back to the financial situation in the High Note example you will see a good example of the difference between cash and profit. After all, the business has sold $/£/€60,000 worth of goods that it paid only $/£/€30,000 for, so it has a substantial profit margin to play with. While $/£/€39,108 has been paid to suppliers, only $/£/€30,000 of goods at cost have been sold,

TABLE 1.5 Un-audited condensed cash-flow statement for XYZ plc (for the 6 months ended 30 June 2011)

	Half year to 30 June 2011 $/£/€'000	Half year to 30 June 2010 $/£/€'000	Year 31 Dec 2010 $/£/€'000
Net cash flows from operating activities	2,242	3,879	1,171
Cash flows from investing activities			
Purchases of property, plant and equipment	(603)	(464)	(701)
Proceeds from sale of property, plant and equip	345	–	–
Purchase of intangible assets	(55)	(87)	(193)
Purchase of investments	(35)	–	–
Interest received	28	58	107
Net cash used in investing activities	(320)	(493)	(787)
Cash flows from financing activities			
Dividends paid	(310)	(283)	(422)
Proceeds from issue of shares	13	–	128
Net cash used in financing activities	(297)	(283)	(294)
Net increase in cash and cash equivalents	1,625	3,103	90
Cash and cash equivalents at beginning of period	2,126	2,036	2,036
Cash and cash equivalents at the end of period	3,751	5,139	2,126

meaning that $/£/€9,108 worth of instruments, sheet music and CDs are still in stock. A similar situation exists with sales. We have billed for $/£/€60,000 but been paid for only $/£/€48,000; the balance is owed by debtors. The bald figure at the end of the cash-flow projection showing High Note to be in the red to the tune of $/£/€4,908 seems to be missing some important facts.

The difference between profit and cash

Cash is immediate and takes account of nothing else. Profit, however, is a measurement of economic activity that considers other factors that can be assigned a value or cost. The accounting principle that governs profit is known as the 'matching principle', which means that income and expenditure are matched to the time period in which they occur. (Look back to earlier in the chapter where realization and accruals are explained.)

So for High Note the profit and loss account for the first six months would be as shown in Table 1.6.

The structure of the profit and loss statement

This account is set out in more detail for a business in order to make it more useful when it comes to understanding how a business is performing. For example, although the profit shown in our worked example is $/£/€8,700, in fact it would be rather lower. As money has been borrowed to finance cash flow there would be interest due, as there would be on the longer-term loan of $/£/€10,000.

TABLE 1.6   Profit and loss account for High Note for the six months Apr–Sept

	$/£/€	$/£/€
Sales		60,000
Less cost of goods to be sold		30,000
Gross profit		30,000
Less expenses:		
Heat, electric, telephone, internet etc	6,000	
Wages	6,000	
Advertising	9,300	
Total expenses		21,300
Profit before tax, interest and depreciation charges		8,700

TABLE 1.7   High Note extended profit and loss account

	$/£/€
Sales	60,000
Less the cost of goods to be sold	30,000
Gross profit	30,000
Less operating expenses	21,300
Operating profit	8,700
Less interest on bank loan and overdraft	600
Profit before tax	8,100
Less tax	1,827
Profit after tax	6,723

In practice we have four levels of profit:

● Gross profit is the profit left after all costs related to making what you sell are deducted from income.

● Operating profit is what's left after you take away the operating expenses from the gross profit.

● Profit before tax is what is left after deducting any financing costs.

● Profit after tax is what is left for the owners to spend or reinvest in the business.

For High Note this could look much as set out in Table 1.7.

A more substantial business than High Note will have taken on a wide range of commitments. For example, as well as the owner's money, there may be a long-term loan to be serviced (interest and capital repayments); parts of the workshop or offices may be sublet, generating 'non-operating income'; and there will certainly be some depreciation expense to deduct. Like any accounting report, it should be prepared in the best form for the user, bearing in mind the requirements of the regulatory authorities. The elements to be included are:

1 sales (and any other revenues from operations);

2 cost of sales (or cost of goods sold);

3 gross profit – the difference between sales and cost of sales;

4 operating expenses – selling, administration, depreciation and other general costs;

5 operating profit – the difference between gross profit and operating expenses;

6 non-operating revenues – other revenues, including interest, rent, etc;

7 non-operating expenses – financial costs and other expenses not directly related to the running of the business;

8 profit before income tax;

9 provision for income tax;

10 net income (or profit or loss).

Profit and loss spreadsheet

There is an online spreadsheet at SCORE's website (**www.score.org** > Business Tools > Template Gallery > Profit and Loss). Download in Excel format and you have a profit and loss account with 30 lines of expenses, the headings of which you can change or delete to meet your particular needs.

The balance sheet

A balance sheet is a snapshot picture at a moment in time. On the one hand it shows the value of assets (possessions) owned by the business and, on the other, it shows who provided the funds with which to finance those assets and to whom the business is ultimately liable.

Assets are of two main types and are classified under the headings of either fixed assets or current assets. Fixed assets come in three forms. First, there are the hardware or physical things used by the business itself and which are not for sale to customers. Examples of fixed assets include buildings, plant, machinery, vehicles, furniture and fittings. Next come intangible fixed assets, such as goodwill, intellectual property etc, and these are also shown under the general heading 'fixed assets'. Finally there are investments in other businesses. Other assets in the process of eventually being turned into cash from customers are called current assets, and include stocks, work in progress, money owed by customers and cash itself.

Total assets = Fixed assets + Current assets

Assets can only be bought with funds provided by the owners or borrowed from someone else, for example bankers or creditors. Owners provide funds by directly investing in the business (say, when they buy shares issued by the company) or indirectly by allowing the company to retain some of the profits in reserves. These sources of money are known collectively as liabilities.

Total liabilities = Share capital and reserves + Borrowings and other creditors

Borrowed capital can take the form of a long-term loan at a fixed rate of interest or a short-term loan, such as a bank overdraft, usually at a variable rate of interest. All short-term liabilities owed by a business and due for payment within 12 months are referred to as creditors falling due within one year, and long-term indebtedness is called creditors falling due after one year.

So far in our High Note example, the money spent on 'capital' items such as the $/£/€12,500 spent on a computer and fixtures and fittings have been ignored, as has the $/£/€9,108 worth of sheet music etc remaining in stock waiting to be sold and the $/£/€12,000 of money owed by customers who have yet to pay up. An assumption has to be made about where the cash deficit will be made up, and the most logical short-term source is a bank overdraft.

For High Note at the end of September the balance sheet is set out in Table 1.8.

Balance sheet structure

The layout of the balance sheet using UK accounting rules is something of a jumble, with assets and liabilities intermingled. In the United States the balance sheet is traditionally set out horizontally, with the assets on one side and the liabilities and owner's equity, the two sources of funds, on the other (see Table 1.9).

Working capital

You will also have noticed in this example that the assets and liabilities have been jumbled together in the middle to net off the current assets and current liabilities and so end up with a figure for the working capital. 'Current' in accounting means within the trading cycle, usually taken to be one year. Stock will be used up and debtors will pay up within the year, and overdraft being repayable on demand also appears as a short-term liability.

There are a number of other items not shown in the working capital section of the example balance sheet that should appear, such as liability for tax and VAT that have not yet been paid, and these should appear as current liabilities.

Intangible fixed assets

There are a number of seemingly invisible items that nevertheless have been acquired for a measurable money cost and so have to be accounted for:

- Goodwill: This is where the price paid for an asset is above its fair market price. This is fairly common in the case of acquisitions where competition for a company can push prices higher.
- Intellectual property such as patents, copyright, designs and logos.

These items too are amortized over their working life. So, for example, if a patent is considered to have a 10-year life and cost £1 million to acquire, it would be written down in the accounts by $/£/€100,000 a year.

TABLE 1.8   High Note balance sheet at 30 September

	$/£/€	$/£/€
Assets		
Fixed assets		
Fixtures, fitting, equipment	11,500	
Computer	1,000	
Total fixed assets		12,500
Working capital		
Current assets		
Stock	9,108	
Debtors	12,000	
Cash	0	
	21,108	
Less current liabilities (creditors falling due within one year)		
Overdraft	4,908	
Creditors	0	
	4,908	
Net current assets [Working capital (CA-CL)]		16,200
Total assets less current liabilities		28,700
Less creditors falling due after one year		
Long-term bank loan		10,000
Net total assets		18,700
Capital and reserves		
Owner's capital introduced	10,000	
Profit retained (from P&L account)	8,700	
Total capital and reserves		18,700

Accounting for stock

Deciding on the stock figure to put into a balance sheet is a tricky calculation. Theoretically it is simple; after all, you know what you paid for it. The rule that stock should be entered in the balance sheet at cost or market-price, whichever is the lower, is also not too difficult to follow. But

TABLE 1.9   High Note balance sheet – US style

Assets		Liabilities and owner's equity	
Cash	0	Accounts payable	0
Accounts receivable (debtors)	12,000	Notes, short term (overdraft)	4,908
Inventory (stock)	9,108	Bank loans, long term	10,000
Fixed assets	12,500	Owner's industrial capital (owner's capital introduced)	10,000
		Retained earnings (profit retained)	8,700
TOTAL	33,608		33,608

in the real world a business keeps on buying in stock so it has product to sell, and the cost can vary every time a purchase is made.

Take the example of a business selling a breakfast cereal. Four pallets of cereal are bought in from various suppliers at prices of $/£/€1,000, $/£/€1,020, $/£/€1,040 and $/£/€1,060 respectively, a total of $/£/€4,120. At the end of the period three pallets have been sold, so logically the cost of goods sold in the profit and loss account will show a figure of $/£/€3,060 ($/£/€1,000 + $/£/€1,020 + $/£/€1,040). The last pallet costing $/£/€1,060 will be the figure to put into the balance sheet, thus ensuring that all $/£/€4,120 of total costs are accounted for.

This method of dealing with stock is known as FIFO (first in first out), for obvious reasons. There are two other popular costing methods that have their own merits. LIFO (last in first out) is based on the argument that if you are staying in business you will have to keep on replacing stock at the latest (higher) price, so you might just as well get used to that sooner by accounting for it in your profit and loss account. In this case the cost of goods sold would be $/£/€3,120 ($/£/€1,060 + $/£/€1,040 + $/£/€1,020), rather than the $/£/€3,060 that FIFO produces.

The third popular costing method is the average cost method, which does what it says on the box. In the above example this would produce a cost midway between those obtained by the other two methods; in this example $/£/€3,090.

All these methods have their merits, but FIFO usually wins the argument as it accommodates the realities that prices rise steadily and goods move in and out of a business in the order in which they are bought. It would be a very badly run grocer's shop that sold its last delivery of cereal before clearing out its existing stocks.

Methods of depreciation

The depreciation is how we show the asset being 'consumed' over its working life. It is simply a bookkeeping record to allow us to allocate some of the cost of an asset to the appropriate time period. The time period will be determined by such factors as how long the working life of the asset is. The principal methods of depreciation used in business are:

- The straight-line method: This assumes that the asset will be 'consumed' evenly throughout its life. If, for example, an asset is being bought for £1,200 and sold at the end of five years for £200, the amount of cost we have to write off is £1,000. Using 20%, so that the whole 100% of cost is allocated, we can work out the 'book value' for each year.

- The declining-balance method: This works in a similar way, but instead of an even depreciation each year we assume the drop will be less. Some assets, motor vehicles for example, will reduce sharply in their first year and less so later on. So at the end of year 1, both these methods of depreciation will result in a £200 fall, but in year 2 the picture starts to change. The straight-line method takes a further fall of £200, while the declining-balance method reduces by 20% (our agreed depreciation rate) of £800 (the balance of £1,000 minus the £200 depreciation so far), which is £160.

- The sum of the digits method: This is more common in the United States than in the UK. While the declining-balance method applies a constant percentage to a declining figure, this method applies a progressively smaller percentage to the initial cost. It involves adding up the individual numbers in the expected life span of the asset to arrive at the denominator of a fraction. The numerator is year number concerned, but in reverse order.

    For example, if our computer asset bought for £1,200 had an expected useful life of 5 years (unlikely), then the denominator in our sum would be 1+2+3+4+5 which equals 15. In year 1 we would depreciate by 5/15 times the initial purchase price of £1,200, which equals £400. In year 2 we would depreciate by 4/15ths and so on.

These are just three of the most common of many ways of depreciating fixed assets. In choosing which method of depreciation to use, and in practice you may have to use different methods with different types of asset, it is useful to remember what you are trying to do. You are aiming to allocate the cost of buying the asset as it should apply to each year of its working life.

Balance sheet and other online tools

SCORE (**www.score.org** > Business Tools > Template Gallery > Balance Sheet (projected)) is an Excel-based spreadsheet you can use for constructing your own balance sheet. You can find guidance on depreciation, on handling stock and on the layout of the balance sheet and profit and loss account as required by the Companies Act from the Accounting Standards Board (**www.frc.org** > ASB > Technical > FRSSE). Accounting Glossary (**www.accountingglossary.net**) and Accounting for Everyone (**www.accountingfor-everyone.com** > Accounting Glossary) have definitions of all the accounting terms you are ever likely to come across in the accounting world.

Package of accounts

The cash-flow statement, the profit and loss account and the balance sheet between them constitute a set of accounts, but conventionally two balance sheets, the opening and closing one, are provided to make a 'package'. By including these balance sheets we can see the full picture of what has happened to the owner's investment in the business.

Table 1.10 shows a simplified package of accounts. We can see from these, that over the year the business has made £600 of profit after tax, and has invested that profit in £200 of additional fixed assets and £400 of working capital such as stock and debtors, balancing that off with the £600 put into reserves from the year's profits.

Filing accounts

A company's financial affairs are in the public domain. As well as keeping the government tax authorities such as The Internal Revenue Service (IRS) and HM Revenue and Customs (HMRC) informed, companies have to file their accounts with Companies House (**www.companieshouse.gov.uk/about/gbhtml/gb3.shtml**). Accounts should be filed within 10 months of the company's financial year-end. Small businesses in the UK (turnover below £5.6 ($8.8/€6.3) million) can file abbreviated accounts that include only very limited balance sheet and profit and loss account information and these do not need to be audited. Businesses can be fined up to £1,000 ($1,570/€1,127) for filing accounts late.

You can find the report and accounts for all companies listed on UK stock markets at Corporate Reports (**www.corporatereports.co.uk**). US company accounts can be obtained from The Securities Exchange Commission (**www.sec.gov**). The Investor Relations Society (**www.irs.org.uk** > IR Best Practice) makes an award each year to the company producing the best set of report and accounts.

TABLE 1.10 A package of accounts

Balance sheet at 31 Dec 2010 $/£/€		P & L for year to 31 Dec 2011 $/£/€		Balance sheet at 2011 $/£/€	
Fixed assets	1,000	Sales	10,000	Fixed assets	1,200
Working capital	1,000	less cost of sales	6,000	Working capital	1,400
	2,000	Gross profit	4,000		2,600
		less expenses	3,000		
		Profit before tax	1,000	Financed by	
Financed by		Tax	400	Owners' equity	2,000
Owners' equity	2,000	Profit after tax	600	Reserves	600
					2,600

Financial ratios

Earlier in this chapter the two important financial statements of profit and loss account and balance sheet were examined. To recap – the trading performance of a company for a period of time is measured in the profit and loss account by deducting running costs from sales income. A balance sheet sets out the financial position of the company at a particular point in time, usually the end of the accounting period. It lists the assets owned by the company at that date matched by an equal list of the sources of finance.

Reading company accounts, with practice, you can get some insight into a company's affairs. Comparing the current year's figure with the previous year's figure can identify changes in some of the key items, but conclusions drawn from this approach can be misleading. Consider the situation shown in Table 1.11.

You can see that the table is nothing more than a simplified profit and loss account on the left and the assets section of the balance sheet on the right. Any change that increases net profit (more sales, lower expenses, less tax etc), but does not increase the amount of assets employed (lower stocks, fewer debtors etc), will increase the return on assets. Conversely, any change that increases capital employed without increasing profits in proportion will reduce the return on assets.

Now let us suppose that events occur to increase sales by $/£/€25,000 and profits by $/£/€1,000 to $/£/€8,910. Superficially that would look like an improved position. But if we then discover that in order to achieve that extra profit new equipment costing $/£/€5,000 had to be bought and a further $/£/€2,500 had to be tied up in working capital (stock and debtors), the picture might not look so attractive. The return being made on assets employed has dropped from 31 per cent (8,910 / 28,910 × 100) to 27 per cent (9,910 / [28,910 + 5,000 + 2,500] × 100).

TABLE 1.11   Factors that affect profit performance

	$/£/€		$/£/€	$/£/€
Sales	100,000	Fixed assets		12,500
– Cost of sales	50,000			
= Gross profit	50,000	Working capital		
– Expenses	33,000	Current assets	23,100	
= Operating profit	17,000	– Current liabilities	6,690 = 16,410	
– Finance charges	8,090	Total net assets		28,910
= Net profit	8,910			

Analysing accounts

The main analytical approach is to examine the relationship of pairs of figures extracted from the accounts. A pair may be taken from the same statement, or one figure from each of the profit and loss account and balance sheet statements. When brought together, the two figures are called ratios. Miles per gallon, for example, is a useful ratio for drivers checking one aspect of a vehicle's performance. Some financial ratios are meaningful in themselves, but their value mainly lies in their comparison with the equivalent ratio last year, a target ratio, or a competitor's ratio.

Before we can measure and analyse anything about a business's accounts we need some idea of what level or type of performance a business wants to achieve. All businesses have three fundamental objectives in common, which allow us to see how well (or otherwise) they are doing.

Making a satisfactory return on investment

The first of these objectives is to make a satisfactory return (profit) on the money invested in the business.

It is hard to think of a sound argument against this aim. To be satisfactory the return must meet four criteria:

1 It must give a fair return to shareholders, bearing in mind the risk they are taking. If the venture is highly speculative and the profits are less than bank interest rates, your shareholders (yourself included) will not be happy.

2 You must make enough profit to allow the company to grow. If a business wants to expand sales it will need more working capital and eventually more space or equipment. The safest and surest source of new money for this is internally generated profits, retained in the business: reserves. (A business has three sources of new money: share capital or the owner's money; loan capital, put up by banks etc; retained profits, generated by the business.)

3 The return must be good enough to attract new investors or lenders. If investors can get a greater return on their money in some other comparable business, then that is where they will put it.

4 The return must provide enough reserves to keep the real capital intact. This means that you must recognize the impact inflation has on the business. A business retaining enough profits each year to meet a 3% growth is actually contracting by 1% if inflation is running at 4%.

Maintaining a sound financial position

As well as making a satisfactory return, investors, creditors and employees expect the business to be protected from unnecessary risks. Clearly, all businesses are exposed to market risks: competitors, new products and price changes are all part of a healthy commercial environment. The sorts of unnecessary risk that investors and lenders are particularly concerned about are high financial risks, such as overtrading.

Cash-flow problems are not the only threat to a business's financial position. Heavy borrowing can bring a big interest burden to a small business, especially when interest rates rise unexpectedly. This may be acceptable when sales and profits are good; however, when times are bad, bankers, unlike shareholders, cannot be asked to tighten their belts – they expect to be paid all the time. So the position audit is not just about profitability, but about survival capabilities and the practice of sound financial disciplines.

Achieving growth

Making profit and surviving are insufficient achievements in themselves to satisfy either shareholders or directors or ambitious MBAs – they want the business to grow too. But they do not just want the number of people they employ to get larger, or the sales turnover to rise, however nice they may be. They want the firm to become more efficient, to gain economies of scale and to improve the quality of profits.

Accounting ratios

Ratios used in analysing company accounts are clustered under five headings and are usually referred to as 'tests':

- tests of profitability;
- tests of liquidity;
- tests of solvency;
- tests of growth;
- market tests.

The profit and loss account and balance sheet in Tables 1.7 and 1.8 will be used, where possible, to illustrate these ratios.

Tests of profitability

There are six ratios used to measure profit performance. The first four profit ratios are arrived at using only the profit and loss account and the other two use information from both that account and the balance sheet.

Gross profit

This is calculated by dividing the gross profit by sales and multiplying by 100. In this example the sum is 30,000 / 60,000 × 100 = 50%. This is a measure of the value we are adding to the bought-in materials and services we need to 'make' our product or service; the higher the figure the better.

Operating profit

This is calculated by dividing the operating profit by sales and multiplying by 100. In this example the sum is 8,700 / 60,000 × 100 = 14.5%. This is a measure of how efficiently we are running the business, before taking account of financing costs and tax. These are excluded as interest and tax rates change periodically and are outside our direct control. Excluding them makes it easier to compare one period with another or with another business. Once again the rule here is the higher the figure the better.

Net profit before and after tax

Dividing the net profit before and after tax by the sales and multiplying by 100 calculates these next two ratios. In this example the sums are 8,100/60,000 × 100 = 13.5% and 6,723/60,000 × 100 = 11.21%. This is a measure of how efficiently we are running the business, after taking account of financing costs and tax. The last figure shows how successful we are at creating additional money to either invest back in the business or distribute to the owner(s) as either drawings or dividends. Once again the rule here is the higher the figure the better.

Return on equity

This ratio is usually expressed as a percentage in the way we might think of the return on any personal financial investment. Taking the owners' viewpoint, their concern is with the profit earned for them relative to the amount of funds they have invested in the business. The relevant profit here is after interest and tax (and any preference dividends) have been deducted. This is expressed as a percentage of the equity that comprises ordinary share capital and reserves. So in this example the sum is: return on equity = 6,723 / 18,700 × 100 = 36%.

Return on capital employed

This takes a wider view of company performance than return on equity by expressing profit before interest, tax and dividend deductions as a percentage of the total capital employed, irrespective of whether this capital is borrowed or provided by the owners.

Capital employed is defined as share capital plus reserves plus long-term borrowings. Where, say, a bank overdraft is included in current liabilities every year and in effect becomes a source of capital, this may be regarded as part of capital employed. If the bank overdraft varies considerably from year to year, a more reliable ratio could be calculated by averaging the start- and end-year figures. There is no one precise definition used by companies for capital employed. In this example the sum is: return on capital employed = 8,700/18,700 + 10,000 × 100 = 30%.

Tests of liquidity

In order to survive, companies must also watch their liquidity position, by which is meant keeping enough short-term assets to pay short-term debts. Companies go out of business compulsorily when they fail to pay money due to employees, bankers or suppliers.

The liquid money tied up in day-to-day activities is known as working capital, the sum of which is arrived at by subtracting the current liabilities from the current assets. In the case of High Note we have $/£/€21,108 in current assets and $/£/€4,908 in current liabilities, so the working capital is $/£/€16,200.

Current ratio

As a figure the working capital doesn't tell us much. It is rather as if you knew your car had used 20 gallons of petrol but had no idea how far you had travelled. It would be more helpful to know how much larger the current assets are than the current liabilities. That would give us some idea if the funds would be available to pay bills for stock, the tax liability and any other short-term liabilities that may arise. The current ratio, which is arrived at by dividing the current assets by the current liabilities, is the measure used. For High Note this is 21,108/4,908 = 4.30. The convention is to express this as 4.30 : 1 and the aim here is to have a ratio of between 1.5 : 1 and 2 : 1. Any lower and bills can't be met easily; much higher and money is being tied up unnecessarily.

Quick ratio (acid test)

This is a belt and braces ratio used to ensure that a business has sufficient ready cash or near cash to meet all its current liabilities. Items such as stock are stripped out as although these are assets, the money involved is not immediately available to pay bills. In effect the only liquid assets a business has are cash, debtors and any short-term investment such as bank deposits or government securities. For High Note this ratio is: 12,000/4,908 = 2.44 : 1. The ratio should be greater than 1 : 1 for a business to be sufficiently liquid.

Average collection period

We can see that High Note's current ratio is high, which is an indication that some elements of working capital are being used inefficiently. The business has $/£/€12,000 owed by customers on sales of $/£/€60,000 over a six-month period. The average period it takes High Note to collect money owed is calculated by dividing the sales made on credit by the money owed (debtors) and multiplying it by the time period, in days; in this case the sum is as follows: 12,000/60,000 × 182.5 = 36.5 days.

If the credit terms are cash with order or seven days, then something is going seriously wrong. If it is net 30 days then it is probably about right. In this example it has been assumed that all the sales were made on credit.

Average payment period

This ratio shows how long a company is taking on average to pay its suppliers. The calculation is as for average collection period, but substituting creditors for debtors and purchase for sales.

Days stock held

High Note is carrying $/£/€9,108 stock of sheet music, CDs etc and over the period it sold $/£/€30,000 of stock at cost (the cost of sales is $/£/€30,000 to support $/£/€60,000 of invoiced sales as the mark-up in this case is 100 per cent). Using a similar sum as with average collection period we can calculate that the stock being held is sufficient to support 55.41 days sales (9,108/10,000 × 182.5). If High Note's suppliers can make weekly deliveries then this is almost certainly too high a stock figure to hold. Cutting stock back from nearly 8 weeks (55.41 days) to 1 week (7 days) would trim 48.41 days or $/£/€7,957.38 worth of stock out of working capital. This in turn would bring the current ratio down to 2.68 : 1.

Circulation of working capital

This is a measure used to evaluate the overall efficiency with which working capital is being used. That is the sales divided by the working capital (current assets – current liabilities). In this example that sum is: 60,000/16,420 = 3.65 times. In other words, we are turning over the working capital more than three and a half times each year. There are no hard and fast rules as to what is an acceptable ratio. Clearly the more times working capital is turned over, stock sold for example, the more chance a business has to make a profit on that activity.

Tests of solvency

These measures see how a company is managing its long-term liabilities. There are two principal ratios used here.

Gearing

This measures as a percentage the proportion of all borrowing, including long-term loans and bank overdrafts, to the total of shareholders' funds – share capital and all reserves. The gearing ratio is sometimes also known as the debt/equity ratio. For High Note this is: (4,908 + 10,000) / 18,800 = 14,908/18,800 = 0.79 : 1. In other words, for every $/£/€1 the shareholders have invested in High Note they have borrowed a further 79p. This ratio is usually not expected to exceed 1 : 1 for long periods.

Interest cover

This is a measure of the proportion of profit taken up by interest payments and can be found by dividing the annual interest payment into the annual profit before interest, tax and dividend payments. The greater the number, the less vulnerable the company will be to any setback in profits, or rise in interest rates on variable loans. The smaller the number, the more risk that level of borrowing represents to the company. A figure of between 2 and 5 times would be considered acceptable.

Tests of growth

These are arrived at by comparing one year with another, usually for elements of the profit and loss account such as sales and profit. So, for example, if next year High Note achieved sales of $/£/€100,000 and operating profits of $/£/€16,000 the growth ratios would be 67 per cent, that is, $/£/€40,000 of extra sales as a proportion of the first year's sales of $/£/€60,000; and 84 per cent, that is, $/£/€7,300 of extra operating profit as a percentage of the first year's operating profit of $/£/€8,700.

Some additional information can be gleaned from these two ratios. In this example we can see that profits are growing faster than sales, which indicates a healthier trend than if the situation were reversed.

Market tests

This is the name given to stock market measures of performance. Four key ratios here are:

$$\text{Earnings per Share} = \frac{\text{Net Profit}}{\text{Shares Outstanding}}$$

The after-tax profit made by a company divided by the number of ordinary shares it has issued.

$$\text{Price Earnings Ratio} = \frac{\text{Market Price per Share}}{\text{Earnings per Share}}$$

The market price of an ordinary share divided by the earnings per share. The PE ratio expresses the market value placed on the expectation of future earnings, ie the number of years required to earn the price paid for the shares out of profits at the current rate.

$$\text{Yield} = \frac{\text{Dividends per Share}}{\text{Price per Share}}$$

The percentage return a shareholder gets on the 'opportunity' or current value of their investment.

$$\text{Dividend Cover} = \frac{\text{Net Income}}{\text{Dividend}}$$

The number of times the profit exceeds the dividend; the higher the ratio, the more retained profit to finance future growth.

Other ratios

There are a very large number of other ratios that businesses use for measuring aspects of their performance such as:

- sales per £ invested in fixed assets – a measure of the use of those fixed assets;
- sales per employee – showing if your headcount is exceeding your sales growth;
- sales per manager, per support staff etc – showing the effectiveness of overhead spending.

Combined ratios

No one would use a single ratio to decide whether one vehicle was a better or worse buy than another. MPG, MPH, annual depreciation percentage and residual value proportion are just a handful of the ratios that would need to be reviewed. So it is with a business. A combination of ratios can be used to form an opinion on the financial state of affairs at any one time.

The best known of these combination ratios is the Altman Z-Score (**www.creditguru.com/CalcAltZ.shtml**), which uses a combined set of five financial ratios derived from eight variables from a company's financial statements linked to some statistical techniques to predict a company's probability of failure. Entering the figures into the on-screen template at this website produces a score and an explanatory narrative giving a view on the business's financial strengths and weaknesses.

Some problems in using ratios

Finding the information to calculate business ratios is often not the major problem. Being sure of what the ratios are really telling you almost always is. The most common problems lie in the four following areas.

Which way is right?

There is natural feeling with financial ratios to think that high figures are good ones, and an upward trend represents the right direction. This theory

TABLE 1.12   Difficult comparisons

Current assets	1 $/£/€	$/£/€	2 $/£/€	$/£/€
Stock	10,000		22,990	
Debtors	13,000		100	
Cash	100	23,100	10	23,100
Less current liabilities				
Overdraft	5,000		90	
Creditors	1,690	6,690	6,600	6,690
Working capital		16,410		16,410
Current ratio		3.4:1		3.4:1

is, to some extent, encouraged by the personal feeling of wealth that having a lot of cash engenders.

Unfortunately, there is no general rule on which way is right for financial ratios. In some cases a high figure is good, in others a low figure is best. Indeed, there are even circumstances in which ratios of the same value are not as good as each other. Look at the two working capital statements in Table 1.12.

The amount of working capital in each example is the same, $/£/€16,410, as are the current assets and current liabilities, at $/£/€23,100 and $/£/€6,690 respectively. It follows that any ratio using these factors would also be the same. For example, the current ratios in these two examples are both identical, 3.4:1, but in the first case there is a reasonable chance that some cash will come in from debtors, certainly enough to meet the modest creditor position. In the second example there is no possibility of useful amounts of cash coming in from trading, with debtors at only $/£/€100, while creditors at the relatively substantial figure of $/£/€6,600 will pose a real threat to financial stability.

So in this case the current ratios are identical, but the situations being compared are not. In fact, as a general rule, a higher working capital ratio is regarded as a move in the wrong direction. The more money a business has tied up in working capital, the more difficult it is to make a satisfactory return on capital employed, simply because the larger the denominator the lower the return on capital employed.

In some cases the right direction is more obvious. A high return on capital employed is usually better than a low one, but even this situation can be a danger signal, warning that higher risks are being taken. And not all high profit ratios are good: sometimes a higher profit margin can lead to reduced sales volume and so lead to a lower ROCE (return on capital employed).

In general, business performance as measured by ratios is best thought of as lying within a range, liquidity (current ratio), for example, staying between 1.2 : 1 and 1.8 : 1. A change in either direction represents a cause for concern.

Accounting for inflation

Financial ratios all use pounds as the basis for comparison: historical pounds at that. That would not be so bad if all these pounds were from the same date in the past, but that is not so. Comparing one year with one from three or four years ago may not be very meaningful unless we account for the change in value of the pound.

One way of overcoming this problem is to adjust for inflation, perhaps using an index, such as that for consumer prices. Such indices usually take 100 as their base at some time in the past, for example 2000. Then an index value for each subsequent year is produced showing the relative movement in the item being indexed.

Apples and pears

There are particular problems in trying to compare one business's ratios with another. A small new business can achieve quite startling sales growth ratios in the early months and years. Expanding from £10,000 sales in the first six months to £50,000 in the second would not be unusual. To expect a mature business to achieve the same growth would be unrealistic. For Tesco to grow from sales of £10 billion to £50 billion would imply wiping out every other supermarket chain. So some care must be taken to make sure that like is being compared with like, and allowances made for differing circumstances in the businesses being compared (or if the same business, the trading/economic environment of the years being compared).

It is also important to check that one business's idea of an account category, say current assets, is the same as the one you want to compare it with. The concepts and principles used to prepare accounts leave some scope for differences.

Seasonal factors

Many of the ratios that we have looked at make use of information in the balance sheet. Balance sheets are prepared at one moment in time, and reflect the position at that moment; they may not represent the average situation. For example, seasonal factors can cause a business's sales to be particularly high once or twice a year, as with fashion retailers, for example. A balance sheet prepared just before one of these seasonal upturns might show very high stocks, bought in specially to meet this demand. Conversely, a look at the balance sheet just after the upturn might show very high cash and low stocks. If either of those stock figures were to be treated as an average it would give a false picture.

Getting company accounts

It will be very useful to look at other comparable businesses to see their ratios as a yardstick against which to compare your own businesses performance. For publicly quoted and larger businesses whose accounts are audited this should not be too difficult. However, for smaller private companies the position is not quite so simple. In the first place, small companies need only file an abbreviated balance sheet. Even medium-sized businesses can omit turnover from the information filed on their financial performance. Only public companies listed on a stock market and larger companies have to provide full financial statements, though in many cases even the smallest companies choose to provide comfort to suppliers and potential employees.

Despite the limitation, it is still possible to glean some valuable information on financial performance using these sources:

- Companies House (**www.companieshouse.gov.uk**) is the official repository of all company information in the UK. Their WebCHeck service offers a free-of-charge searchable Company Names and Address Index, covering 2 million companies, searchable by either the company's name or its unique company registration number. You can use WebCHeck to purchase a company's latest accounts giving details of sales, profits, margins, directors, shareholders and bank borrowings at a cost of £1 per company.

- Credit reports such as those provided by **www.ukdata.com**, **www.checksure.biz**, **www.business-inc.co.uk** cost around £8, are available online and provide basic business performance ratios.

- FAME (Financial Analysis Made Easy) is a powerful database that contains information on 3.4 million companies in the UK and Ireland. Typically the following information is included: contact information including phone, e-mail and web addresses plus main and other trading addresses, activity details, 29 profit and loss account and 63 balance sheet items, cash flow and ratios, credit score and rating, security and price information (listed companies only), names of bankers, auditors, previous auditors and advisers, details of holdings and subsidiaries (including foreign holdings and subsidiaries), names of current and previous directors with home addresses and shareholder indicator, heads of department, and shareholders. You can compare each company with detailed financials with its peer group based on its activity codes, and the software lets you search for companies that comply with your own criteria, combining as many conditions as you like. FAME is available in business libraries and on CD from the publishers, who also offer a free trial (**www.bvdep.com/en/ companyInformationHome.html** > Company data - national > FAME).

- Keynote (**www.keynote.co.uk**) operates in 18 countries, providing business ratios and trends for 140 industry sectors and sufficient information to assess accurately the financial health of each industry sector. Using this service you can find out how profitable a business sector is and how successful the main companies operating in each sector are. Executive summaries are free, but expect to pay between £250/$392/€282 and £500/$784/€564 for most reports.

- London Stock Exchange's website (**www.londonstockexchange.com**).

- Proshare (**www.proshareclubs.co.uk** > Research Centre > Performance Tables) is an Investment Club website, which, once you have registered, which you can do for free, has a number of tools that crunch public company ratios for you. Select the companies you want to look at, then the ratios you are most interested in: EPS, P/E, ROI, Dividend Yield and so forth. Press the button and in a couple of seconds all is revealed. You can then rank the companies by performance in more or less any way you want.

- Precision IR (**www.precisionir.com** > Annual Reports Service) has direct links to several thousand public companies' 'Report and Accounts' online, so you can save yourself the time and trouble of hunting down company websites.

Ratio analysis spreadsheets

biz/ed (**www.bized.co.uk** > Company Information > Financial Ratio Analysis) and the Harvard Business School (**http://harvardbusinessonline.hbsp.harvard. edu/b02/en/academic/edu_tk_acct_fin_ratio.jhtml**) have free tools that calculate financial ratios from your financial data. They also provide useful introductions to ratio analysis as well as defining each ratio and the formula used to calculate it. You need to register on the Harvard website to be able to download their spreadsheet.

Break-even analysis

A tool for making Cost, volume, pricing and profit decisions

Break-even is a technique that straddles several business disciplines. Marketeers use it for pricing, economists borrow it for demand curves and accountants use it for costing purposes. Break-even analysis had started to appear by 1962 (*Break-Even Analysis: Its Uses and Misuses*, by Howard F Stettler, 1962, American Accounting Association). But most managers still have barely heard of this tool and those who have don't know how to use it. This gives the MBA a powerful edge and allows them to muscle into decisions that are normally the prerogative of those several pay grades higher and in different departments to boot!

Working out the cost of making a product or delivering a service and consequently how much to charge doesn't seem too complicated. At first glance the problem is simple. You just add up all the costs and charge a bit more. The more you charge above your costs, provided the customers will keep on buying, the more profit you make. Unfortunately as soon as you start to do the sums the problem gets a little more complex. For a start, not all costs have the same characteristics. Some costs, for example, do not change however much you sell. If you are running a shop, the rent and rates are relatively constant figures, completely independent of the volume of your sales. On the other hand, the cost of the products sold from the shop is completely dependent on volume. The more you sell, the more it costs you to buy in stock.

	£/$/€
Rent and rates for shop	2,500
Cost of 1,000 units of volume of product	1,000
Total costs	3,500

You can't really add up those two types of costs until you have made an assumption about volume – how much you plan to sell. Look at the simple example above. Until we decide to buy, and we hope sell, 1,000 units of our product, we cannot total the costs. With the volume hypothesized we can arrive at a cost per unit of product of:

Total costs ÷ Number of units = £/$/€3,500 ÷ 1,000 = £/$/€3.50

Now, provided we sell out all the above at £/$/€3.50, we shall always be profitable. But will we? Suppose we do not sell all the 1,000 units, what then? With a selling price of £/$/€4.50 we could, in theory, make a profit of £/$/€1,000 if we sell all 1,000 units. That is a total sales revenue of £/$/€4,500, minus total costs of £/$/€3,500. But if we only sell 500 units, our total revenue drops to £/$/€2,250 and we actually lose £/$/€1,250 (total revenue £/$/€2,250 – total costs £/$/€3,500). So at one level of sales a selling price of £/$/€4.50 is satisfactory, and at another it is a disaster. This very simple example shows that all those decisions are intertwined. Costs, sales volume, selling prices and profits are all linked together. A decision taken in any one of these areas has an impact on the other areas. To understand the relationship between these factors, we need a picture or model of how they link up. Before we can build up this model, we need some more information on each of the component parts of cost.

The compontents of cost

Understanding the behaviour of costs as the trading patterns in a business change is an area of vital importance to decision makers. It is this 'dynamic' nature in every business that makes good costing decisions the key to survival and provides the MBA with a wealth of opportunities to demonstrate their skills and knowledge.

The last example showed that if the situation was static and predictable, a profit was certain, but if any one component in the equation was not a certainty (in that example it was volume), then the situation was quite different. To see how costs behave under changing conditions we first have to identify the different types of cost.

Fixed costs

Fixed costs are costs that happen, by and large, whatever the level of activity. For example, the cost of buying a car is the same whether it is driven 100 miles a year or 20,000 miles. The same is also true of the road tax, the insurance and any extras, such as a stereo system or navigator.

In a business, as well as the cost of buying cars, there are other fixed costs such as plant, equipment, computers, desks and answering machines. But certain less tangible items can also be fixed costs, for example, rent, rates, insurance, etc, which are usually set quite independent of how successful – or otherwise – a business is.

Costs such as most of those mentioned above are fixed irrespective of the timescale under consideration. Other costs, such as those of employing people, while theoretically variable in the short term, in practice are fixed. In other words, if sales demand goes down and a business needs fewer people, the costs cannot be shed for several weeks (notice, holiday pay, redundancy, etc). Also, if the people involved are highly skilled or expensive to recruit and train (or in some other way particularly valuable) and the downturn looks a short one, it may not be cost effective to reduce those short-run costs in line with falling demand. So viewed over a period of weeks and months, labour is a fixed cost. Over a longer period it may not be fixed.

We could draw a simple chart showing how fixed costs behave as the 'dynamic' volume changes. The first phase of our cost model is shown in Figure 1.1. This shows a static level of fixed costs over a particular range of output. To return to a previous example, this could show the fixed cost, rent and rates for a shop to be constant over a wide range of sales levels. Once the shop owner has reached a satisfactory sales and profit level in one shop, he or she may decide to rent another one, in which case the fixed costs will 'step' up. This can be shown in the variation on the fixed cost model in Figure 1.2.

FIGURE 1.1   Cost model 1: showing fixed costs

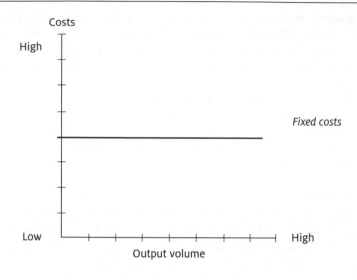

FIGURE 1.2   Variation on cost model 1: showing
a step up in fixed costs

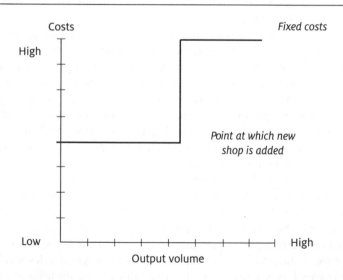

Variable costs

These are costs that change in line with output. Raw materials for production, packaging materials, bonuses, piece rates, sales commission and postage are some examples. The important characteristic of a variable cost is that it rises or falls in direct proportion to any growth or decline in output

FIGURE 1.3 Cost model 2: showing behaviour of variable costs as volume changes

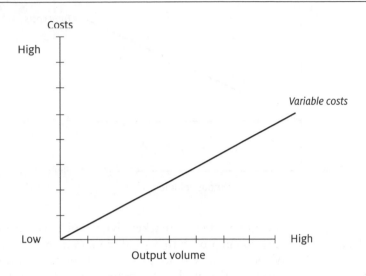

volumes. We can now draw a chart showing how variable costs behave as volume changes. The second phase of our cost model will look like Figure 1.3. There is a popular misconception that defines fixed costs as those costs that are predictable, and variable costs as those that are subject to change at any moment. The definitions already given are the only valid ones for costing purposes.

Semi-variable costs

Unfortunately not all costs fit easily into either the fixed or variable category. Some costs have both a fixed and a variable element. For example, a mobile phone has a monthly rental cost which is fixed, and a cost per unit consumed over and above a set usage rate which is variable. In this particular example low consumers can be seriously penalized. If only a few calls are made each month, their total cost per call (fixed rental + cost per unit ÷ number of calls) can be several pounds.

Other examples of this dual-component cost are photocopier rentals, electricity and gas.

These semi-variable costs must be split into their fixed and variable elements. For most small businesses this will be a fairly simple process, nevertheless it is essential to do it accurately or else much of the purpose and benefits of this method of cost analysis will be wasted.

Bringing both fixed and variable costs together we can build a costing model that shows how total costs behave for different levels of output (Figure 1.4).

FIGURE 1.4   Cost model showing total costs and fixed costs

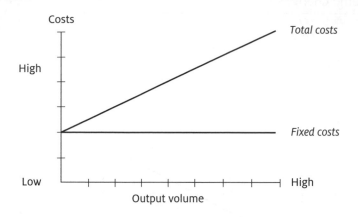

So any company capturing a sizeable market share will have an implied cost advantage over any competitor with a smaller market share. That cost advantage can then be used to make more profit, lower prices and compete for an even greater share of the market or invest in making the product better and so stealing a march on competitors. By starting the variable costs from the plateau of the fixed costs, we can produce a line showing the total costs. Taking vertical and horizontal lines from any point in the total cost line will give the total costs for any chosen output volume. This is an essential feature of the costing model that lets us see how costs change with different output volumes: in other words, accommodating the dynamic nature of a business. It is to be hoped that we are not simply producing things and creating costs. We are also selling things and creating income. So a further line can be added to the model to show sales revenue as it comes in. To help bring the model to life, let's add some figures, for illustration purposes only.

Figure 1.5 shows the break-even point (BEP). Perhaps the most important single calculation in the whole costing exercise is to find the point at which real profits start to be made. The point where the sales revenue line crosses the total costs line is the break-even point. It is only after that point has been reached that a business can start to make a profit. We can work this out by drawing a graph, such as the example in the figure, or by using a simple formula. The advantage of using the formula as well is that you can experiment by changing the values of some of the elements in the model quickly.

The equation for the BEP is:

$$\text{BEP} = \frac{\text{Fixed costs}}{\text{Unit selling price} - \text{Variable costs per unit}}$$

This is quite logical. Before you can reach profits you must pay for the variable costs. This is done by deducting those costs from the unit selling price.

FIGURE 1.5   Cost model showing break-even point

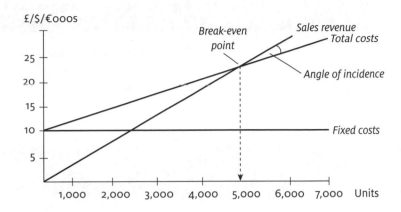

What is left (usually called the unit contribution) is available to meet the fixed costs. Once enough units have been sold to meet these fixed costs, the BEP has been reached. Let's try the sum out, given the following information shown on the break-even chart:

Fixed costs = £/$/€10,000
Selling price = £/$/€5 per unit
Variable cost = £/$/€3 per unit

$$\text{So BEP} = \frac{\text{£/\$/€}10,000}{\text{£/\$/€}5 - \text{£/\$/€}3} = \frac{\text{£/\$/€}10,000}{\text{£/\$/€}2} = 5{,}000 \text{ units}$$

Now we can see that 5,000 units must be sold at £/$/€5 each before we can start to make a profit. We can also see that if 7,000 is our maximum output we have only 2,000 units available to make our required profit target. Obviously, the more units we have available for sale (ie the maximum output that can realistically be sold) after our break-even point, the better. The relationship between total sales and the break-even point is called the margin of safety.

Margin of safety

This is usually expressed as a percentage and can be calculated as shown in Table 1.13. Clearly, the lower this percentage, the lower the business's capacity for generating profits. A low margin of safety might signal the need to rethink fixed costs, selling price or the maximum output of the business. The angle formed at the BEP between the sales revenue line and the total costs line is called the angle of incidence. The size of the angle shows the rate at which profit is made after the break-even point. A large angle means a high rate of profit per unit sold after the BEP.

TABLE 1.13   Calculating a margin of safety

	£/$/€	
Total sales	35,000	(7,000 units × £/$/€5 selling price)
Minus break-even point	25,000	(5,000 units × £/$/€5 selling price)
Margin of safety	10,000	
Margin of safety as a percentage of sales	29%	(10,000 ÷ 35,000)

Meeting profit objectives

By adding in the final element, desired profits, we can have a comprehensive model to help us with costing and pricing decisions. Supposing in the previous example we knew that we had to make £/$/€10,000 profits to achieve a satisfactory return on the capital invested in the business, we could amend our BEP formula to take account of this objective:

$$\text{BEPP (break-even profit point)} = \frac{\text{Fixed costs} + \text{Profit objective}}{\text{Unit selling price} - \text{Variable costs per unit}}$$

Putting some figures from our last example into this equation, and choosing £/$/€10,000 as our profit objective, we can see how it works. Unfortunately, without further investment in fixed costs, the maximum output in our example is only 7,000 units, so unless we change something the profit objective will not be met.

$$\text{BEPP} = \frac{£/\$/€10,000 + £/\$/€10,000}{£/\$/€5 - £/\$/€3} = \frac{20,000}{2} = 10,000 \text{ units}$$

The great strength of this model is that each element can be changed in turn, on an experimental basis, to arrive at a satisfactory and achievable result. Let us return to this example. We could start our experimenting by seeing what the selling price would have to be to meet our profit objective. In this case we leave the selling price as the unknown, but we have to decide the BEP in advance (you cannot solve a single equation with more than one unknown). It would not be unreasonable to say that we would be prepared to sell our total output to meet the profit objective. So the equation now works out as follows:

$$7,000 = \frac{20,000}{£/\$/€ \text{ Unit selling price} - £/\$/€3}$$

Moving the unknown over to the left-hand side of the equation we get:

$$£/\$/€ \text{ Unit selling price} = £/\$/€3 + \frac{20{,}000}{7{,}000} = £/\$/€3 + 2.86 = £/\$/€5.86$$

We now know that with a maximum capacity of 7,000 units and a profit objective of £/\$/€10,000, we have to sell at £/\$/€5.86 per unit. Now if the market will stand that price, then this is a satisfactory result. If it will not, then we are back to experimenting with the other variables. We must find ways of decreasing the fixed or variable costs, or increasing the output of the plant, by an amount sufficient to meet our profit objective.

Negotiating special deals

Managers are frequently laid open to the temptation of taking a particularly big order at a 'cut-throat' price and it is the MBA's role to make sure that however attractive the proposition may look at first glance, certain conditions must be met before the order can be safely accepted. Let us look at an example – a slight variation on the last one. Your company has a maximum output of 10,000 units, without any major investment in fixed costs. At present you are just not prepared to invest more money until the business has proved itself. The background information is:

Maximum output	10,000 units
Output to meet profit objective	7,000 units
Selling price	£/\$/€5.86
Fixed costs	£/\$/€10,000
Unit variable cost	£/\$/€3.00
Profitability objective	£/\$/€10,000

The break-even chart will look like Figure 1.6.

FIGURE 1.6 Break-even chart for special deals

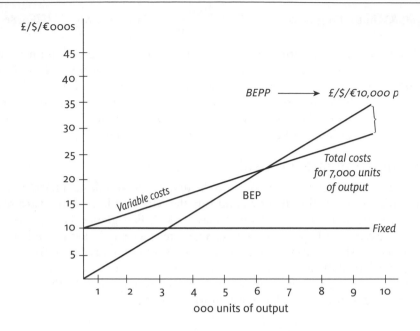

The managers you are advising are fairly confident that they can sell 7,000 units at £/$/€5.86 each, but that still leaves 3,000 units unsold – should they decide to produce them. Out of the blue an enquiry comes in for about 3,000 units, but a strong hint is given that nothing less than a 33 per cent discount will clinch the deal. What should you recommend? Using the costing information assembled so far, you can show the present breakdown of costs and arrive at your selling price.

	£/$/€
Unit cost breakdown	3.00
Variable costs	1.43 (£/$/€10,000 fixed costs ÷ 7,000 units)
Contribution to fixed costs	
Contribution to meet profit objective	1.43 (£/$/€10,000 prof object ÷ 7,000 units)
Selling price	5.86

As all fixed costs are met on the 7,000 units sold (or to be sold), the remaining units can be sold at a price that covers both variable costs and the profitability contribution, so you can negotiate at the same level of profitability, down to £/$/€4.43, just under 25 per cent off the current selling price. However, any selling price above the £/$/€3.00 variable cost will generate extra profits, but these sales will be at the expense of your profit margin. A lower profit margin in itself is not necessarily a bad thing if it results in a higher return on capital employed, but first you must do the sums. There is a great danger with negotiating orders at marginal costs, as these costs are called, in that you do not achieve your break-even point and so perpetuate losses.

Dealing with multiple products and services

The examples used to illustrate the break-even profit point model were fairly simple. Few if any businesses sell only one product or service, so a more general equation may be more useful to deal with real world situations.

In such a business, to calculate your break-even point you must first establish your gross profit. This is calculated by deducting the money paid out to suppliers from the money received from customers. For example, if you are aiming for a 40 per cent gross profit, expressed in decimals as 0.4, your fixed costs are £/$/€10,000 and your overall profit objective is £/$/€4,000, then the sum will be as follows:

$$\text{BEPP} = \frac{10,000 + 4,000}{0.4} = \frac{14,000}{0.4} = £/\$/€35,000$$

So, to reach the target you must achieve a £/$/€35,000 turnover. (You can check this out for yourself: look back to the previous example where the BEPP was 7,000 units and the selling price was £/$/€5 each. Multiplying those figures out gives a turnover of £/$/€35,000. The gross profit in that example was 2/5, or 40 per cent, also.)

02

Finance

- Where business gets its money
- The difference between debt and shareholders' investment
- Understanding the role of private equity
- Floating on a stock market
- Calculating the cost of capital
- Budgeting for the future

The dividing line between accounting and finance is blurred. In basic terms accounting is considered to be everything concerned with the process of recording financial events and ensuring that such recordings are in compliance with the prevailing rules. Finance is the area concerned with where the money to run a business actually comes from in order to be accounted for. In order to be able to understand and interpret the accounts using such tools as ratios you need a reasonable grasp of both these areas, though the ratios themselves are generally considered to be in the accounting domain. In this book the accounting and finance chapters have been placed next to each other to eliminate the need for debate on boundaries.

In many business schools you will find an array of options in addition to the core elements of this discipline. At the London Business School, for example, you will find asset pricing, corporate finance, hedge funds, corporate governance, investments, mergers and acquisitions, capital markets and international finance on the menu. Members of the Finance Group also run the BNP Paribas Hedge Fund Centre, the Centre for Corporate Governance, the Private Equity Institute and the London Share Price Database. At Cass Business School, City of London, you will find options on behavioural finance, dealing with financial crime, and derivatives. In this chapter there is all that you would find in the core teaching that you need to understand and sufficient to move on to more esoteric aspects of finance should the need ever arise.

Sources of funds

There are many sources of funds available to businesses; however, not all of them are equally appropriate to all businesses at all times. These different sources of finance carry very different obligations, responsibilities and opportunities for profitable business. Having some appreciation of these differences will enable managers and directors to make an informed choice.

Most businesses initially, and often until they go public, floating their shares on a stock market, confine their financial strategy to bank loans, either long term or short term, viewing the other financing methods as either too complex or too risky. In many respects the reverse is true. Almost every finance source other than banks will to a greater or lesser extent share some of the risks of doing business with the recipient of the funds.

Debt vs equity

Despite the esoteric names – debentures, convertible loan stock, preference shares – businesses have access to only two fundamentally different sorts of money. Equity, or owner's capital, including retained earnings, is money that is not a risk to the business. If no profits are made, then the owner and other shareholders simply do not get dividends. They may not be pleased, but they cannot usually sue, and even where they can sue, the advisers who recommended the share purchase will be first in line.

Debt capital is money borrowed by the business from outside sources; it puts the business at financial risk and is also risky for the lenders. In return for taking that risk they expect an interest payment every year, irrespective of the performance of the business. High gearing is the name given when a business has a high proportion of outside money to inside money. High gearing has considerable attractions to a business that wants to make high returns on shareholders' capital.

Figure 2.1 shows the funding appetite of various sources of funds. VCs, business angels and indeed any source of share capital will only be attracted to propositions that combine high growth potential with a high risk/reward potential. Banks and other lenders will be attracted to almost the opposite profile, looking instead to a stable less risky proposition that at least offers some security to the capital sum they are putting up.

How gearing works

Table 2.1 shows an example of a business that is assumed to need $/£/€60,000 capital to generate $/£/€10,000 operating profits. Four different capital structures are considered. They range from all share capital (no gearing) at one end to nearly all loan capital at the other. The loan capital has to be 'serviced',

FIGURE 2.1   Funding appetite

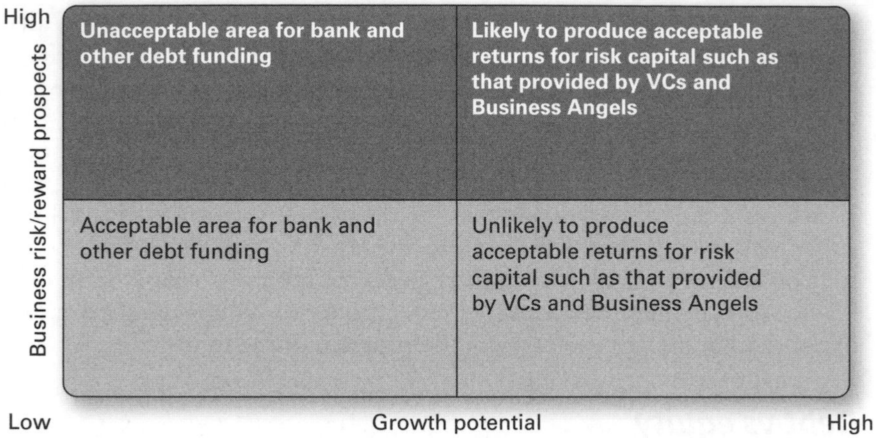

High	Unacceptable area for bank and other debt funding	Likely to produce acceptable returns for risk capital such as that provided by VCs and Business Angels
Business risk/reward prospects	Acceptable area for bank and other debt funding	Unlikely to produce acceptable returns for risk capital such as that provided by VCs and Business Angels
Low	Growth potential	High

TABLE 2.1   The effect of gearing on shareholders' returns

Capital structure	No gearing N/A $/£/€	Average gearing 1:1 $/£/€	High gearing 2:1 $/£/€	Very high gearing 3:1 $/£/€
Share capital	60,000	30,000	20,000	15,000
Loan capital (at 12%)	–	30,000	40,000	45,000
Total capital	60,000	60,000	60,000	60,000
Profits				
Operating profit	10,000	10,000	10,000	10,000
Less interest on loan	None	3,600	4,800	5,400
Net profit	10,000	6,400	5,200	4,600
Return on share capital =	10,000	6,400	5,200	4,400
	60,000	30,000	20,000	15,000
=	16.6%	21.3%	26%	30.7%
Times interest earned =	N/A	10,000	10,000	10,000
		3,600	4,800	5,400
=	N/A	2.8 times	2.1 times	1.8 times

that is, interest of 12 per cent has to be paid. The loan itself can be relatively indefinite, simply being replaced by another one at market interest rates when the first loan expires.

Following the tables through, you can see that return on the shareholders' money (arrived at by dividing the profit by the shareholders' investment and multiplying by 100 to get a percentage) grows from 16.6 to 30.7 per cent by virtue of the changed gearing. If the interest on the loan were lower, the ROSC, the term used to describe return on shareholders' capital, would be even more improved by high gearing, and the higher the interest, the lower the relative improvement in ROSC. So in times of low interest, businesses tend to go for increased borrowings rather than raising more equity, that is, money from shareholders.

At first sight this looks like a perpetual profit-growth machine. Naturally, shareholders and those managing a business whose bonus depends on shareholders' returns would rather have someone else 'lend' them the money for the business than ask shareholders for more money, especially if by doing so they increase the return on investment. The problem comes if the business does not produce $/£/€10,000 operating profits. Very often a drop in sales of 20 per cent means profits are halved. If profits were halved in this example, the business could not meet the interest payments on its loan. That would make the business insolvent, and so not in a 'sound financial position'; in other words, failing to meet one of the two primary business objectives.

Bankers tend to favour 1:1 gearing as the maximum for a business, although they have been known to go much higher. As well as looking at the gearing, lenders will study the business's capacity to pay interest. They do this by using another ratio called 'times interest earned'. This is calculated by dividing the operating profit by the loan interest. It shows how many times the loan interest is covered, and gives the lender some idea of the safety margin. The ratio for this example is given at the end of Table 2.1. Once again rules are hard to make, but much less than 3× interest earned is unlikely to give lenders confidence. (See Chapter 1 for a comprehensive explanation of the use of ratios.)

Borrowed money

Towards the lower-risk end of the financing spectrum are the various organizations that lend money to businesses. They all try hard to take little or no risk, but expect some reward irrespective of performance. They want interest payments on money lent, usually from day one, though sometimes they are content to roll interest payments up until some future date. While they hope the management is competent, they are more interested in securing a charge against any assets the business or its managers may own. At the end of the day they want all their money back. It would be more prudent to think of these organizations as people who will help you turn a proportion of an illiquid asset, such as property, stock in trade or customers who have not yet paid up, into a more liquid asset such as cash, but of course at some discount.

Any decisions about gearing levels have to be taken with the level of business risk involved. Certain categories of venture are intrinsically more risky than others. Businesses selling staple food products where little innovation is required are generally less prone to face financial difficulties than, say, internet start-ups, where the technology may be unproven with a short shelf life and the markets themselves uncertain. See Figure 2.2 below.

FIGURE 2.2   Risk and gearing

Prudent	**Very dangerous under most circumstances**
Prudent, perhaps too much so as missing opportunity to improve shareholder returns	Risky, but acceptable under all but worst of economic circumstances – eg a credit crunch

Business risk — High / Low

Gearing level — Low ... High

Banks

Banks are the principal, and frequently the only, source of finance for 9 out of every 10 unquoted businesses. Firms around the world rely on banks for their funding. In the UK, for example, they have borrowed nearly £55 ($86/€62) billion from the banks, a substantial rise over the past few years. When this figure is compared with the £48 ($75/€54) billion that firms have on deposit at any one time, the net amount borrowed is around £7 billion.

Bankers, and indeed any other sources of debt capital, are looking for asset security to back their loan and provide a near-certainty of getting their money back. They will also charge an interest rate that reflects current market conditions and their view of the risk level of the proposal; usually anything from 0.25 per cent to upwards of 3 or 4 per cent for more risky or smaller firms.

Bankers like to speak of the 'five Cs' of credit analysis, factors they look at when they evaluate a loan request. When applying to a bank for a loan, be prepared to address the following points:

- Character: Bankers lend money to borrowers who appear honest and who have a good credit history. Before you apply for a loan, it makes sense to obtain a copy of your credit report and clean up any problems.

- Capacity: This is a prediction of the borrower's ability to repay the loan. For a new business, bankers look at the business plan. For an existing business, bankers consider financial statements and industry trends.

- Collateral: Bankers generally want a borrower to pledge an asset that can be sold to pay off the loan if the borrower lacks funds.

- Capital: Bankers scrutinize a borrower's net worth, the amount by which assets exceed debts.

- Conditions: Whether bankers give a loan can be influenced by the current economic climate as well as by the amount.

Types of bank funding

Banks usually offer three types of loan:

- Overdrafts: Though technically short-term money as they can be called in at a moment's notice, these tend to form a part of the permanent capital of a business, albeit a fluctuating one.
- Term loans: Offered for set periods.
- Government-backed loans: These are available to some types of business, usually small or new ventures, where the banker's normal criteria might not be met, but the government would like to encourage the sector.

Overdrafts/notes payable

The principal form of short-term bank funding is an overdraft, secured by a charge over the assets of the business. A little over a quarter of all bank finance for small firms is in the form of an overdraft. If you are starting out in a contract cleaning business, say, with a major contract, you need sufficient funds initially to buy the mop and bucket. Three months into the contract they will have been paid for, and so there is no point in getting a five-year bank loan to cover this, as within a year you will have cash in the bank and a loan with an early redemption penalty!

However, if your bank account does not get out of the red at any stage during the year, you will need to re-examine your financing. All too often companies utilize an overdraft to acquire long-term assets, and that overdraft never seems to disappear, eventually constraining the business.

The attraction of overdrafts is that they are very easy to arrange and take little time to set up. That is also their inherent weakness. The key words in the arrangement document are 'repayable on demand', which leaves the bank free to make and change the rules as it sees fit. (This term is under constant review, and some banks may remove it from the arrangement.) With other forms of borrowing, as long as you stick to the terms and conditions, the loan is yours for the duration. It is not so with overdrafts.

Term loans

Term loans, as long-term bank borrowings are generally known, are funds provided by a bank for a number of years.

The interest can either be variable, changing with general interest rates, or fixed for a number of years ahead. The proportion of fixed-rate loans has increased from a third of all term loans to around one in two. In some cases it may be possible to move between having a fixed interest rate and a variable one at certain intervals. It may even be possible to have a moratorium on interest payments for a short period, to give the business some breathing space. Provided the conditions of the loan are met in such matters as repayment, interest and security cover, the money is available for the period of the loan. Unlike in the case of an overdraft, the bank cannot pull the rug from under you if circumstances (or the local manager) change.

Just over a third of all term loans are for periods greater than 10 years, and a quarter are for 3 years or less.

Government Loan Guarantee Schemes

Banks operate loan guarantees at the instigation of governments in the United Kingdom, and in Australia, the United States and elsewhere. These schemes guarantee loans from banks and other financial institutions for small businesses with viable business proposals that have tried and failed to obtain a conventional loan because of a lack of security.

The Enterprise Finance Guarantee Scheme operated by the banks at the behest of the UK government is typical of such interventions. This is aimed at businesses with a turnover up to £25 million with viable business proposals that have tried and failed to obtain a conventional loan because of a lack of security. Loans are available for periods between two and 10 years on sums from £1,000 ($1,500/€1,126) to £1 ($1.5/€1.1) million.

The government guarantees 75 per cent of the loan. In return for the guarantee, the borrower pays a premium of 1–2 per cent per year on the outstanding amount of the loan. The commercial aspects of the loan are matters between the borrower and the lender. You can find out more about the details of the scheme on the Business Link website (**www.businesslink. gov.uk** > Finance and grants > Borrowing > Loans and overdrafts > Enterprise Finance Guarantee).

Bonds, debentures and mortgages

Bonds, debentures and mortgages are all kinds of borrowing with different rights and obligations for the parties concerned. For a business a mortgage is much the same as for an individual. The loan is for a specific event: buying a particular property asset such as a factory, office or warehouse. Interest is payable and the loan itself is secured against the property, so should the business fail the mortgage can substantially be redeemed.

Companies wanting to raise funds for general business purposes, rather than as with a mortgage where a particular property is being bought, issue debentures or bonds. These run for a number of years, typically three years and upwards, with the bond or debenture holder receiving interest over the life of the loan with the capital returned at the end of the period.

The key difference between debentures and bonds lies in their security and ranking. Debentures are unsecured and so in the event of the company being unable to pay interest or repay loans they may well get little or nothing back. Bonds are secured against specific assets and so rank ahead of debentures for any payout.

Unlike bank loans, which are usually held by the issuing bank, though even that assumption is being challenged by the escalation of securitization of debt being packaged up and sold on, bonds and debentures are sold to the public in much the same way as shares. The interest demanded will be a factor of the prevailing market conditions and the financial strength of the borrower.

Categories of bond

There are several general categories of bond that companies can tap into:

- Standard bonds pay interest, a coupon, half-yearly on the principal amount, known as the face or par value. At the maturity date the principal is repaid. The value of bonds fluctuates dependent on market conditions, the length of time to maturity and the likelihood of the borrower defaulting. None of these matters are of immediate concern to the recipient of the funds, as long as they can service the interest. The risk is for the bondholder who can see the value of their investment alter over time.

- Zero coupon bonds pay no interest over their life but pay a lump sum at maturity equivalent to the value of the interest such an investment would normally bear. The buyer of the bond receives a return by the gradual appreciation of the bond's price in the marketplace. This could be an attractive financing strategy for a business making an investment which itself will not bear fruit for a number of years.

- Junk bonds are bonds usually subordinated to, that is, put below others in the pecking order of who gets paid in tough times, other regular bonds. Such bonds carry a higher interest burden.

- Callable bonds are used when an issuer wants to retain the option to buy back their bonds from the public if general interest rates fall sharply after the issue date. The issuer notifies bondholders that after a certain date no further interest will be paid, leaving the holders with no reason to keep the bond. The company issuing the bond can then go out to the market and launch a new bond at a lower rate of interest and so lower its cost of capital. This process is also known as refinancing.

Asset-backed financiers

The banks are more covert when it comes to looking for security for money lent. Two other major sources of funds are less circumspect; indeed their whole prospectus is predicated on a precise relationship between what a business has or will shortly have by way of assets, and what they are prepared to advance. Both groups play an important role in financing growing businesses.

Leasing companies

Physical assets such as cars, vans, computers, office equipment and the like can usually be financed by leasing them, rather as a house or flat may be rented. Alternatively, they can be bought on hire purchase. This leaves other funds free to cover the less tangible elements in your cash flow.

Leasing is a way of getting the use of vehicles, plant and equipment without paying the full cost all at once. Operating leases are taken out where you will use the equipment (for example a car, photocopier, vending machine or kitchen equipment) for less than its full economic life. The lessor takes the risk of the equipment becoming obsolete, and assumes responsibility for repairs, maintenance and insurance. As you, the lessee, are paying for this service, it is more expensive than a finance lease, where you lease the equipment for most of its economic life and maintain and insure it yourself. Leases can normally be extended, often for fairly nominal sums, in the latter years.

Hire purchase differs from leasing in that you have the option to eventually become the owner of the asset, after a series of payments. You can find a leasing company via The Finance and Leasing Association (**www.fla.org** > For Businesses > Business Finance Directory), which gives details of all UK-based businesses offering this type of finance. The website also has general information on terms of trade and code of conduct.

Discounting and factoring

Customers often take time to pay up. In the meantime you have to pay those who work for you and your less patient suppliers. So, the more you grow, the more funds you need. It is often possible to 'factor' your creditworthy customers' bills to a financial institution, receiving some of the funds as your goods leave the door, hence speeding up cash flow.

Factoring is generally only available to a business that invoices other business customers, either in its home market or internationally, for its services. Factoring can be made available to new businesses, although its services are usually of most value during the early stages of growth. It is an arrangement that allows you to receive up to 80 per cent of the cash due from your customers more quickly than they would normally pay. The factoring company in effect buys your trade debts, and can also provide a debtor accounting and administration service. You will, of course, have to pay for factoring services. Having the cash before your customers pay will cost you a little more than normal overdraft rates. The factoring service will cost between 0.5 and 3.5 per cent of the turnover, depending on volume of work, the number of debtors, average invoice amount and other related factors. You can get up to 80 per cent of the value of your invoice in advance, with the remainder paid when your customer settles up, less the various charges just mentioned.

If you sell direct to the public, sell complex and expensive capital equipment, or expect progress payments on long-term projects, then factoring is not for you. If you are expanding more rapidly than other sources of finance will allow, this may be a useful service that is worth exploring.

Invoice discounting is a variation on the same theme where you are responsible for collecting the money from debtors; this is not a service available to new or very small businesses. You can find an invoice discounter or factor through The Asset Based Finance Association (**www.thefda.org.uk/public/membersList.asp**), the association representing the UK's 41 factoring and invoice discounting businesses.

Equity

Businesses operating as a limited company or limited partnership have a potentially valuable opportunity to raise relatively risk-free money. It is risk-free to the business but risky, sometimes extremely so, to anyone investing. Essentially this type of capital, known collectively as equity, consists of the issued share capital and reserves of various kinds. It represents the amount of money that shareholders have invested directly into the company by buying shares, together with retained profits that belong to shareholders but which the company uses as additional capital. As with debt, equity comes in a number of different forms with differing rights and privileges.

Ordinary shares form the bulk of the shares issued by most companies and are the shares that carry the ordinary risks associated with being in business. All the profits of the business, including past retained profits, belong to the ordinary shareholders once any preference share dividends have been deducted. Ordinary shares have no fixed rate of dividend; indeed over half the companies listed on US stock markets pay no or virtually no dividend. These include high-growth companies such as Google and Microsoft, which argue that by retaining and reinvesting all their profits they can create better value for shareholders than by distributing dividends. A company does not have to issue all its share capital at once. The total amount it is authorized to issue must be shown somewhere in the accounts, but only the issued share capital is counted in the balance sheet. Although shares can be partly paid, this is a rare occurrence.

Preference shares get their name for two reasons. First, they receive their fixed rate of dividend before ordinary shareholders. Second, in the event of a winding up of the company, any funds remaining go to repay preference share capital before any ordinary share capital. In a forced liquidation this may be of little comfort, as shareholders of any type come last in the queue after all other claims from creditors have been met.

Class A and Class B shares are cases where categories of shareholder are singled out for more or less favourable treatment. For example, class A shares are often given up to five votes per share, while class B gets one. In extreme cases class B shareholders can get no votes at all. Companies will often try to disguise the disadvantages associated with owning shares with fewer voting rights by naming those shares. One of the most famous examples was their use by the Savoy Hotel Group to ward off an unwanted takeover by Trusthouse Forte. While Trusthouse was able to buy 70 per cent of Savoy shares on the open market, they could secure only 42 per cent of the voting rights as they were only able to buy class B shares, the A shares being in the hands of the Savoy family and allies.

Reserves, a typically misleading term in all accounting, means profits of various kinds that have been retained in the company as extra capital. Also important is what the term reserves does not mean. It does not mean actual money held back in reserve in bank accounts or elsewhere. Reserves come from retained profits over many years but are reinvested in buildings, equipment, stocks or company debts, just like any other source of capital, and are rarely held in cash.

The main categories of reserves are as follows:

- Profit and loss account, ie cumulative retained profits from ordinary trading activities.
- Revaluation reserves, being the paper-profit that can arise if certain assets are revalued to current price levels without the assets concerned being sold.
- Share premium account, ie the excess over the original par value of a share when new shares are offered for sale at an enhanced price. Only the original par value is ever shown as issued share capital.

Sources of equity capital

There are two broad sources of equity: private equity, usually put in by individuals or small groups of individuals who for hopefully the prospects of greater returns will take on greater risks; or public capital through a share issue on a stock market.

Private equity

There are three main sources of private equity: business angels, venture capital firms and corporate venture funding.

Business angels

One likely first source of equity or risk capital will be a private individual with his or her own funds, and perhaps some knowledge of your type of business. In return for a share in the business, such investors will put in money at their own risk. They have been christened 'business angels', a term first coined to describe private wealthy individuals who back a play on Broadway or in London's West End.

Most angels are determined upon some involvement beyond merely signing a cheque and may hope to play a part in your business in some way. They are hoping for big rewards – one angel who backed Sage with £10,000 ($15,700/€11,230) in its first round of £250,000 ($392,000/€280,800) financing saw his stake rise to £40 ($63/€45) million.

These angels frequently operate through managed networks, usually on the internet. In the UK and the United States there are hundreds of networks, with tens of thousands of business angels prepared to put up several billion pounds each year into new or small businesses.

Finding a business angel The World Business Angels Association (**www.wbaa.biz/Directory.html**) provides links to Angels and Angel Associations around the globe. The British Business Angels Association (**www.bbaa.org.uk**) has an online directory of UK business angels. The European Business Angels Network (eban) has directories of national business angel associations both inside and outside of Europe at (**www.eban.org** > Members) from which you can find individual business angels.

Venture capital

Venture capital (VC) providers are investing other people's money, often from pension funds. They have a different agenda from that of business angels, and are more likely to be interested in investing more money for a larger stake.

In general, VCs expect their investment to have paid off within seven years, but they are hardened realists. Two in every 10 investments they make are total write-offs, and six perform averagely well at best. So, the one star in every 10 investments they make has to cover a lot of duds. VCs have a target rate of return of 30 per cent plus, to cover this poor hit rate.

Raising venture capital is not a cheap option and deals are not quick to arrange either. Six months is not unusual, and over a year has been known. Every VC has a deal done in six weeks in its portfolio, but that truly is the exception.

Finding venture capital The British Venture Capital Association (**www.bvca.co.uk**) and the European Venture Capital Association (**www.evca.com**) both have online directories giving details of hundreds of venture capital providers. Ernst & Young (**www.ey.com**/GL/en/Services/Strategic-Growth-Markets) provide an overview of the risk capital market on this website. The National Venture Capital Association in the United States has directories of international venture capital associations both inside and outside the United States (**www.nvca.org** > Resources).

You can see how those negotiating with or receiving venture capital rate the firm in question at The Funded website (**www.thefunded.com**) in terms of the deal offered, the firm's apparent competence and how good they are managing the relationship. There is also a link to the VC's website. The Funded has 2,500 members.

Corporate venturing

Venture capital firms often get their hands dirty taking a hand in the management of the businesses they invest in. Another type of business is also in the risk capital business, without it necessarily being their main line of business. These firms, known as corporate venturers, usually want an inside track to new developments in and around the edges of their own fields of interest. For example, Microsoft, Cisco and Apple have billions of dollars invested in hundreds of small entrepreneurial firms, taking stakes from a few hundred thousand dollars up to hundreds of million.

And it's not just high-tech business that takes this approach. McDonald's held a 33 per cent stake in Prêt à Manger while it worked out where to take its business after saturating the burger market. HM Revenue and Customs (**www.hmrc.gov.uk/guidance/cvs.htm**) has a useful guide entitled 'The Corporate Venturing Scheme', explaining the scheme, tax implications and sources of further information.

Private capital preliminaries

Two important stages will be gone through before a private investor will put cash into a business. The emphasis put on these stages will vary according to the complexity of the deal, the amount of money and the legal ownership of the funds concerned. For example, a business angel investing on their own account can accept greater uncertainty than, say, a venture capital fund using a pension fund's money.

Due diligence Usually, after a private equity firm signs a letter of intent to provide capital and you accept, it will conduct a due diligence investigation of both the management and the company. During this period the private equity firm will have access to all financial and other records, facilities, employees etc to investigate before finalizing the deal. The material to be examined will include copies of all leases, contracts and loan agreements in addition to copious financial records and statements. It will want to see any management reports, such as sales reports, inventory records, detailed lists of assets, facility maintenance records, aged receivables and payables reports, employee organization charts, payroll and benefits records, customer records and marketing materials. It will want to know about any pending litigation, tax audits or insurance disputes. Depending on the nature of the business, it might also consider getting an environmental audit and an insurance check-up. The sting in the due diligence tail is that the current owners of the business will be required to personally warrant that everything they have said or revealed is both true and complete. In the event that proves not to be so, they will be personally liable to the extent of any loss incurred by those buying the shares.

Term sheet A term sheet is a funding offer from a capital provider. It lays out the amount of an investment and the conditions under which the new investors expect the business owners to work using their money.

The first page of the term sheet states the amount offered and the form of the funds (a bond, common stock, preferred stock, a promissory note or a combination of these). A price, either per $/£/€1,000 unit of debt or per share of stock, is quoted to set the cost basis for investors 'getting in' on your company. Later that starting price will be very important in deciding capital gains and any taxes due at acquisition, IPO (initial public offering) or shares/ units transferred.

Another key component of the term sheet is the 'post-closing capitalization'. That is the proposed cash value of the venture on the day the terms are accepted. For example, investors may offer $/£/€500,000 in Series A preferred stock at 50 pence per share (1 million shares) with a post-closing cap of $/£/€2 million. This translates into a 25 per cent ownership stake in the firm ($/£/€500,000 divided by $/£/€2 million).

The next section of the term sheet is typically a table that summarizes the capital structure of your company. Investors generally start with preferred stock in order to gain a priority of distribution, should the enterprise fail and the liquidation of assets occur. The typical way to handle this is to have the preferred stock be convertible into common stock on a 1 : 1 ratio at the investors' option, such that the preferred position is essentially a common stock position, but with priority of repayment over the founders' own common-stock position.

Other terms included on the sheet could cover rents, equipment, levels of debt vs equity, minimum and maximum time periods associated with the transfer of shares, vesting in additional shares, and option periods for making subsequent investments and having 'right of first refusal' when other rounds of funding are sought in the future.

Public capital

Stock markets are the place where serious businesses raise serious money. It's possible to raise anything from a few million to tens of billions; expect the costs and efforts in getting listed to match those stellar figures. The basic idea is that owners sell shares in their businesses that in effect bring in a whole raft of new 'owners' who in turn have a stake in the businesses' future profits. When they want out, they sell their shares on to other investors. The share price moves up and down to ensure that there are as many buyers as sellers at any one time.

Going public also puts a stamp of respectability on you and your company. It will enhance the status and credibility of your business, and it will enable you to borrow more against the 'security' provided by your new shareholders, should you so wish. Your shares will also provide an attractive way to retain and motivate key staff. If they are given, or rather are allowed to earn, share options at discounted prices, they too can participate in the capital gains you are making. With a public share listing you can now join in the takeover and asset-stripping game. When your share price is high and things are going well you can look out for weaker firms to gobble up – and all you have to do is to offer them more of your shares in return for theirs. You do not even have to find real money. But of course this is a two-sided game and you also may now become the target of a hostile bid.

You may find that being in the public eye not only cramps your style but fills up your engagement diary too. Most CEOs of public companies find that they have to spend up to a quarter of their time 'in the City' explaining their strategies, in the months preceding and the first years following their going public. It is not unusual for so much management time to have been devoted to answering accountants' and stockbrokers' questions that there is not enough time to run the day-to-day business, and profits drop as a direct consequence.

The City also creates its own 'pressure' both to seduce companies onto the market and then by expecting them to perform beyond any reasonable expectation. There have been a number of high-profile examples of companies that have floated their shares on a stock market then changed their minds and withdrawn, buying out all outside shareholders. The rationale for taking a company private is that the buyer feels that they can run the company better without the need to justify their decisions to other shareholders, or the complex and burdensome regulations that public companies must comply with.

The Saga saga

The name that is synonymous with providing holidays exclusively for the over-50s is undoubtedly Saga's. Reporting its first results under the ownership of Acromas Holdings in 2009 it reported strong growth despite difficult trading conditions. The business, started in 1951 with the daunting name of 'Old People's Travel Bureau', was an experiment by Folkestone hotelier Sidney De Haan. He believed that older holidaymakers would appreciate a quieter off-season break by the sea, charging just £6.10s ($9.6/€6.9), including travel, full board and three excursions. Over the next decade the company chartered trains, planes and finally bought its own charter boat, the *Saga Rose*. Along the way it launched a magazine, insurance business and a clutch of FM radio stations. Over a third of the UK's over-50s are on Saga's database, which holds 7 million individuals of whom over 2 million actively buy from Saga each year. By January 2010 the company was making around £200 ($314/€225) million in profits and employing some 4,000 people worldwide.

The company's financing history has been something of a rollercoaster. Initially financed using family money and bank debt, the firm was floated on the stock market in 1978. Saga was not a hit with investors though, partly because of the weakening UK holiday market. The De Haan family took the group private in 1990, buying out all the other investors. By 2004 the company was preparing to go back onto the stock market when the private equity firm, Charterhouse Capital Partners, paid £1.35 ($2.12/€1.52) billion to take control of the group and they pulled their IPO at the last minute. The acquisition was by way of a buyout, with Charterhouse taking an 80 per cent stake and the management the remainder. Charterhouse funded the acquisition of Saga with £500 ($784/€562) million of equity. The remainder was funded with debt, which it has since refinanced.

In January 2007, just three years later, the company, then thought to be worth between £2.5 ($9.64/€6.9) billion and £3 ($4.7/€3.4) billion, was again exploring its financing strategy. A sale or flotation could value the 20 per cent stake held by staff and senior management at £500 ($784/€562) million, with the 8 per cent stake of Andrew Goodsell, Saga's chief executive, worth about £200 million. Mr Goodsell stated, 'We've smashed through all of our plans, repaid large amounts of debt and [Charterhouse] has achieved what it wanted to achieve.' Once again stock-market flotation was on the cards, but a very different opportunity emerged. In June 2007 Permira and CVC, the two private equity firms that owned the bulk of the AA, approached Saga's majority owner, Charterhouse, to ask it to consider a merger. The result was a £6.15 ($9.64/€6.9) billion surprise move that created one of the country's largest private-equity-backed companies.

Initial public offer (IPO) – criteria for getting a stock market listing

The rules vary from market to market but these are the conditions that are likely to apply to get a company listed on an exchange:

1 Getting listed on a major stock exchange calls for a track record of making substantial profits with decent seven-figure sums being made in the year you plan to float, as this process is known. A listing also calls for a large proportion, usually at least 25 per cent, of the company's shares to be put up for sale at the outset. In addition, you would be expected to have 100 shareholders now and be able to demonstrate that 100 more will come on board as a result of the listing.

2 As you draw up your flotation plan and timetable you should have the following matters in mind:

   – Advisers: You will need to be supported by a team which will include a sponsor, stockbroker, reporting accountant and solicitor. These should be respected firms, active in flotation work and familiar with the company's type of business. You and your company may be judged by the company you keep, so choose advisers of good repute and make sure that the personalities work effectively together. It is very unlikely that a small local firm of accountants, however satisfactory, will be up to this task.

   – Sponsor: You will need to appoint a financial institution, usually a merchant banker, to fill this important role. If you do not already have a merchant bank in mind, your accountant will offer guidance. The job of the sponsor is to coordinate and drive the project forward.

   – Timetable: It is essential to have a timetable for the final months during the run-up to a float – and to adhere to it. The company's directors and senior staff will be fully occupied in providing information and attending meetings. They will have to delegate and there must be sufficient backup support to ensure that the business does not suffer.

   – Management team: A potential investor will want to be satisfied that your company is well managed, at board level and below. It is important to ensure succession, perhaps by offering key directors and managers service agreements and share options. It is wise to draw on the experience of well-qualified non-executive directors.

   – Accounts: The objective is to have a profit record which is rising but, in achieving this, you will need to take into account directors' remuneration, pension contributions and the elimination of any expenditure which might be acceptable in a privately owned company but would not be acceptable in a public company, namely excessive perks such as yachts, luxury cars, lavish expense accounts and holiday homes.

     Accounts must be consolidated and audited to appropriate accounting standards and the audit reports must not contain any major qualifications. The auditors will need to be satisfied that there are proper stock records and a consistent basis of valuing stock during the years prior to flotation. Accounts for the last three years will need to be disclosed and the date of the last accounts must be within six months of the issue.

AIM

London's Alternative Investment Market (AIM) was formed in the mid-to-late 1990s specifically to provide risk capital for new rather than established ventures. AIM raised £15.7bn in 2007 – a 76 per cent leap from the previous year – and a record number of companies floated on the exchange, bringing the total to 1,634.

AIM is particularly attractive to any dynamic company of any size, age or business sector that has rapid growth in mind. The smallest firm on AIM entered at under £1 million capitalization and the largest at over £500 million. The formalities are minimal, but the costs of entry are high and you must have a nominated adviser, such as a major accountancy firm, stockbroker or banker. The survey showed that costs of floating on the junior market is around 6.5 per cent of all funds raised and companies valued at less than £2m can expect to shell out a quarter of funds raised in costs alone. The market is regulated by the London Stock Exchange (**www.londonstockexchange.com** > AIM).

You can check out all the world stock markets from Australia to Zagreb on Stock Exchanges World Wide Links (**www.tdd.lt/slnews/Stock_Exchanges/ Stock.Exchanges.htm**), maintained by Aldas Kirvaitis of Lithuania, and at World Wide Tax.com (**www.worldwide-tax.com** > World Stock Exchanges). Once in the stock exchange website, almost all of which have pages in English, look out for a term such as 'Listing Center', 'Listing' or 'Rules'. There you will find the latest criteria for floating a company on that particular exchange.

PLUS

One rung down from AIM is PLUS-Quoted Market whose roots lie in the market formerly known as Ofex. It began life in November 2004 and was granted Recognised Investment Exchange (RIE) status by the Financial Services Authority (FSA) in 2007. Aimed at smaller companies wanting to raise up to £10 million it draws on a pool of capital primarily from private investors. The market is regulated, but requirements are not as stringent as those of AIM or the main market and the costs of flotation and ongoing costs are lower. Keycom used this market to raise £4.4 million in September 2008 to buy out a competitor to give them a combined contract to provide broadband access to 40,000 student rooms in UK universities. There are 174 companies quoted on PLUS with a combined market capitalization of £2.3 billion. Even in 2009/10, a particularly bad period for stock market activity, 30 companies applied for entry to PLUS and 18 were admitted. You can find out more about PLUS at **www.plusmarketsgroup.com**.

Share buyback

Companies can buy back their shares, which reduces the number of shares outstanding, giving each remaining shareholder a larger percentage ownership of the company. This is usually considered a sign that the company's management believes its share price is undervalued. Other reasons for buybacks include putting unused cash to use, raising earnings per share and obtaining stock for employee stock option plans or pension plans.

Hybrids

A number of financing methods straddle the debt and equity boundary. These try to mitigate taking a bit more risk for the potential of a bit more return than would be usual with debt financing. But they also limit the upside that might be expected from pure equity, which would retain all of any increase in value from the outset:

- Convertible preference shares operate like preference shares, in that their holders rank before ordinary shareholders for dividend payment, or return of funds in the case of failure. They also have the option, at some specified date in the future, to convert to ordinary shares and so enjoy all of any increase in value.
- Mezzanine finance has one or all of these characteristics: it ranks after other forms of debt, but before equity, for any payout in the event of a business failing; it pays higher, often significantly higher, interest than other debt; it can be held for up to 10 years; it can be converted into ordinary shares. It is popular with VCs for management buyouts.

Grants

Government agencies at both national and local government level as well as some extra-governmental bodies such as the EU offer grants, effectively free or nearly free money in return for certain behaviour. It may be to encourage research into a particular field, stimulate innovation or employment or to persuade a company to locate in a particular area. Grants are constantly being introduced (and withdrawn), but there is no system that lets you know automatically. You have to keep yourself informed.

You can find out about International Grants and Funding at Proposalwriter.com (**www.proposalwriter.com/intgrants.html**), as well as advice on writing a proposal.

Business Link (**www.businesslink.gov.uk** > Finance and grants > Grants and government support) has advice on how to apply for a grant as well as a directory of grants on offer. European Union Grant Advisor (**www. eugrantadvisor.com**) has a search facility to help you find which of the

6,000 grants on offer might suit your business needs. Grants.Gov (**www. grants.gov**) is a guide to how to apply for over 1,000 federal government grants in the United States.

Cost of capital

A business needs to keep track of how much it is paying for the capital it uses, as that is the minimum hurdle rate for any investment it may make. Also, it needs to be aware that if new money being raised is more costly than that already in the business, it will only be profitable if it raises the hurdle rate for new projects accordingly.

Cost of debt

This can be very straightforward. If a company takes out a bank loan at a fixed rate of interest of say, 8 per cent, then this is the cost before any tax relief. Taking tax relief at 40 per cent into account, the net cost of debt comes down to 4.8 per cent. In the case of a public offer for bonds or debentures, the rate of interest which has to be paid on new loans to get them taken up by investors at par can be regarded as the cost of borrowed capital.

Cost of equity

Put simply, the cost of equity is the return shareholders expect the company to earn on their money. It is their estimation, often not scientifically calculated, of the rate of return that will be obtained both from future dividends and an increased share value.

Dividend valuation model

One approach to finding the cost of equity is to take the current gross dividend yield for a company and add the expected annual growth.

Example For example, XYZ plc has forecast payment of a gross equivalent dividend of 10p on each ordinary share in the coming year. The company's shares are quoted on the Stock Exchange and currently trade at \$/£/€2.00. Growth of profits and dividends has averaged 15 per cent over the past few years. The cost of equity for XYZ plc can be calculated as:

Cost of equity capital = Current dividend (gross) % + Growth rate %
Current market price = (\$/£/€0.10 × 100) % + 15% = 20% = \$/£/€2

With this method, dividends are assumed to grow in the future at the constant rate achieved by averaging the last few years' performance.

Capital asset pricing model (CAPM)

Before turning to the next method, we need to clarify some aspects of risk. There are two broad types of risk:

- Specific risk: This applies to one particular business. It includes, for example, the risk of losing the chief executive; the risk of someone else bringing out a similar or better product; or the risk of labour problems. Shareholders are expected not to want compensation for this type of risk as it can be diversified away by holding a sufficient number of investments in their portfolios.

- Systematic risk: This derives from global or macroeconomic events that can damage all investments to some extent and therefore holders require compensation for this risk to their wealth. This compensation takes the form of a higher required rate of return.

A slightly more complicated approach to the cost of equity tries to take the systematic risk element into account. It is known as the capital asset pricing model or CAPM for short. Put simply, CAPM states that investors' required rate of return on a share is composed of two parts: a risk-free rate similar to that obtainable on a risk-free investment in short-term government securities; and an additional premium to compensate for the systematic risk involved in investing in shares.

This systematic risk for a company's shares is measured by the size of its beta factor. A beta the size of 1.0 for a company means that its shares have the same systematic risk as the average for the whole market. If the beta is 1.4 then systematic risk for the share is 40 per cent higher than the market average. A company's share beta is applied to the market premium that is obtained from the excess of the return on a market portfolio of shares over the risk-free rate of return. The formula to calculate cost of equity capital using CAPM is:

$$Ke = Rf + B(Rm - Rf)$$

Where: Ke = cost of equity, Rf = risk-free return, Rm = return on market portfolio of shares and B = beta factor.

Example If the risk-free rate of return is 5.5 per cent and the return on a market portfolio is 12 per cent, then for a company with a beta of 0.7 for its ordinary shares calculate its cost of equity.

$$Ke = Rf + B(Rm - Rf)$$
$$= 5.5\% + 0.7(12\% - 5.5\%)$$
$$= 10.05\%$$

Of the two methods described for finding the cost of equity for a company, the latter CAPM method is the more scientific. Ideally, the risk-free and market rates of return should reflect the future, but current rates of return are used as substitutes. Beta factors measure how sensitive each company's share price movements are relative to market movements over a period of a few years.

The weakness of CAPM is that it assumes all investors are rational and well informed, that markets are perfect and that there is an unlimited supply of risk-free money. There are even more complex models for calculating the cost of equity capital, but none are without their critics.

Weighted average cost of capital

Having identified the cost of equity and the cost of borrowed capital (and that of any other long-term source of finance such as hire purchase or mortgages), we need to combine them into one overall cost of capital. This is primarily for use in project appraisals as justification of those that yield a return in excess of their cost of capital.

An average cost is required because we do not usually identify each individual project with one particular source of finance. Because equity and debt capital have very different costs, we would make illogical decisions and accept a project financed by debt capital only to reject a similar project next time round when it was financed by equity capital. Generally businesses take the view that all projects have been financed from a common pool of money except for the relatively rare case when project-specific finance is raised. The weightings used in the calculations should be based on the market value of the securities and not on their book or balance sheet values.

Example Assume your company intends to keep the gearing ratio of borrowed capital to equity in the proportion of 20 : 80. The nominal cost of new capital from these sources has been assessed, say, at 10 per cent and 15 per cent respectively and corporation tax is 30 per cent. The calculation of the overall weighted average cost is as follows:

Type of capital	Proportion (a)	After-tax cost (b)	Weighted cost (a × b)
10% loan capital	0.20	7.0%	1.4%
Equity	0.80	15.0%	12.0%
			13.4%

The resulting weighted average cost of 13.4 per cent is the minimum rate that this company should accept on proposed investments. Any investment that is not expected to achieve this return is not a viable proposition. Risk has been allowed for in the calculation of the beta factor used in the CAPM method of identifying the cost of equity. This relates to the risk of the existing whole business. If a company embarks on a project of significantly different risk, or has a divisional structure of activities of varying risk levels, then a single cost of equity for the whole company is inappropriate. In this situation, the average beta of proxy companies operating in the same field as a division can be used.

Investment decisions

The cost of capital is an important figure as it is in essence the threshold for future investments. Taking the figures shown above, if our weighted average cost of capital is 13.4 per cent then taking on any new activity that makes a lower profit ratio will be lowering the performance, hardly an MBA type of activity.

Investment decisions, where the decisions have cost and revenue implications for years, perhaps even decades, fall into a number of categories:

- Bolt-on investments: These are where an investment will be supporting and enhancing an existing operation. For example, if part of a production process is being slowed down for want of some new equipment to eliminate a bottleneck.

- Standalone single project: This involves a simple accept or reject decision.

- Competing projects: This requires a choice of which produces the best results, either because only one can be pursued or because of limited finance. In the latter case this is described as capital rationing.

CASE STUDY Cobra Beer

In 1990, Cambridge-educated and recently qualified accountant Karan Bilimoria started importing and distributing Cobra beer, a name he chose because it appeared to work well in lots of different languages. He initially supplied his beer to complement Indian restaurant food in the UK. Lord Bilimoria, as he now is, started out with debts of £20,000, but from a small flat in Fulham and with just a Citroen CV by way of assets he has grown his business to sales of over £100 million a year. Three factors have been key to its success. Cobra was originally sold in large 660ml bottles and so were more likely to be shared by diners. Also, as Cobra is less fizzy than European lagers, drinkers are less likely to feel bloated and can eat and drink more. The third factor was Bilimoria's extensive knowledge, through his training as an accountant, of sources of finance for a growing business. He was fortunate in having an old-style bank manager who had such belief in Cobra that he agreed a loan of £30,000, but since then he has had to tap into every possible type of funding (see Figure 2.3), including selling a 28 per cent stake in his firm in 1995.

FIGURE 2.3 Cobra Beer's financing strategy

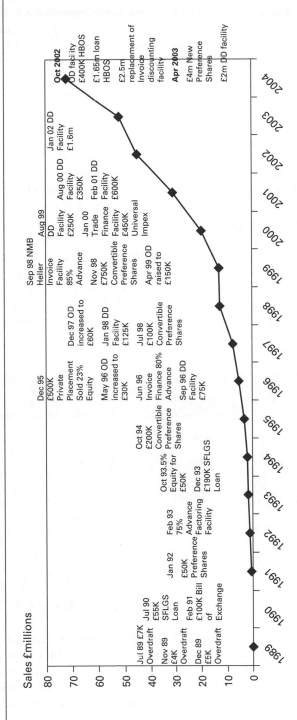

What follows is an examination of the financial aspects of investment decisions. There may well be other strategic reasons for taking investment decisions, including those that might be more important than finance alone. For example, it could be imperative to deny a competitor a particular opportunity; or if part of achieving a national or global strategy calls for disproportionate expenses in one or more areas. However, there are NO circumstances when any investment decision should not be subjected to proper financial appraisal and so at least see the cost of accepting a lower return than required by the cost of capital being used.

Also, it's important to note that any methodology for appraising investments requires that cash is used rather than profits, for reasons that will become apparent as the techniques are explained. Profit is not ignored; it is simply allowed to work its way through in the timing of events.

Payback period

The most popular method for evaluating investment decisions is the payback method. To arrive at the payback period you have to work out how many years it takes to recover your cash investment. Table 2.2 shows two investment projects that require respectively $/£/€20,000 and $/£/€40,000 cash now in order to get a series of cash returns spread over the next five years.

TABLE 2.2   The payback method

	Investment A $/£/€	Investment B $/£/€
Initial cash cost NOW (Year 0)	20,000	40,000
Net cash flows		
Year 1	1,000	10,000
Year 2	4,000	10,000
Year 3	8,000	16,000
Year 4	7,000	4,000
Year 5	5,000	28,000
Total cash in over period	25,000	68,000
Cash surplus	5,000	28,000

Although both propositions call for different amounts of cash to be invested, we can see that both recover all their cash outlays by year 4. So we can say these investments have a four-year payback. But as a matter of fact Investment B produces a much bigger surplus than the other project and it returns half our initial cash outlay in two years. Investment A has returned only a quarter of our cash over that time period.

Payback may be simple, but it is not much use when it comes to dealing with the timing or with comparing different investment amounts.

Discounted cash flow

We know intuitively that getting cash in sooner is better than getting it in later. In other words, a pound received now is worth more than a pound that will arrive in one, two or more years in the future because of what we could do with that money ourselves, or because of what we ourselves have to pay out to have use of that money (see Cost of capital above). To make sound investment decisions we need to ascribe a value to a future stream of earnings to arrive at what is known as the present value. If we know we could earn 20 per cent on any money we have, then the maximum we would be prepared to pay for a pound coming in one year hence would be around 80p. If we were to pay one pound now to get a pound back in a year's time we would in effect be losing money.

The technique used to handle this is known as discounting. The process is termed discounted cash flow (DCF) and the residual discounted cash is called the net present value.

The first column in Table 2.3 shows the simple cash-flow implications of an investment proposition; a surplus of $/£/€5,000 comes after five years from putting $/£/€20,000 into a project. But if we accept the proposition that future cash is worth less than current cash, the only question we need to answer is how much less. If we take our weighted average cost of capital as a sensible starting point, we would select 13.4 per cent as an appropriate

TABLE 2.3 Using discounted cash flow (DCF)

	$/£/€ Cash flow A	Discount factor at 15% B	Discounted cash flow A × B
Initial cash cost NOW (Year 0)	20,000	1.00	20,000
Net cash flows			
Year 1	1,000	0.8695	870
Year 2	4,000	0.7561	3,024
Year 3	8,000	0.6575	5,260
Year 4	7,000	0.5717	4,002
Year 5	5,000	0.4972	2,486
Total	25,000		15,642
Cash surplus	5,000	Net present value	(4,358)

rate at which to discount future cash flows. To keep the numbers simple and to add a small margin of safety, let's assume that 15 per cent is the rate we have selected (this doesn't matter too much, as you will see in the section on internal rate of return).

The formula for calculating what a pound received at some future date is:

$$\text{Present Value (PV)} = \$/€/£P \times 1/(1 + r)^n$$

where $\$/£/€P$ is the initial cash cost, r is the interest rate expressed in decimals and n is the year in which the cash will arrive. So if we decide on a discount rate of 15 per cent, the present value of a pound received in one year's time is:

$$\begin{aligned}\text{Present Value} \\ = \$/€/£1 \times 1/(1 + 0.15)^1 \\ = 0.87 \text{ (rounded to two decimal places)}\end{aligned}$$

So we can see that our $\$/£/€1,000$ arriving at the end of year 1 has a present value of $\$/£/€870$; the $\$/£/€4,000$ in year 2 has a present value of $\$/£/€3,024$ and by year 5 present value reduces cash flows to barely half their original figure. In fact, far from having a real payback in year 4 and generating a cash surplus of $\$/£/€5,000$, this project will make us $\$/£/€4,358$ worse off than we had hoped to be if we required to make a return of 15 per cent. The project, in other words, fails to meet our criteria using DCF but might well have been pursued using payback.

Internal rate of return (IRR)

DCF is a useful starting point but does not give us any definitive information. For example, all we know about the above project is that it doesn't make a return of 15 per cent. In order to know the actual rate of return we need to choose a discount rate that produces a net present value of the entire cash flow of zero, known as the internal rate of return. The maths is time consuming but Solutions Matrix website (**www.solutionmatrix.com**) has a tool for working out payback, discounted cash flow, internal rate of return, and a whole lot more calculations relating to capital budgeting. You have to register on the site first before downloading their free capital budgeting spreadsheet suite and tutorial. From the home page you should click on 'Download Center' and 'Download Financial Metrics Lite for Microsoft Excel'.

Using this spreadsheet you will see that the IRR for the project in question is slightly under 7 per cent, not much better than bank interest and certainly insufficient to warrant taking any risks for.

Budgets and variances

Budgeting is the principal interface between the operating business units and the finance department. As a staff function (see Chapter 4 for more on line and staff functions), the finance department will assist managers in preparing a detailed budget for the year ahead for every area of the organization and is in effect the first year of the business plan. MBAs are invariably expected to play a role in facilitating the process within their departments. Budgets are usually reviewed at least halfway through the year and often quarterly. At that review a further quarter or half year can be added to the budget to maintain a one-year budget horizon. This is known as a 'rolling quarterly (half yearly) budget'.

Budget guidelines

Budgets should adhere to the following general principles:

- The budget must be based on realistic but challenging goals.
  Those goals are arrived at by both a top-down 'aspiration' of senior management and a bottom-up forecast of what the department concerned sees as possible.
- The budget should be prepared by those responsible for delivering the results – the salespeople should prepare the sales budget and the production people the production budget. Senior managers must maintain the communication process so that everyone knows what other parties are planning for.
- Agreement to the budget should be explicit. During the budgeting process, several versions of a particular budget should be discussed. For example, the boss may want a sales figure of $/£/€2 million, but the sales team's initial forecast is for $/£/€1.75 million.
- After some debate, $/£/€1.9 million may be the figure agreed upon. Once a figure is agreed, a virtual contract exists that declares a commitment from employees to achieve the target and commitments from the employer to be satisfied with the target and to supply resources in order to achieve it. It makes sense for this contract to be in writing.
- The budget needs to be finalized at least a month before the start of the year and not weeks or months into the year.
- The budget should undergo fundamental reviews periodically throughout the year to make sure all the basic assumptions that underpin it still hold good.
- Accurate information to review performance against budgets should be available 7 to 10 working days before the month's end.

Variance analysis

Explaining variances is also an MBA-type task so performance needs to be carefully monitored and compared against the budget as the year proceeds, and corrective action must be taken where necessary. This has to be done on a monthly basis (or using shorter time intervals if required), showing both the company's performance during the month in question and throughout the year so far.

Looking at Table 2.4, we can see at a glance that the business is behind on sales for this month, but ahead on the yearly target. The convention is to put all unfavourable variations in brackets. Hence, a higher-than-budgeted sales figure does not have brackets, while a higher materials cost does. We can also see that, while profit is running ahead of budget, the profit margin is slightly behind (−0.30 per cent).

This is partly because other direct costs, such as labour and distribution in this example, are running well ahead of budget.

TABLE 2.4   The fixed budget ($/£/€ooo's)

Heading	Month			Year to date		
	Budget	Actual	Variance	Budget	Actual	Variance
Sales	805	753	(52)	6,358	7,314	956
Materials	627	567	60	4,942	5,704	(762)
Materials margin	178	186	8	1,416	1,610	194
Direct costs	74	79	(5)	595	689	(94)
Gross profit	104	107	3	820	921	101
Percentage	12.92	14.21	1.29	12.90	12.60	(0.30)

Flexing the budget

A budget is based on a particular set of sales goals, few of which are likely to be exactly met in practice. Table 2.4 shows a company that has used $/£/€762,000 more materials than budgeted. As more has been sold, this is hardly surprising. The way to manage this situation is to flex the budget to show what, given the sales that actually occurred, would be expected to happen to expenses. Applying the budget ratios to the actual data does this. For example, materials were planned to be 22.11 per cent of sales in the budget. By applying that to the actual month's sales, a materials cost of $/£/€587,000 is arrived at.

Looking at the flexed budget in Table 2.5, we can see that the company has spent $/£/€19,000 more than expected on the material given the level of sales actually achieved, rather than the $/£/€762,000 overspend shown in the fixed budget.

TABLE 2.5　The flexed budget ($/£/€000's)

Heading	Month			Year to date		
	Budget	Actual	Variance	Budget	Actual	Variance
Sales	753	753	–	7,314	7,314	–
Materials	587	567	20	5,685	5,704	(19)
Materials margin	166	186	20	1,629	1,610	(19)
Direct costs	69	79	(10)	685	689	(4)
Gross profit	97	107	10	944	921	(23)
Percentage	12.92	14.21	1.29	12.90	12.60	(0.30)

The same principle holds for other direct costs, which appear to be running $/£/€94,000 over budget for the year. When we take into account the extra sales shown in the flexed budget, we can see that the company has actually spent $/£/€4,000 over budget on direct costs. While this is serious, it is not as serious as the fixed budget suggests.

The flexed budget allows you to concentrate your efforts on dealing with true variances in performance.

The following website, SCORE (**www.score.org** > Business Tools > Template Gallery > Sales Forecast), has a downloadable Excel spreadsheet from which you can make sales and cost projections on a trial and error basis. Once you are satisfied with your projection, use the profit and loss projection (**www.score.org** > Business Tools > Template Gallery > Profit and Loss Projection (3 Years)) to complete your budget.

Seasonality and trends

The figures shown for each period of the budget are not the same. For example, a sales budget of $/£/€1.2 million for the year does not translate to $/£/€100,000 a month. The exact figure depends on two factors:

- The projected trend may forecast that, while sales at the start of the year are $/£/€80,000 a month, they will change to $/£/€120,000 a month by the end of the year. The average would be $/£/€100,000.
- By virtue of seasonal factors, each month may also be adjusted up or down from the underlying trend. You could expect the sales of heating oil, for example, to peak in the autumn and tail off in the late spring.

See also Chapter 11, Quantitative and qualitative research and analysis, for more on forecasting.

Marketing

- Measuring markets
- Assessing strengths and weaknesses
- Understanding customers
- Segmenting markets
- The marketing mix
- Selling
- Researching markets

Business schools didn't invent marketing but they certainly ensured its pre-eminence as an academic discipline. *Principles of Marketing* and *Marketing Management*, seminal books on the subject by Philip Kotler (*et al*) of Kellogg School of Management at Northwestern University, have been core reading on management programmes the world over for decades. The School's marketing department has rated at the top in all national and international ranking surveys conducted during the past 15 years. [You can see Kotler lecture at this link: **www.anaheim.ed** > CEO Webcast]

Marketing is defined as the process that ensures the right products and services get to the right markets at the right time and at the right price. The devil in that sentence lies in the use of the word 'right'. The deal has to work for the customer, because if they don't want what you have to offer the game is over before you begin. You have to offer value and satisfaction, otherwise people will either choose an apparently superior competitor or, if they do buy from you and are dissatisfied, they won't buy again. Worse still, they may bad-mouth you to a lot of other people. For you the marketer, being right means that there have to be enough people wanting your product or service to make the venture profitable; and ideally those numbers should be getting bigger rather than smaller.

So inevitably marketing is something of a voyage of discovery for both supplier and consumer, from which both parties learn something and hopefully improve. The boundaries of marketing stretch from inside the mind of the customer, perhaps uncovering emotions they were themselves barely aware of, out to the logistic support systems that get the product or service into customers' hands. Each part of the value chain from company to consumer has the potential to add value or kill the deal. For example, at the heart of the Amazon business proposition are a superlatively efficient warehousing and delivery system and a simple zero-cost way for customers to return products they don't want and get immediate refunds. These factors are every bit as important as elements of Amazon's marketing strategy as are its product range, website structure, Google placement or its competitive pricing.

Marketing is also a circuitous activity. As you explore the topics below, you will see that you need the answers to some questions before you can move on, and indeed once you have some answers you may have to go back a step to review an earlier stage. For example, your opinion as to the size of the relevant market may be influenced by the results achieved when you segment the market and assess your competitive position.

Getting the measure of markets

The starting point in marketing is definition of the scope of the market you are in or are aiming for. This comes from the business objectives, mission and vision that form the heart of the strategy of the enterprise. These are topics covered in Chapter 12 on strategy. For most MBAs for most of the time these will be a 'given' and as such will not inhibit your ability to apply the marketing concepts explored in this chapter. So, for example, if you are working in, say, Body Shop, McDonald's, IBM, a Hospital Trust or the Prison Service, the broad market thrust of your current business will be self-evident. Later you may want or need to change strategic direction, but effective marketing is concerned fundamentally with dealing with a defined product (service)/market scope. These concepts apply to any marketing activity, but you will find that understanding them is made easier by applying them to the business you are in, or have some appreciation of.

Assessing the relevant market

Much of marketing is concerned with achieving goals such as selling a specific quantity of a product or service or capturing market share. MBAs are frequently set the challenging task of measuring the size of the market. Now in principle this is not too difficult. Desk research (see in 'Market research' later in this chapter) will yield a sizeable harvest of statistics of varying degrees of reliability. You will be able to discover that the consumption, say, of bread in Europe is £10 ($16/€11) billion a year. But first you need a definition of bread. The industry-wide definition of Bakery includes sliced and un-sliced bread, rolls, bakery snacks and speciality breads. It covers plant-baked products; those that are baked by in-store bakers; and products sold through craft bakers.

Assessing the relevant market then involves refining global statistics down to provide the real scope of your market. If your business operates only in the UK the market is worth over £2.7 ($4.2/€3.03) billion, equivalent to 12 million loaves a day, one of the largest sectors in Food. If you are operating only in the craft bakery segment then the relevant market shrinks to £13.5 ($21.16/€15.16) million; this contracts still further to £9.7 ($15.2/€10.9) million if you are, say, operating only within the radius of the M25 ring road.

The importance of market share

The relevant market will be shared by various competing businesses in different proportions. Typically there will be a market leader, a couple of market followers and a host of businesses trailing in their wake. The slice that each competitor has of a market is its market share. You will find that marketing people are fixated on market share, perhaps even more so than on absolute sales. That may appear little more than a rational desire to beat the 'enemy' and appear higher in rankings, but it has a much more deep-seated and profound logic.

Back in the 1960s a firm of US management consultants observed a consistent relationship between the cost of producing an item (or delivering a service) and the total quantity produced over the life of the product concerned. They noticed that total unit costs (labour and materials) fell by between 20 and 30 per cent for every doubling of the cumulative quantity produced. (See Chapter 12 for more on the experience curve effect.)

So any company capturing a sizeable market share will have an implied cost advantage over any competitor with a smaller market share. That cost advantage can then be used to make more profit, lower prices and compete for an even greater share of the market, or invest in making the product better and so stealing a march on competitors.

Figure 3.1 demonstrates clearly the advantage of market share in the supermarket business. Tesco makes £3 ($4.7/€3.4) billion of profit with a 31 per cent share of the market. That implies every percentage point of market share is worth £0.1 ($0.15/€0.11) billion. Sainsbury's, with profits of £0.5 ($0.78/€0.56) billion, only generates £0.03 ($0.05/€0.04) billion for each per cent of market share. In other words, for each percentage point in market share Tesco's superior position allows it to generate 3.33 times more profit than Sainsbury's.

FIGURE 3.1 Market share UK supermarkets June 2010

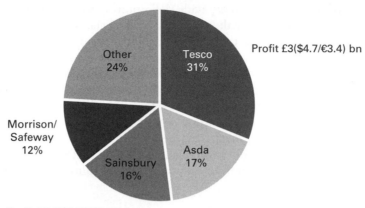

Profit £3($4.7/€3.4) bn

Profit £0.5($0.78/€0.56) bn

Competitive position

It follows that if market share and relative size are important marketing goals, you need to assess your products' and services' positions relative to the competition in your relevant market. The techniques most used to carry out this analysis are SWOT and perceptual mapping.

Strengths, weaknesses, opportunities and threats (SWOT)

This is a general-purpose tool developed in the late 1960s at Harvard by Learned, Christensen, Andrews and Guth, and published in their seminal book, *Business Policy, Text and Cases* (Richard D Irwin, 1969). The SWOT framework consists of a cross, with space in each quadrant to summarize your observations, as in Figure 3.2.

FIGURE 3.2 Example SWOT chart for a hypothetical Cobra Beer competitor

Strengths	*Weaknesses*
1. Beginning to get brand recognition 2. Established strongly in Indian restaurants	1. Don't have own production 2. Need more equity finance to be able to advertise more strongly
Opportunities	*Threats*
1. We could capitalize more on our relationships in Indian restaurants 2. We are only in the UK – so have the world to go for	1. We are vulnerable to a big player targeting our niche 2. Our sector looks like being the target of major tax rises which could reduce overall demand

In this example the SWOT analysis is restricted to a handful of areas, though in practice the list might run to a dozen or more areas within each of the four quadrants. The purpose of the SWOT analysis is to suggest possible ways to improve the competitive position and hence market share while minimizing the dangers of perceived threats. A strategy that this SWOT would suggest as being worth pursuing could be to launch a low-alcohol product (and sidestep the tax threat) that would appeal to all restaurants, rather than just Indian (widen the market). The company could also start selling in India using the international cachet of being a UK brand. That would open up the market still further and limit the damage that larger UK competitors could inflict.

SWOT is also used as a tool in strategic analysis and indeed it was so used by General Electric in the 1980s. While it is a useful way of pulling together a large amount of information in a way that is easy for managers to assimilate, it can be most effective when used in individual market segments, as a strength in one segment could be a weakness in another. For example, giving a product features that would enhance its appeal, say, to the retirees market may reduce its appeal to other market segments.

Perceptual mapping

Perceptual or positioning maps are much used by marketing executives to position products and services relative to competitors on two dimensions. In Figure 3.3 the positions of companies competing in a particular industry are compared on price and quality, on a spectrum from low to high.

Similar maps can be produced for any combination of variables that are of importance to customers – availability, product range, after-sales support, market image and so on. The technique is used in a variety of ways,

FIGURE 3.3 Perceptual mapping

including highlighting possible market gaps when one quadrant is devoid of players, suggesting areas to be built on or extended; or where a USP (see below) is required to create a competitive edge.

Understanding customers

Without customers no business can get off the ground, let alone survive. Knowing something about your customers, what they need, how much they can 'consume', who they buy from now, all seems such elementary information that it is hard to believe so many people could start without those insights: and yet they do.

There is an old business maxim that says the customer is always right. But that does not mean they are necessarily right for you. So as well as knowing who to sell to, you also need to know the sorts of people who are not right for you and accept that trying to interest them will be a waste of scarce resources on your part.

Recognizing needs

The founder of a successful cosmetics firm, when asked what he did, replied: 'In the factories we make perfume, in the shops we sell dreams.'

Those of us in business usually start by defining our business in physical terms. Customers, on the other hand, see businesses having as their primary value the ability to satisfy their needs. Even firms that adopt customer satisfaction, or even delight, as their stated maxim often find it a more complex goal than it at first appears. Take Blooming Marvellous (see below). It made clothes for the mother-to-be, sure enough: but the primary customer need it was aiming to satisfy was neither to preserve their modesty nor to keep them warm. The need it was aiming for was much higher: it was ensuring that its customers would feel fashionably dressed, which is about the way people interact with each other and how they feel about themselves. Just splashing, say, a Tog rating showing the thermal properties of the fabric, as you would, say, a duvet, would cut no ice with the Blooming Marvellous potential market.

Until you have clearly defined the needs of your market(s) you cannot begin to assemble a product or service to satisfy them. Fortunately, help is at hand. An American psychologist, Abraham Maslow, who taught at Brandeis University, Boston and whose International Business School now ranks highly in the *Economist*'s survey of top business schools (see the Appendix for more on business school rankings), demonstrated in his research that 'all customers are goal seekers who gratify their needs by purchase and consumption'. He then went a bit further and classified consumer needs into a five-stage pyramid he called the hierarchy of needs.

Self-actualization

This is the summit of Maslow's hierarchy, in which people are looking for truth, wisdom, justice and purpose. It's a need that is never fully satisfied and according to Maslow only a very small percentage of people ever reach the point where they are prepared to pay much money to satisfy such needs. It is left to the likes of Bill Gates and Sir Tom Hunter to give away billions to form foundations to dispose of their wealth on worthy causes. The rest of us scrabble around further down the hierarchy.

Esteem

Here people are concerned with such matters as self-respect, achievement, attention, recognition and reputation. The benefits that customers are looking for include the feeling that others will think better of them if they have a particular product. Much of brand marketing is aimed at making consumers believe that by conspicuously wearing the maker's label or logo so that others can see it, it will earn them 'respect'. Understanding how this part of Maslow's hierarchy works was vital to the founders of Responsibletravel.com (**www.responsibletravel.com**). Founded six years ago with backing from the late Anita Roddick (Body Shop) in Justin Francis's front room in Brighton, with his partner Harold Goodwin, it set out to be the world's first company to offer environmentally responsible travel and holidays. It was one of the first companies to offer carbon offset schemes for travellers and it boasts that it turns away more tour companies trying to list on its site than it accepts. It appeals to consumers who want to be recognized in their communities as being socially responsible.

Social needs

The need for friends, belonging to associations, clubs or other groups and the need to give and get love are all social needs. After 'lower' needs have been met, these needs, which relate to interacting with other people, come to the fore. Hotel Chocolat (**www.hotelchocolat.co.uk**), founded by Angus Thirlwell and Peter Harris in their kitchen, is a good example of a business based on meeting social needs. It markets home-delivered luxury chocolates but generates sales by having Tasting Clubs to check out products each month. The concept of the club is that you invite friends round and use the firm's scoring system to rate and give feedback on the chocolates.

Safety

The second most basic need of consumers is to feel safe and secure. People who feel they are in harm's way, either through their general environment or because of the product or service on offer, will not be over-interested in having their higher needs met. When Charles Rigby set up World Challenge (**www.world-challenge.co.uk**) to market challenging expeditions to exotic locations around the world, with the aim of taking young people up to around 19 out of their comfort zones and teaching them how to overcome adversity, he knew he had a challenge of his own on his hands: how to make an activity simultaneously exciting and apparently dangerous to teenagers, while being safe enough for the parents writing the cheques to feel comfortable. Six full sections on its website are devoted to explaining the safety measures that the company takes to ensure that unacceptable risks are eliminated as far as is humanly possible.

Physiological needs

Air, water, sleep and food are all absolutely essential to sustain life. Until these basic needs are satisfied, higher needs such as self-esteem will not be considered.

You can read more about Maslow's needs hierarchy and how to take it into account in understanding customers on the Net MBA website (**www. netmba.com** > Management > Maslow's Hierarchy of Needs).

Features, benefits and proofs

While understanding customer needs is vital, it is not sufficient on its own to help put together a saleable proposition. Before you can do that, you have to understand the benefits that customers will get when they purchase. Features are what a product or service has or is, and benefits are what the product does for the customer. When Nigel Apperley founded his business Internet Cameras Direct, now Internet Direct (**www.internetdirect.co.uk**) and part of the AIM-listed eXpansy plc, while a student at business school, he knew there was no point in telling customers about SLRs or shutter speeds. These are not the end product that customers want; they are looking for the convenience and economy of buying direct, so he planned to follow the Dell Computer direct sales model and show good pictures. Within three years Apperley had annual turnover in excess of £20m and had moved a long way from his home-based beginnings.

Look at the example of product features and benefits (Table 3.1), which has been extended to include proofs showing how the benefits will be delivered. The essential element to remember here is that the customer only wants to pay for benefits while the seller has to pick up the tab for all the features whether the customers sees them as valuable or not. Benefits will provide the 'copy' for a business's advertising and promotional activities.

Product/service adoption cycle – who will buy first?

Customers do not sit and wait for a new business to open its doors. Word spreads slowly as the message is diffused throughout the various customer groups. Even then it is noticeable that generally it is the more adventurous types who first buy from a new business. Only after these people have given

TABLE 3.1 Example showing product features, benefits and proofs

Features	Benefits	Proofs
Our maternity clothes are designed by fashion experts	You get to look and feel great	See the press comments in fashion magazines
Our bookkeeping system is approved by HM Revenue and Customs	You can sleep at night	Our system is rated No1 by the Evaluation centre (**www.evaluationcenter. com**>accounting software)

TABLE 3.2 The product/service adoption cycle

Innovators	2.5% of the overall market
Early adopters	13.5% of the overall market
Early majority	34.0% of the overall market
Late majority	34.0% of the overall market
Laggards	16.0% of the overall market
Total market	100%

their seal of approval do the 'followers' come along. Research shows that this adoption process, as it is known, moves through five distinct customer characteristics, from innovators to laggards, with the overall population being different for each group. (See Table 3.2.)

Let's suppose you have identified the market for your internet gift service. Initially your market has been constrained to affluent professionals within 5 miles of your home to keep delivery costs low. So if market research shows that there are 100,000 people that meet the profile of your ideal customer and they have regular access to the internet, the market open for exploitation at the outset may be as low as 2,500, which is the 2.5 per cent of innovators.

This adoption process, from the 2.5 per cent of innovators who make up a new business's first customers through to the laggards who won't buy from anyone until they have been in business for 20 years, is most noticeable with truly innovative and relatively costly goods and services, but the general trend is true for all businesses. Until you have sold to the innovators, significant sales cannot be achieved. So, an important first task is to identify these customers. The moral is: the more you know about your potential customers at the outset, the better your chances of success.

One further issue to keep in mind when shaping your marketing strategy is that innovators, early adopters and all the other sub-segments don't necessarily use the same media, websites, magazines and newspapers or respond to the same images and messages. So they need to be marketed to in very different ways.

Segmenting markets

Having established that customers have different needs means that we need to organize our marketing effort so as to address those individually. However, trying to satisfy everyone may mean that we end up satisfying no one fully. The marketing process that helps us deal with this seemingly impossible task is market segmentation. This is the name given to the process whereby customers and potential customers are organized into clusters or groups of 'similar' types. For example, a carpet/upholstery cleaning business has private individuals and business clients running restaurants and guesthouses, for example.

These two segments are fundamentally different, with one segment being more focused on cost and the other more concerned that the work is carried out with the least disruption to their business. Also, each of these customer groups is motivated to buy for different reasons and your selling message has to be modified accordingly.

Worthwhile criteria

These are four useful rules to help decide if a market segment is worth trying to sell into:

- Measurability: Can you estimate how many customers are in the segment? Are there enough to make it worth offering something 'different'?

- Accessibility: Can you communicate with these customers, preferably in a way that reaches them on an individual basis? For example, you could reach the over-50s by advertising in a specialist 'older people's' magazine, with reasonable confidence that young people will not read it. So if you were trying to promote Scrabble with tiles 50 per cent larger, you might prefer that young people did not hear about it. If they did, it might give the product an old-fashioned image.

- Open to profitable development: The customers must have money to spend on the benefits that you propose to offer.

- Size: A segment has to be large enough to be worth your exploiting it, but perhaps not so large as to attract larger competitors.

One example of a market segment that has not been open to development for hundreds of years is the sale of goods and services to retired people. Several factors made this a particularly unappealing segment. First, retired people were perceived as 'old' and less adventurous; second, they had a short life expectancy; and finally, the knockout blow was that they had no money. In the past decade or so that has all changed: people retire early, live longer and many have relatively large pensions. The result is that travel firms, house builders, magazine publishers and insurance companies have rushed out a stream of products and services aimed particularly at this market segment.

Segmentation is an important marketing process, as it helps to bring customers more sharply into focus, classifies them into manageable groups and allows you to focus on one or more niches. It has wide-ranging implications for other marketing decisions. For example, the same product can be priced differently according to the intensity of customers' needs. The first- and second-class post is one example, off-peak rail travel another.

It is also a continuous process that needs to be carried out periodically, for example when strategies are being reviewed.

Methods of segmentation

These are some of the ways by which markets can be segmented:

- Psychographic segmentation divides individual consumers into social groups such as 'yuppies' (young, upwardly mobile professionals), 'bumps' (borrowed-to-the-hilt, upwardly mobile, professional show-offs) and 'jollies' (jet-setting oldies with lots of loot). These categories try to show how social behaviour influences buyer behaviour. Forrester Research, an internet research house, claims that when it comes to determining whether consumers will or will not go on the internet, how much they'll spend and what they'll buy, demographic factors such as age, race and gender don't matter anywhere near as much as the consumers' attitudes towards technology. Forrester uses this concept, together with its research, to produce Technographics® market segments as an aid to understanding people's behaviour as digital consumers. Forrester has used two categories: technology optimists and technology pessimists, and has used these alongside income and what it calls 'primary motivation' – career, family and entertainment – to divide up the whole market. Each segment is given a new name – 'Techno-strivers', 'Digital Hopefuls' and so forth – followed by a chapter explaining how to identify them, how to tell whether they are likely to be right for your product or service, and providing some pointers as to what marketing strategies might get favourable responses from each group.

- Benefit segmentation recognizes that different people can get different satisfaction from the same product or service. Lastminute.com claims two quite distinctive benefits for its users. First, it aims to offer people bargains that appeal because of price and value. Second, the company has recently been laying more emphasis on the benefit of immediacy. This idea is rather akin to the impulse-buy products placed at checkout tills, which you never thought of buying until you bumped into them on your way out. Whether 10 days on a beach in Goa or a trip to Istanbul are the type of things people 'pop in their baskets' before turning off their computers, time will tell.

- Geographic segmentation arises when different locations have different needs. For example, an inner-city location may be a heavy user of motorcycle dispatch services, but a light user of gardening products. Internet companies have been slow to extend their reach beyond their own back yard, which is surprising considering the supposed global reach of the service. Microsoft exports only 20 per cent of its total sales beyond US borders, and fewer than 16 per cent of AOL's subscribers live outside the United States. However, the figure for AOL greatly overstates the company's true export performance. In reality, AOL does virtually no business with overseas subscribers, but instead serves them through affiliate relationships. Few of the recent batch of internet IPOs have registered much overseas activity in their filing details. By way of contrast, the Japanese liquid crystal display industry exports more than 70 per cent of its entire output.

- Industrial segmentation groups together commercial customers according to a combination of their geographic location, principal business activity, relative size, frequency of product use, buying policies and a range of other factors. Logical Holdings is an e-business solutions and service company that floated for over £1 ($1.6/€1.12) billion on the London Stock Exchange and TechMark index, making it one of the UK's biggest IT companies. It was formed from about 30 acquisitions of small (ish) businesses. The company was founded by Rikke Helms, formerly head of IBM's E-Commerce Solutions portfolio. Her company split the market into three segments: Small, Medium-Sized and Big, tailoring its services specifically for each.

- Multivariant segmentation is where more than one variable is used. This can give a more precise picture of a market than using just one factor.

Specifiers, users and customers

When analysing market segments it is important to keep in mind that there are at least three major categories of people who have a role to play in the buying decisions and whose needs have to be considered in any analysis of a market:

- The user, or end customer, will be the recipient of any final benefits associated with the product.

- The specifier will want to be sure that the end user's needs are met in terms of performance, delivery and any other important parameters. Their 'customer' is both the end user and the budget holder of the cost centre concerned. There may even be conflict between the two (or more) 'customer' groups. For example, in the case of, say, hotel toiletries, those responsible for marketing the rooms will want high-quality products to enhance their offer, while the hotel manager will have cost concerns close to the top of their concerns and the people responsible for actually putting the product in place will be interested only in any handling and packaging issues.

- The non-consuming buyer, who places the order, also has individual needs. Some of their needs are similar to those of a specifier, except

CASE STUDY

In just 18 years, Dawn Gibbons MBE, co-founder of Flowcrete (**www.flowcrete.com**), took the company from a 400-square-foot unit (the size of a double garage) with £2,000 ($3,140/€2,250) capital to a plc with a turnover of £52 ($82/€58) million in the field of floor-screeding technology and clients including household names such as Cadbury, Sainsbury's, Unilever, Marks & Spencer, Barclays and Ford. Part of Flowcrete's success was down to a continuing focus on technical superiority. This attribute was engendered by Dawn's father, a well-respected industrial chemist with an interest in resin technology.

But arguably Dawn's skills contributed as much if not more to the firm's success. 'We want to be champions of change,' Gibbons claims. 'We have restructured a dozen times, focusing on new trends.' Markets and market segmentation are a vital part of any restructuring process – indeed, the best companies restructure around their customers' changing needs.

The first reappraisal came after seven years in business when Flowcrete realized that its market was no longer those firms that laid floors; it now had to become an installer itself. Changes in the market meant that to maintain growth Flowcrete had to appoint proven specialist contractors, train their staff, write specifications and carry out audits to ensure quality.

that they will have price at or near the top of their needs. A particular category here is those buying gifts. Once again their needs and those of the recipient may be dissimilar. For example, those buying gifts are as concerned with packaging as with content. Watches, pens, perfumes and fine wines are all gifts whose packaging is paramount at the point of purchase. Yet for the user they are often things to be immediately discarded.

The marketing mix

The term 'marketing mix' has a pedigree going back to the late 1940s when marketing managers referred to mixing ingredients to create strategies. The concept was formalized by E Jerome McCarthy, a marketing professor at Michigan State University, in 1960. The mix of ingredients with which marketing strategy can be developed and implemented is price, product (or/and service), promotion and place. A fifth 'P', people, is often added. Just as with cooking, taking the same or similar ingredients in different proportions can result in very different 'products'. A change in the way these elements are put together can produce an offering tailored to meet the needs of a specific market segment.

The ingredients in the marketing mix represent only the elements that are largely, though not entirely, within a firm's control. Uncontrollable ingredients include the state of the economy, changes in legislation, new and powerful market entrants and rapid changes in technology. The effects of these external elements are covered in the chapter on strategy, though many of the concepts discussed there apply to marketing as well as to wider aspects of a firm's operations.

Product/service

When the term 'marketing mix' was first coined, the bulk of valuable trade was concerned with physical goods. Certainly services existed, but these were mostly supplied by professions such as law, accountancy, insurance and finance where the concept of marketing was in any event taboo; today, a product is generally accepted as the whole bundle of 'satisfactions', either tangible such as a physical product, or intangible such as warranties, guarantees or customer support that support that product. Generally the terms product and service will be used synonymously in this part of this chapter.

The bundle that makes up a successful product includes:

- design;
- specification and functionality;
- brand name/image;

- performance and reliability;
- quality;
- safety;
- packaging;
- presentation and appearance;
- after-sales service;
- availability;
- delivery;
- colour/flavour/odour/touch;
- payment terms.

The principal tools that marketing managers use to manage product issues are as follows.

Product/service life cycle

The idea that business products and services have a life cycle much as any being was first seen in management literature as far back as 1922, when researchers looking back at the growth of the US automobile industry observed a bell-shaped pattern for the sales of individual cars. Over the following four decades various practitioners and researchers, adding, substituting and renaming the stages in the life cycle to arrive at the five steps in Figure 3.4, carried out further work. The length of a product's lifetime can be weeks or months in the case of fads such as the hula-hoop or the Rubik's cube:

- Product development: This stage is typified by cash outlays only, and can last from decades in the case of medical products down to a few months or even weeks to launch a simple consumer product.

FIGURE 3.4 The product life cycle

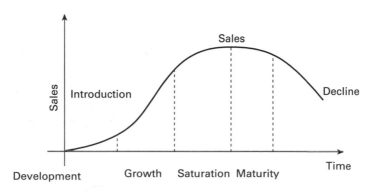

- Introduction: Here the product is brought to market, perhaps just to one initial segment, and it may comprise little more than a test marketing activity. Once again costs are high; advertising and selling costs have to be borne up front and sales revenues will be minimal.

- Growth: This stage sees the product sold across the whole range of a company's market segments, gaining market acceptance and becoming profitable.

- Maturity and saturation: Sales peak as the limit of customers' capacity to consume is reached and competitors or substitute products enter the market. Profits start to tail off as prices drop and advertising is stepped up to beat off competitors.

- Decline: Sales and profits fall away as competition becomes heavy and better and more competitive or technologically advanced products come into the market.

The usefulness of the product life cycle as a marketing tool is as an aid to deciding on the appropriate strategy to adopt. For example, at the introduction stage the goal for advertising and promotion may be to inform and educate, during the growth stage differences need to be stressed to keep competitors at bay, and during maturity customers need to be reminded that you are still around and it's time to buy again. During decline it's probable that advertising budgets could be cut and prices lowered. As all major costs associated with the product will have been covered at this stage, this should still be a profitable stage.

These, of course, are only examples of possible strategies rather than rules to be followed. For example, many products are successfully relaunched during the decline stage by changing an element of the marketing mix or by repositioning into a different marketplace. Cigarette manufacturers are responding to declining markets in the developed economies by targeting markets such as Africa and China, even setting up production there and buying up local brands to extend their range of products.

Unique positioning proposition

This used to be known as the unique selling proposition (USP) and still is in the sales field. For marketers the term is synonymous with the idea of a slogan or strap line that captures the value of the product in the mind of the user. It should position your product against competitors in a manner that is hard to emulate or dislodge. John Lewis, for example, has 'never knowingly undersold' as its powerful message to consumers that they can safely set price considerations to one side when they come to making their choice.

Another strategy is to set out to own the word and turn it into an adjective. Hoover with vacuum cleaners and FedEx with overnight delivery are examples of this approach.

Product range

Being a single-product business is generally considered too dangerous a position except for very small or start-up businesses. The two options to consider are:

- Depth of line: This is the situation when a company has many products within a particular category. Washing powders and breakfast cereals are classic examples of businesses that offer scores of products into the same marketplace. The benefit to the company is that the same channels of distribution and buyers are being used. The weakness is that all these products are subject to similar threats and dangers. However 'deep' your beers and spirits range, for example, you will always face the threat of higher taxes or the opprobrium of those who think you are damaging people's health.

- Breadth of line: This is where a company has a variety of products of different types such as Marlboro with cigarettes and fashion clothing, or 3M with its extensive variety of adhesives extending out to the Post-It Note.

Branding

Since the first edition of this book the world of brands has been transformed in ways not seen since the term itself, derived from the Old Norse brandr, meaning 'to burn', entered the business lexicon. For a start, 2010 saw thirteen brands from so called developing countries, including those from the BRIC countries – Brazil, Russia, India and China – enter the ranks of the world's top 100 most valuable brands. Brandr refers to the custom of owners burning their mark (or brand) onto their goods, but burning of a different kind has swept over brands and their owners for reasons linked more or less to the recent global economic catastrophes. Whilst long-established companies such as Lehman Brothers, respected and feared in equal measure on Wall Street since before 1929, have been swept away, a host of new names have sprung up to take their place. Bank of China, first listed on the Hong Kong stock market in 2002, became the world's 24th most valuable brand in 2010, just behind HSBC, but well ahead of Citibank. That same year ICICI, India's largest bank by market capitalization, entered the listings as the 45th most valuable brand. So for the first time since its inception in 2006, the BrandZ Top 100, who provide an objective annual study of brand value and positioning, include brands from all four of the BRIC countries.

Why branding matters

This is considered the holy grail of the product/service aspect of the marketing mix. A brand encompasses not just what a product is or does but all the elements such as logo, symbols, image, reputation and associations. The McDonald's arches represent its brand as a welcoming beacon drawing customers in. Branding is an intangible way of differentiating a product in a way that captures and retains markets through loyalty to that brand. Coca-Cola tastes little different from a supermarket brand, but the promotion that supports the brand confers on the consumer the chance to share the attractive lifestyle of those 'cool' people in the adverts. Apple's iPod is differentiated from just any old MP3 player in much the same way. Intel and Audi are examples of branding designed to reassure consumers in unfamiliar territory that a product will deliver. Body Shop International exudes ethics and concern for the environment, where other cosmetics concentrate on how they will make the wearer look beautiful.

Building a brand takes time and a considerable advertising budget to build. But by creating brand value, that is the price premium commanded by that product over its unbranded or less appealing competitors, a business can end up with a valuable asset. Superbrands (**www.superbrands.com**) has a listing of the top brands by country, often with a case study supporting the top brands in any country.

Alongside this dramatic position jostling the global meltdown has revealed some important facts about the economic resilience of established brands. Warren Buffet's statement 'it's not until the tide goes out that you can see who is swimming naked' could be aptly applied here. The share prices of the top 100 brands as identified in the BrandZ study have outperformed the S&P 500 by over 30 per cent over the period 2005–10. In fact whilst companies in the S&P 500 lost 11.5 per cent in value, those of the top 100 brands gained 18.5 per cent. The reasons for this outperformance in hard times seem to be:

- A brand generates trust, a fact that appears to transcend business sectors. Consumers are as loyal to Coca-Cola, Procter & Gamble and WalMart as business users are to Cisco, HSBC and Goldman Sachs for a company, for its products, and for its services. According to BrandZ consideration of brand in the purchase decision has risen by 20 percentage points since 2005 so in uncertain economic conditions people turn to something they can trust – an established brand.

- Brands are established in almost every corner of the globe. In China, India and Russia brands are as prevalent as in France, the United Kingdom or in the United States. Today over a dozen emerging market economies now have world class brands, where there were none at all in 2000. This global dimension allows businesses with top brands to keep growing across economic cycles. So while the Western economies shrank between 2008 and 2010, China, India, Brazil and much of South America were powering ahead.

- The population of top brands is relatively stable, and that in turn allows them the luxury of formulating and implementing long-term strategy, rather than being buffeted by turbulence. Seven of the same brands are present in both the 2006 and the 2010 BrandZ rankings. True, some positions have changed with Google now number 1 brand up from 7th in 2006 and IBM in the second slot up from 8th. This resilience means that firms such as Starbucks, Samsung, Toyota and Exxon had the ability to recover from difficulties relatively quickly. Exxon, for example, a virtual pariah after the Valdez oil spill disaster in 1989, was back in the top rankings in under a decade, coming in at 39th in the world, ahead of Disney, Orange and Colgate in 2010. It remains to be seen if BP is as fortunate.

CASE STUDY Tata Nano, India – the People's brand

On 17 July 2010 Mr Ashok Raghunath Vichare of Mumbai became the first customer in India to take delivery of the Tata Nano LX (Lunar Silver) from the Chairman of Tata Sons and Tata Motors, Mr Ratan N Tata, at the company's dealership, Concorde Motors. Tata, the Indian conglomerate that took over Jaguar and Land Rover, launched its Nano, the 'People's Car' in concept form in 2008, with a basic model aimed at the local and Chinese markets. Models with air-conditioning and a range of extras that will double its price were scheduled for its launch on the European market at an unspecified later date. The Nano mission began back in 2003, when Tata Motors set itself the challenge to build a 'people's car'. Tata gave an engineering team, led by 32-year-old star engineer Girish Wagh, three goals for the new vehicle; it should be low-cost, adhere to regulatory requirements, and achieve performance targets such as fuel efficiency and acceleration capacity. The Nano is a four-door car with a 623-cc engine that gets 50 miles to the gallon and seats up to five. It's nearly a tenth smaller in outer length than its closest rival, Suzuki's Maruti 800, but has a fifth more useful interior space. Costing around $2,800 (£1,800/€2,154) it is the most inexpensive car in the world.

Tata Motors is India's largest automobile company, with consolidated revenues of Rs 92,519 crores (£10 million/$20 billion) in 2009–10. It is the leader in commercial vehicles, among the top three in passenger vehicles, the world's fourth largest truck manufacturer, and the world's second largest bus manufacturer.

The car has three powerful strengths as a brand. Tata Nano's safety performance exceeds current regulatory requirements – it passes the roll-over test and offset impact, which are not regulated in India. It's affordable in the local market. Tata Motors has entered into agreements with 15 banks for a financing deal that enables a car to be reserved by paying just Rs 2,999 (£41/$64/€50). Internationally the car is a steal. For the price of a new Range Rover, the top brand in the Tata Motors stable, you could buy 60 Nano's, one for every week of the year with a few left over. The brand is generating attention by winning awards. In 2010 the Tata Nano won the prestigious Indian Car of the Year (ICOTY) award ahead of the Chevrolet Cruze, Honda Jazz, Fiat Linea, Fiat Grande Punto, Maruti Suzuki Ritz, Mahindra Xylo, Skoda Superb and Toyota Fortuner.

Branding pitfalls

Brands have global visibility and as a consequence problems can appear to be on some distant horizon yet suddenly become amplified and virtually omnipresent with unfortunate consequences. Nowhere has this capacity to suffer global reputation for local or narrow specific problems been more in evidence than the fall from grace in 2010 of two of the world's most successful brands, BP ranked 34th and Toyota ranked 26th in the top 100 brands of 2009/10. Both brands suffered catastrophic, though perhaps not terminal, blows to their reputations for quality, integrity and honesty. Whilst BP tussled with leaking oil in the Gulf of Mexico it received four times as many mentions in the world press as it did two years earlier on 29 July 2008 when it announced record profits of £3.5 billion ($5.53 billion) for a single quarter. Though the brand may survive on the international arena a survey running on a local Gulf website puts 48 per cent in favour of adopting Amoco for US gas stations, a brand it abandoned when that company was acquired by BP. Toyota and its near invisible chairman Akio Toyoda, also found themselves the centre of a storm of unwelcome public visibility when the company had to recall a few million cars for a variety of reasons – ranging from sticking accelerator peddles to steering lock defects.

Price

Seemingly the simplest of the marketing choices, it is often the most agonizing decision that MBAs are faced with. The subject transcends almost every area of a business. The economists get the ball rolling with ideas around the elasticity of demand. Set too high a price and no one comes to the dance; too low and your budget for bouncers will go off the Richter scale. The accounts and production teams are concerned that sales will at least be sufficient to reach break-even in reasonable time. The strategists are worried about the signals in terms of corporate positioning that prices can send. However profitable a certain price may be for the business, it may just be so low that it devalues other products in your range. Apple, for example, has a position fairly and squarely at the innovator end of the product adoption cycle. Their customers expect to pay high prices for the privilege of being the first users of a new product. The iPod was positioned above the Walkman in price terms, though as the market for pocket sound devices was already mature there was scope to come into the market lower down the price spectrum.

Skim vs penetrate

You need to decide between two generic pricing strategies before you can fine-tune your plans. Skimming involves setting a price at the high end of what you believe the market will bear. This would be a strategy to pursue if you have a very limited amount of product available for sale and would rather 'ration' than disappoint customers. It is also a way to target the 'innovators' in your market who are happy to pay a premium to be among the first to have a new product. To be successful with this strategy you would need to be sure that competitors can't just step in and soak up the demand that you have created.

Penetration pricing is the mirror image; prices are set at the low end, while being above your costs. Prices are competitive, with the deliberate intention of eliminating your customers' need to shop around. Slogans such as 'everyday low prices' are used to emphasize this policy. The aim here is to grab as much of the market as you can before competitors arrive on the scene and hopefully lock them out. The danger here is that you need a lot of volume either of product or hours sold before you can make a decent profit. This in turn means tying up more money for longer before you break even.

Dragon Lock (the executive puzzle makers), who were Cranfield enterprise programme participants, adopted a skim strategy when they launched their new product. Their product was easy to copy and impossible to patent, so they chose a low price as a strategy to discourage competitors and to swallow up the market quickly.

Danger of low pricing

Aside from the obvious possible problems of the cash-flow implications of stretching out the break-even horizon and quality/image issues, it is an immutable law that raising prices is a whole lot more difficult than lowering them. It is less of a problem if the market as a whole is moving up, but raising a price because you set it too low in the first place is a challenge to say the least.

Value pricing

Another consideration when setting your prices is the value of the product or service in the customer's mind. His or her opinion of price may have little or no relation to the cost, and he or she may be ignorant of the price charged by the competition, especially if the product or service is a new one. In fact, many consumers perceive price as a reliable guide to the value they can expect to receive. The more you pay, the more you get. With this in mind, had Dyson launched its revolutionary vacuum cleaner, with its claims of superior performance, at a price below that of its peers, then some potential customers might have questioned those claims. In its literature Dyson cites as the inspiration for the new vacuum cleaner the inferior performance of existing products in the same price band. A product at six times the Dyson price is the one whose performance Dyson seeks to emulate. The image created is that, although the price is at the high end of general run-of-the-mill products, the performance is disproportionately greater. The runaway success of Dyson's vacuum cleaner would tend to endorse this argument.

Real-time pricing

The stock market works by gathering information on supply and demand. If more people want to buy a share than sell it, the price goes up until supply and demand are matched. If the information is perfect (that is, every buyer and seller knows what is going on), the price is optimized. For most businesses this is not a practical proposition. Their customers expect the same price every time for the same product or service – they have no accurate idea what the demand is at any given moment.

However, for businesses selling on the internet, computer networks have made it possible to see how much consumer demand exists for a given product at any time. Anyone with a point-of-sale till could do the same, but the reports might come in weeks later. This means that online companies could change their prices hundreds of times each day, tailoring them to certain circumstances or certain markets, and so improve profits dramatically. easyJet.com, a budget airline, does just this. It prices to fill its planes, and you could pay anything from £30 ($47/€34) to £200 ($313/€223) (including airport taxes) for the same trip, depending on the demand for that flight. Ryanair and Eurotunnel have similar price ranges based on the basic rule – discounted low fares for early reservations and full fares for desperate late callers!

Internet auction pricing

Once the prerogative of the fine art and antiques markets, auctioning is a fast-growing pricing strategy for a whole host of very different types of business. The theory of auctioning is simple. Have as many interested potential buyers as possible see an item, set a time limit for the transaction to be completed and let them fight it out. The highest bidder wins and, in general, you can get higher prices than by selling through traditional pricing strategies. eBay was a pioneer in the new auction house sector and is still perhaps the best known. But there are dozens of others covering this area and other auction houses you can plug into:

- eBay.com (**www.ebay.co.uk/university**) has its own 'university' training 160,000 or so people in the UK, PowerSellers as they are known, in the art of successful auctioning.

- IBidFree.com (**www.ibidfree.com**), set up by Shane McCormack, a former eBay seller, with the proposition that you can have all the features of eBay but for free. IBidFree.com was created as a perfect opportunity for the person working from home trying to market their products without all of their profits being swallowed up by charges and fees. The rules are few and, unlike eBay, sellers are encouraged to place a link in their auctions back to their own websites. They are also allowed to e-mail each other directly to allow for better communication.

- UBid.com (**www.ubid.com**), founded in 1997, went public in 2005. Its online marketplace provides merchants with an efficient and economical channel for selling on their surplus merchandise. UBid currently carries over 200,000 items for auction/sale each day. You have to become a certified merchant to sell on the site, which cuts down on fraud. The fees are no sale, no fee, and then from 12.5% down to 2.5% on sales of over $1,000.

You could consider starting your own online auction house. The case study example below is a good one, with an interesting twist. To lend a bit of extra credibility, the products being sold can be seen in the showroom.

Pay-what-you-like pricing

This strategy is based on the auction concept but buyers set their own price. The twist is that there is no limit on supply, so everyone can have one at the price they want to pay. Radiohead, the band, released its seventh album *In Rainbows* in October 2007 as a download on its website where fans could pay what they wished, from nothing to £99.99 ($157/€112). Estimates by the online survey group comScore indicate that of the 1.2 million visitors to Radiohead's website, three out of five downloaders paid nothing and the payers averaged £3 ($4.7/€3.37) per album, so allowing for the freeloaders the band realized £1.11 ($1.74/€1.25) per album. The band reckons that was more than they would have made in a traditional label deal. In fact the version of the album released in this way was not the definitive one; that was released three months later in CD format, debuting at No 1 in the United States and the UK.

A number of restaurateurs have experimented with this pricing strategy with some success, but as yet it is in its infancy. Still, eBay is only a 'baby' in the business model world, so watch this space, as they say in the marketing world.

CASE STUDY

Founded in 2006 by Allison Earl Woessner, Auction Atrium (**www.auctionatrium.com**) is an auction company for fine art, antiques and collectables in the £30 ($47/€34) to £3,000 ($4,700/€3,400) price bracket. Auctions run for 7–10 days and bidders can come and inspect lots downstairs in the company's Notting Hill showroom. Julian Costley, former CEO of E*Trade, joined the company as a non-executive director in September 2007 and the business is gearing up for expansion.

Promotion and advertising

The answers to these five questions underpin all advertising and promotional strategies:

- What do you want to happen?
- If that happens, how much is it worth?
- What message will make it happen?
- What media will work best?
- How will you measure the effectiveness of your effort and expense?

What do you want to happen?

Do you want prospective customers to visit your website; phone, write to you or e-mail you; return a card; or send an order in the post? Do you expect them to have an immediate need to which you want them to respond now, or is it that you want them to remember you at some future date when they have a need for whatever it is you are selling?

The more you are able to identify a specific response in terms of orders, visits, phone calls or requests for literature, the better your promotional effort will be tailored to achieve your objective, and the more clearly you will be able to assess the effectiveness of your promotion and its cost versus its yield.

How much is that worth to you?

Once you know what you want a particular promotional activity to achieve, it becomes a little easier to estimate its cost. Suppose a $/£/€1,000 advertisement is expected to generate 100 enquiries for your product. If experience tells you that on average 10 per cent of enquiries result in orders, and your profit margin is $/£/€200 per product, then you can expect an extra $/£/€2,000 profit. That 'benefit' is much greater than the $/£/€1,000 cost of the advertisement, so it seems a worthwhile investment. Then, with your target in mind, decide how much to spend on advertising each month, revising that figure in the light of experience.

Deciding the message

Your promotional message must be built around facts about the company and about the product. The stress here is on the word 'fact', and while there may be many types of fact surrounding you and your products, your customers are interested in only two: the facts that influence their buying decisions, and the ways in which your business and its products stand out from the competition.

These facts must be translated into benefits. (See also 'Features, benefits and proofs' in this chapter.) There is sometimes an assumption that everyone buys only for obvious, logical reasons, when we all know of innumerable examples showing this is not so. Do people buy new clothes only when the old ones are worn out? Do bosses have desks that are bigger than their subordinates' because they have more papers to put on them?

The message should follow the AIDA formula: get Attention, capture Interest, create Desire and encourage Action. Looking at each in turn:

- Getting attention requires a hook. Colour, humour and design are tools used to focus people on your offer and away from the masses of distracting clutter that occupy minds.

- Interest is achieved by involving people in some aspect of the product, perhaps by posing a question such as one diet company does with its challenge 'would you like to loose 2 kg in 2 weeks?'.

- Desire is about showing people the end result they could achieve by having or using your product. Every speedboat advertisement has a beautiful bikini-clad girl posing on the bow, the inference being that if you owned the boat you would be sure to get the girl too.

- Action means provoking a painless way for people to start the buying process. Free trial, money-back guarantee, offer only lasts this week and so forth are examples of the strategies used to achieve this result.

UACCA – Unawareness, Awareness, Comprehension, Conviction, Action is another acronym used in this context.

Choosing the media

Your market research (see below) should produce a clear understanding of who your potential customer group are, which in turn will provide pointers as to how to reach them. But even when you know whom you want to reach with your advertising message it's not always plain sailing. The *Fishing Times*, for example, will be effective at reaching fishermen but less so at reaching their partners who might be persuaded to buy them fishing tackle for Christmas or birthdays. Also, the *Fishing Times* will be jam packed with competitors. It might just conceivably be worth considering a web ad on a page giving tide tables to avoid going head to head with competitors, or getting into a gift catalogue to grab that market's attention.

If a consumer already knows what they want to buy and are just looking for a supplier then, according to statistics, around 60 per cent will turn to print Yellow Pages (or similar); 12 per cent will use a search engine; 11 per cent will use telephone directory enquiries; and 7 per cent online Yellow Pages. Only 3 per cent will turn to a friend. But if you are trying to persuade consumers to think about buying a product or service at a particular time then a leaflet or flyer may be a better option. Once again it's back to your objectives in advertising. The more explicit they are the easier it will be to choose media.

Above or below the line

Advertising media are usually clustered under two headings, above the line and below the line. It has to be said that the line is becoming increasingly indistinct but it is still a term that is part of the lexicon in setting the advertising budget.

Above the line Above the line (ATL) involves using conventional impersonal mass media to promote products and services, talking at the consumer. Major above-the-line techniques include:

- TV, cinema and radio advertising: The vast array of local newspapers, TV channels and digital radio stations can make this a more targeted advertising strategy than has been the case.

- Print advertising in newspapers, magazines, directories and classified ads: Print of all forms has the merit of having a long life, so it can be used for handling more complex messages than, say, radio or TV.

- Internet banner ads act as a point of entry for a more detailed advert.

- Search engines: Search engine advertising comes in two main forms. PPC (pay per click) is where you buy options on certain key words so that someone searching for a product will see your 'advertisement' to the side of the natural search results. Google, for example, offers a deal where you pay only when someone clicks on your ad and you can set a daily budget stating how much you are prepared to spend, with $5 a day as the starting price.

- Podcasts, where internet users can download sound and video free, are now an important part of the E-advertising armoury.

- Posters and billboards.

Below the line Below the line (BTL) talks to the consumer in a more personal way using such media as:

- Direct mail – leaflets, flyers, brochures: Response rates are notoriously low, often less than 1 per cent resulting in sale, but direct mail has the merit of being a proven method of reaching specific targeted market segments.

- Direct e-mail and viral marketing: The latter is the process of creating something so hot that the recipients will pass it on to friends and colleagues, creating extra demand as it rolls out. Jokes, games, pictures, quizzes and surveys are examples.

- Sales promotions, including point of sales material: Activities carried out in this area include free samples, try before you buy, discounts, coupons, incentives and rebates, contests, and special events such as fairs and exhibitions.

- PR (public relations): This is about presenting yourself and your business in a favourable light to your various 'publics' – at little or no cost. It is also a more influential method of communication than general advertising – people believe editorials. There may also be times when you have to deal with the press – anything from when you are trying to get attention for a new product to handling an adverse situation, say if your product has to be recalled for quality reasons, or worse.

- Letterheads, stationery and business cards are often overlooked in the battle for customer attention, but are in fact often the first and perhaps only way in which a business's image is projected.

- Blogs, where the opinions and experiences of particular groups of people are shared using online communities such as MySpace, for example, are an extension of this idea. Neilson NetRatings reported in 2008 that over 2 billion community sites are viewed every month in the UK alone.

Push or pull Like above or below the line, push and pull are different advertising strategies used for achieving different results. Pull advertising is geared to drawing visitors into your net if they are actively looking for your type of product or service. Search engines, listings in on- and off-line directories, Yellow Pages and shopping portals are examples here.

Push advertising tries to get the word out to groups of potential customers in the hope that some of them will be considering making a purchase at about that time. Magazines, newspapers, TV, banner ads and direct mail both on- and off-line are examples here.

As with above and below the line, the distinctions are fast becoming blurred, but the message used in your advertising will be different. With pull there is the assumption that people want to buy, and they just need convincing that they should buy from you. Push calls for a different message convincing them of their need and desire in the first place.

Measuring results

A glance at the advertising analysis in Table 3.3 will show how to tackle the problem. It shows the advertising results for a small business course run in London. At first glance the Sunday paper produced the most enquiries. Although it cost the most, \$/£/€3,400, the cost per enquiry was only slightly more than for the other media used. But the objective of this advertising was not simply to create interest; it was intended to sell places on the course. In fact, only 10 of the 75 enquiries were converted into orders – an advertising cost of \$/£/€340 per head. On this basis the Sunday paper was between 2.5 and 3.5 times more expensive than any other medium.

Judy Lever, co-founder of Blooming Marvellous, the upmarket maternity-wear company, believes strongly not only in evaluating the results of

TABLE 3.3   Measuring advertising effectiveness

Media used	Cost per advert $/£/€	Number of enquiries	Cost per enquiry $/£/€	Number of customers	Advertising cost per customer $/£/€
Sunday paper	3,400	75	45	10	340
Daily paper	2,340	55	43	17	138
Posters	1,250	30	42	10	125
Local weekly paper	400	10	40	4	100

advertising, but in monitoring a particular media capacity to reach her customers:

> We start off with one-sixteenth of a page ads in the specialist press, then once the medium has proved itself we progress gradually to half a page, which experience shows to be our optimum size. On average there are 700,000 pregnancies a year, but the circulation of specialist magazines is only around the 300,000 mark. We have yet to discover a way of reaching all our potential customers at the right time – in other words, early on in their pregnancies.

Place (distribution and logistics)

Place is the fourth 'P' in the marketing mix. This aspect of marketing strategy is about how products and services are actually delivered into the customers' hands.

If you are a retailer, restaurant or hotel chain, for example, then your customers will come to you. Here, your physical location will most probably be the key to success. For businesses in the manufacturing field it is more likely that you will go out to 'find' customers. In this case it will be your channels of distribution that are the vital link. For many businesses delivering a service the internet will be both the ordering and fulfilment vehicle.

The following are the factors to take into account in this area.

Channels of distribution

If your customers don't come to you, then you have the following options in getting your product or service to them:

- Retail stores: This general name covers the great range of outlets from the corner shop to Harrods. Some offer speciality goods such as hi-fi equipment, where the customer expects professional help from the staff. Others, such as Marks & Spencer and Tesco, are mostly self-service, with customers making up their own mind on choice of product.

- Wholesalers and distributors: The pattern of wholesale distribution has changed out of all recognition over the past two decades. It is still an extremely important channel where physical distribution, stock holding, finance and breaking bulk are still profitable functions.

- Cash and carry: This slightly confusing route has replaced the traditional wholesaler as a source of supply for smaller retailers. In return for your paying cash and picking up the goods yourself, the 'wholesaler' shares part of his or her profit margin with you. The attraction for the wholesaler is improved cash flow and for the retailer a bigger margin and a wide product range. Hypermarkets and discount stores also fit somewhere between the manufacturer and the marketplace.

- Mail order: This specialized technique provides a direct channel to the customer, and is an increasingly popular route for new small businesses.

- Internet: Revenue generation via the internet is big business and getting bigger. For some sectors, such as advertising, books, music and video, it has become the dominant route to market. There is no longer any serious argument about whether 'bricks' or 'clicks' is the way forward, or if service businesses work better on the web than physical products. Almost every sector has a major part to play and it is increasingly unlikely that any serious 'bricks' business will not either have or being building an internet trading platform too. Dixon's, a major electrical retailer, has shifted emphasis from the high street to the web and Tesco has built a £ billion-plus home delivery business on the back of its store structure. Amazon, the sector's pioneer, now has in effect the first online department store, with a neat sideline in selling on second-hand items once the customer has finished with the product.

- Door-to-door selling: Traditionally used by vacuum cleaner distributors and encyclopaedia companies, this is now used by insurance companies, cavity-wall insulation firms, double-glazing firms and others. Many use hard-sell techniques, giving door-to-door selling a bad name. However, companies such as Avon Cosmetics have managed to sell successfully door-to-door without attracting the stigma of unethical selling practices.

- Party-plan selling: This is a variation on door-to-door selling that is on the increase, with new party-plan ideas arriving from the United States. Agents enrolled by the company invite their friends to a get-together where the products are demonstrated and orders are invited. The agent gets a commission. Party plan has worked very well for Avon and other firms that sell this way.

Selecting distribution channels

These are the factors you should consider when choosing channels of distribution for your particular business:

1 Does it meet your customers' needs? You have to find out how your customers expect their product or service to be delivered to them and why they need that particular route.

2 Will the product itself survive? Fresh vegetables, for example, need to be moved quickly from where they are grown to where they are consumed.

3 Is it compatible with your image? If you are selling a luxury product, then door-to-door selling may spoil the impression you are trying to create in the rest of your marketing effort.

4 How do your competitors distribute? If they have been around for a while and are obviously successful, it is well worth looking at how your competitors distribute and using that knowledge to your advantage.

5 Will the channel be cost-effective? A small manufacturer may not find it cost-effective to sell to retailers over a certain distance because the direct 'drop' size – that is, the load per order – is too small to be worthwhile.

6 Will the mark-up be enough? If your product cannot bear at least a 100% mark-up, then it is unlikely that you will be able to sell it through department stores. Your distribution channel has to be able to make a profit from selling your product too.

7 Push–pull: Moving a product through a distribution channel calls for two sorts of selling activity. 'Push' is the name given to selling your product in, for example, a shop. 'Pull' is the effort that you carry out on the shop's behalf to help it to sell your product out of that shop. That pull may be caused by your national advertising, a merchandising activity or the uniqueness of your product. You need to know how much push and pull are needed for the channel you are considering. If you are not geared up to help retailers to sell your product, and they need that help, then this could be a poor channel.

8 Physical distribution: The way in which you have to move your product to your end customer is also an important factor to weigh up when choosing a channel. As well as such factors as the cost of carriage, you will also have to decide about packaging materials, warehousing and storage. As a rough rule of thumb, the more stages in the distribution channel, the more robust and expensive your packaging will have to be.

9 Cash flow. Not all channels of distribution settle their bills promptly. Mail-order customers, for example, will pay in advance, but retailers can take up to 90 days or more. You need to take account of this settlement period in your cash-flow forecast.

Logistics The goal of a marketing logistics system is to manage the whole process of getting products to customers in an efficient and cost-effective manner to meet marketing goals; and to get faulty or unwanted products back. This interfaces with a host of related areas of business, including physical transportation, warehousing, relationships with suppliers, and inventory and stock management. Some important considerations in logistics include:

- Just in time (JIT) aims to reduce the need for warehousing through accurate sales forecasting. All parties in the distribution channel carry minimum stock and share information on demand levels.
- Vendor managed inventory (VMI) and continuous inventory replenishment systems (CIRS) require customers to share real-time data on sales demand and inventory levels with suppliers.

Both supplier and customers, while benefiting from cooperation, have mutually conflicting goals in that they want to shift costs onto the other party. Their capacity for doing so depends on their relative strengths. For example, giant retailers such as Tesco and Marks & Spencer have been very successful in getting their suppliers to carry a major part of the cost of stockholding.

Selling

Marketing is the thinking process behind selling; in other words, finding the right people to buy your product or service and making them aware that you are able to meet their needs at a competitive price. But just because customers know you are in the market is not in itself sufficient to make them buy from you. Even if you have a superior product at a competitive price they can escape your net.

Getting customers to sign on the dotted line almost invariably involves selling. This is a process that business people have to use in many situations other than in persuading customers to buy. MBAs have to 'sell' bank managers the idea that lending their business money is worthwhile, that shareholders should invest, that employees by working for them are making a good career move or that their boss should back one of their proposals.

Though essential, selling on its own is an inefficient method of getting potential customers to the point of buying. Understanding the 'ascending ladder of influence', as marketers call it, puts the salesperson's role in perspective. This is a method to rank the 'warm bodies' a customer will encounter in the selling process in the order in which it is most likely to influence your customers favourably. At the top of the scale is the personal recommenda-tion of someone whose opinion is trusted and who is known to be unbiased. An example here is the endorsement of an industry expert who is not on the payroll, such as an existing user of the goods or services who is in the same line of business as the prospective customer. While highly effective, this method is hard to achieve and can be expensive and time consuming. Further down the scale is an approach by you in your role as a salesperson. While you may be seen to be knowledgeable, you clearly stand to gain if a sale is made. So you can hardly be unbiased. Sales calls, however they are made, are an expensive way to reach customers, especially if their orders are likely to be small and infrequent.

How selling works

There is an erroneous view that salespeople, like artists and musicians, are born, not made. Selling can be learnt, improved and enhanced just like any other business activity. First, you need to understand selling's three elements:

- Selling is a process moving through certain stages if the best results are to be achieved. First, you need to listen to the customers to learn what they want to achieve from buying your product or service; then you should demonstrate how you can meet their needs. The next stage is handling questions or objections; a good sign as it shows that the customer is sufficiently interested to engage. Finally comes 'closing the sale'. This is little more than asking for the order with a degree of subtlety.

CASE STUDY

When Sumir Karayi started up in business in the spare room of his flat in West Ealing, London, he wanted his business to be distinctive. He was a technical expert at Microsoft and with two colleagues he set up 1E (**www.1e.com**) as a commune aiming to be the top technical experts in their field. The business name comes from the message that appears on your screen when your computer has crashed. Within a year of starting up the team had learnt two important lessons. Businesses need leaders, not communes, if they are to grow fast and prosper; and they need someone to sell.

On the recommendation of an adviser Karayi went on a selling course and within months had won the first of what became a string of blue chip clients. The company is now one of the 10 fastest-growing companies in the Thames Valley, with annual turnover approaching £15 ($23.5/€16.85) million, profits of 30 per cent and partners and reseller partners worldwide.

- Selling requires planning in that you need to keep records and information on customers and potential customers so you know when they might be ready to buy or reorder.

- Selling is a skill that can be learnt and enhanced by training and practice, as shown in the case study above. The Sales Training Directory (**www.sales-training-courses.co.uk**>Directory) lists sales course providers in the UK.

Negotiating

Like selling, negotiating, of which it usually forms a part, is as much a science as an art. There are a few immutable rules, easily understood but invariably difficult to execute:

- Aim high at the outset. Unless you can find the point of resistance, you can't find the outer limits of your negotiating range.

- You must be prepared to walk away from a deal and make that evident, if you are to have any negotiating leverage. To achieve this you must have prepared plans B and C ready to execute if the terms you want can't be achieved. For example, when negotiating to buy out a competitor, have other businesses in the frame too; or have plans to enter that market without them.

- Search out a range of variables to negotiate other than price. Delivery date, payment terms, quantities, currencies, shared future profits, know-how swaps are just a handful of areas rich in negotiating possibilities.

- Never give a concession away. Anything given for nothing is seen as being worth nothing. Instead, trade concessions and always put the highest value possible on the concession. 'We will pay 30% upfront rather than the 20% you're asking for (a gain for the seller) if you bring the price down to $/£/€1.2m rather than the $/£/€1.3m you're asking' (a gain for the buyer) is the place to start if you hope to hit a $/£/€1.25m final price.

- Talk as little as possible. The less you say the less you can give away.

- Once you have put a proposition on the table, shut up. The first to blink is the loser.

Market research

The purpose of market research is to ensure you have sufficient information on customers, competitors and markets so that you can be reasonably confident that enough people want to buy what you want to sell at a price that will give you a viable business proposition.

You do not have to launch a product or enter a market to prove there are no customers for your goods or services; frequently, even some modest market research beforehand can give clear guidance as to whether your venture will succeed or not.

While big businesses may employ market research agencies to design and execute their research, an MBA should both understand the process and be able to carry out elementary research themselves quickly and on a low budget.

The fundamental goals of market research

The purpose of market research from an MBA's perspective is twofold:

1 To build credibility for a business proposition. The MBA must demonstrate, first to his or her own satisfaction, and later to colleagues, superiors and eventually to financiers, a thorough understanding of the marketplace for the new product, service or strategy. This will be vital if resources are to be attracted to execute the proposal.

2 To develop a realistic market entry strategy for the proposed course of action, based on a clear understanding of genuine customer needs and ensuring that product quality, price, promotional methods and the distribution chain are mutually supportive and clearly focused on target customers.

You will need to research in particular:

- Your customers: Who will buy your goods and services? What particular customer needs will your business meet? How many of them are there?

- Your competitors: Which established companies are already meeting the needs of your potential customers? What are their strengths and weaknesses?

- Your product or service: How should it be tailored to meet customer needs?

- What price should you charge to be perceived as giving value for money?

- What promotional material is needed to reach customers; which newspapers, journals do they read?

- Whether or not your operational base is satisfactorily located to reach your customers most easily, at minimum cost.

Seven steps to successful market research

Researching the market need not be a complex process, nor need it be very expensive. The amount of effort and expenditure needs to be related in some way to the costs and risks associated with the proposition. The market research needs to be conducted systematically following these seven stages:

1 Formulate the problem: Before embarking on your market research you should first set clear and precise objectives, rather than just setting out to find interesting general information about the market.

   So, for example, if you are planning on selling to young fashion-conscious women, among others, your research objective could be: to find out how many women aged 18 to 28, with an income of over £35,000 ($54,800/€39,700) a year, live or work within your catchment area. That would give you some idea whether the market could support a venture such as this.

2 Determine the information needs: Knowing the size of the market, in the example given above, may require several different pieces of information. For example, you would need to know the size of the resident population, which might be fairly easy to find out, but you might also want to know something about people who come into the catchment area to work or stay on holiday or for any other major purpose. There might, for example, be a hospital, library, railway station or school nearby that also pulled potential customers to that particular area.

3 Where can you get the information? This will involve either desk research in libraries or on the internet, or field research, which you can do yourself or get help in doing. Some of the most important of these areas are covered later in this chapter.

   Field research, that is, getting out and asking questions yourself, is the most fruitful way of gathering original information that can provide competitive advantage

4 Decide the budget: Market research will not be free even if you do it yourself. At the very least there will be your time. There may well be the cost of journals, phone calls, letters and field visits to plan for. At the top of the scale could be the costs of employing a professional market research firm.

   Starting at this end of the scale, a business-to-business survey comprising 200 interviews with executives responsible for office equipment purchasing decisions cost one company £12,000 ($18,800/€13,500). Twenty in-depth interviews with consumers who are regular users of certain banking services cost £8,000 ($12,500/€9,000). Using the internet for web surveys is another possibility, but that can impose too much of your agenda onto the recipients and turn them away from you.

Check out companies such as Free Online Surveys (**http://free-online-surveys.co.uk**) and Zoomerang (**www.zoomerang.com/web/signup/Basic.aspx**) which provide software that lets you carry out online surveys and analyse the data quickly. Most of these organizations offer free trials.

Doing the research yourself may save costs but may limit the objectivity of the research. If time is your scarcest commodity, it may make more sense to get an outside agency to do the work. Using a reference librarian or university student to do some of the spadework need not be prohibitively expensive. Another argument for getting professional research is that it may carry more clout with investors.

Whatever the cost of research, you need to assess its value to you when you are setting your budget. If getting it wrong would cost £100,000, then £5,000 spent on market research might be a good investment.

5 Select the research technique: If you cannot find the data you require from desk research, you will need to go out and find the data yourself. The options for such research are described later in this section, under 'Field research'.

6 Construct the research sample population: It is rarely possible or even desirable to include every possible customer or competitor in your research. So, you have to decide how big a sample you need to give you a reliable indication of how the whole population will behave.

7 Process and analyse the data: The raw market research data needs to be analysed and turned into information to guide your decisions on price, promotion and location, and the shape, design and scope of the product or service itself.

Desk research

There is increasingly a great deal of secondary data available in published form and accessible either online or via business sections of public libraries throughout the UK to enable new home business starters both to quantify the size of market sectors they are entering and to determine trends in those markets. In addition to populations of cities and towns (helping to start quantification of markets), libraries frequently purchase Mintel reports, involving studies of growth in different business sectors. Government statistics, showing trends in the economy, are also held (Annual Abstracts for the economy as a whole, Business Monitor for individual sectors).

If you plan to sell to companies or shops, Kompass and Kelly's directories list all company names and addresses (including buyers' telephone numbers). Many industrial sectors are represented by trade associations, which can provide information (see Directory of British Associations, CBD

Research), while Chambers of Commerce are good sources of reference for import/export markets.

These are some readily available sources of desk research data that an MBA can use without tapping deeply into the corporate budget:

- Applegate (**www.applegate.co.uk**) has information on 237,165 companies cross-referenced to 57,089 products in the UK and Ireland. It has a neat facility that allows you to search out the top businesses and people in any industry.

- Business.com (**www.business.com**): Contains some 400,000 listings in 25,000 industry, product and service sub-categories. Useful for general industry background or details about a particular product line.

- Chambers of Commerce (**www.chamberonline.co.uk** > International Trade > International Chambers) run import/export clubs, international trade contacts and provide market research and online intelligence through a 150-country local network of chambers. Their Link2Exports (**www.link2exports.co.uk**) website provides specific information on export markets by industry sector by country.

- Companies House (**www.companieshouse.gov.uk**) is the official repository of all company information in the UK. Their WebCHeck service offers a free-of-charge searchable Company Names and Address Index which covers 2 million companies either by name or by their unique company registration number. You can use WebCHeck to purchase a company's latest accounts giving details of sales, profits, margins, directors, shareholders and bank borrowings at a cost of £1 ($1.57/€1.12) per company.

- Corporate Information (**www.corporateinformation.com** > TOOLS > Research Links) is a business information site covering the main world economies, offering plenty of free information. This link takes you to sources of business information in over 100 countries.

- Easy Searcher 2 (**www.easysearcher.com**) is a collection of 400 search engines, both general and specialist, available on drop-down menus, listed by category.

- Euro Info Centres (**www.euro-info.org.uk**) is a network of 250 centres across Europe providing local access to a range of specialist information and advisory services to help business owners expand. Their services include advice on funding as well as help with market information through their network contacts and specialist information services.

- Kelly's (**www.kellysearch.co.uk**) lists information on 200,000 product and service categories across 200 countries. Business contact details, basic product and service details and online catalogues are provided.

- Key Note Ltd (**www.keynote.co.uk**) has built a reputation as an expert provider of market information, producing highly respected off-the-shelf publications that cover a comprehensive range of market sectors, from commercial and industrial to service and consumer titles. Its report gallery has a listing of literally hundreds of reports covering everything from Activity Holidays to Women's Magazines. The executive summary, a generous 1,000 words plus a full index, is available free on every report, which should make it clear if the report is worth buying, or worth a trip to a major reference library that may well have a copy to view. Reports are priced from around £300 ($470/€340) upwards, with most in the £500 to £700 range.

- Kompass (**www.kompass.com**) claims to have details of 1.6 million UK companies, 23 million key product and service references, 3.2 million executive names, 744,000 trade and brand names and 50,000 Kompass classification codes in its UK directory. It also creates directory information in over 70 countries. Its website has a free access area that users may access without registration.

- LexisNexis (**www.lexis-nexis.com**) has literally dozens of databases covering every sector you can think of, but most useful for researching competitors is Company Analyser, which creates comprehensive company reports drawn from 36 separate sources, with up to 250 documents per source providing access to accurate information about a company.

- Mintel (**www.mintel.com**) publishes over 400 reports every year examining every conceivable consumer market. Reports cost several hundred pounds, but you can view the introduction and main headings. Most are available free in business libraries. Mintel also offers a number of reports on the US and European markets.

- National Statistics (**www.statistics.gov.uk**) contains a vast range of official UK statistics and information about statistics, which can be accessed and downloaded free. There are 13 separate themes. Each one deals with a distinct and easily recognizable area of national life. So, whether you are looking to access the very latest statistics on the UK's economy, or research and survey information released by the government, or want to study popular trends and facts, click on one of these themes and explore!

- Online Newspapers (**www.onlinenewspapers.com**). Newspapers and magazines are a source of considerable information on companies, markets and products in that sphere of interest. Virtually every online newspaper in the world is listed here. You can search straight from the homepage, either by continent or country. You can also find the 50 most popular online newspapers from a link in the top centre of the homepage. There is also a separate site for online magazines (**www.onlinenewspapers.com/SiteMap/magazines-sitemap.htm**).

- Research and Markets (**www.researchandmarkets.co.uk**) is a one-stop shop that holds nearly 400,000 market research reports listed in a hundred or so categories and across over 70 countries. Reports are priced from £20 ($31.50/€22.50) upwards.

- The Wholesaler UK (**www.thewholesaler.co.uk**) is a directory for a wide range of products. It is intended for businesses looking for additional suppliers but as such provides a valuable first sift to see who is the market.

- Thomas Global Register (**www.thomasglobal.com**) is an online directory in 11 languages with details of over 700,000 suppliers in 28 countries. It can be searched by industry sub-sector or name either for the world or by country.

- World Market Research Associations (**www.mrweb.com**), while not quite the world, does have web addresses for over 65 national market research associations and a hundred or so other bodies such as the Mystery Shopping Providers Association, which in turn has over 150 members, companies worldwide.

Using the internet

The internet is a rich source of market data, much of it free and immediately available. But you can't always be certain that the information is reliable or free of bias, as it can be difficult if not impossible to always work out who exactly is providing it. That being said, you can get some valuable pointers as to whether or not what you plan to sell has a market, how big that market is and who else trades in that space. The following sources should be your starting point:

- Google Trends (**www.google.co.uk/Trends**) provides a snapshot on what the world is most interested in at any one moment. For example, if you are thinking of starting a bookkeeping service, entering that into the search pane produces a snazzy graph showing how interest measured by the number of searches is growing (or contracting) since January 2004 when they started collecting the data. You can also see that South Africa has the greatest interest and the Netherlands the lowest. You can tweak the graph to show seasonality, thus showing that Croydon registers the greatest interest in the UK overall and 'demand' peaks in September and bottoms out in November.

- Google News (**www.google.com**), which you can tap into by selecting 'News' on the horizontal menu at the top of the page under the Google banner. Here you will find links to any newspaper article anywhere in the world covering a particular topic over the past decade or so listed by year. Asking for information on baby clothes will reveal recent articles on how much the average family spends on baby clothes, the launch of a thrift store specializing in second-hand baby clothes and the launch of an Organic baby clothes catalogue.

- Microsoft (**http://adlab.microsoft.com/Demographics-Prediction**) is testing a product that can give you masses of data on market demographics (age, sex, income etc), purchase intentions and a search funnel tool that helps you understand how your market searches the internet. Using the demographics tool, you can find that 76% of people showing an interest in baby clothes are female and surprisingly 24% are male. The peak age group is the 25–34-year-olds and the lowest is the under-18s followed by the over-50s.

- Inventory Overture (**http://inventory.overture.com/d/ searchinventory/suggestion/**) is a search tool showing how many people searched Yahoo for a particular item. So, for example, while 10,837 looked for either baby or baby and toddler clothing, only 927 searched for organic baby clothing, 167 for used baby clothing and 141 for cheap baby clothing: facts that give useful pointers as to the likely price sensitivity in this market.

- Blogs are sites where people, informed and ignorant, converse about a particular topic. The information on blogs is more straw in the wind than fact. Globe of Blogs (**www.globeofblogs.com**), launched in 2002, claims to be the first comprehensive world weblog directory, which links up to over 58,100 blogs, searchable by country, topic and just about any other criteria you care to name. Google (**http:// blogsearch.google.com**) is also a search engine to the world's blogs.

- Trade Association Forum (**www.taforum.org** > Directories > Association Directory) is the directory of Trade Associations on whose websites are links to industry-relevant online research sources. For example, you will find The Baby Products Association listed, at whose website you can find details of the 238 companies operating in the sector, including their contact details.

- The Internet Public Library (**www.ipl.org**) is run by a consortium of US universities whose aim is to provide internet users help with finding information online. There are extensive sections on business, computers, education, leisure and health.

- Find Articles.com (**www.findarticles.com**) aims to provide credible, freely available information you can trust. It has over 10 million articles from thousands of resources, archived dating back to 1984, on its website. You can see a summary of all articles and most are free, though in some cases you may need a modest subscription, rarely more than a few pounds. You can restrict your search to those articles that are free by selecting 'free articles only' from the right-hand pull-down menu.

Field research

Most fieldwork carried out consists of interviews, with the interviewer putting questions to a respondent. The more popular forms of interview are currently:

- personal (face-to-face) interview: 45% (especially for the consumer markets);
- telephone, e-mail and web surveys: 42% (especially for surveying companies);
- post: 6% (especially for industrial markets);
- test and discussion group: 7%.

Personal interviews, web surveys and postal surveys are clearly less expensive than getting together panels of interested parties or using expensive telephone time. Telephone interviewing requires a very positive attitude, courtesy, an ability not to talk too quickly, and listening while sticking to a rigid questionnaire. Low response rates on postal services (less than 10 per cent is normal) can be improved by accompanying letters explaining the questionnaire's purpose and why respondents should reply, by offering rewards for completed questionnaires (small gift), by sending reminder letters and, of course, by providing pre-paid reply envelopes. Personally addressed e-mail questionnaires have secured higher response rates – as high as 10–15 per cent – as recipients have a greater tendency to read and respond to e-mail received in their private e-mail boxes. However, unsolicited e-mails ('spam') can cause vehement reactions: the key to success is the same as with postal surveys – the mailing should feature an explanatory letter and incentives for the recipient to 'open' the questionnaire.

There are the basic rules for good questionnaire design, however the questions are to be administered:

1 Keep the number of questions to a minimum.
2 Keep the questions simple! Answers should be either 'Yes/No/Don't know' or offer at least four alternatives.
3 Avoid ambiguity – make sure the respondent really understands the question (avoid 'generally', 'usually', 'regularly').
4 Seek factual answers, avoid opinions.
5 Make sure that at the beginning you have a cut-out question to eliminate unsuitable respondents (eg those who never use the product/service).
6 At the end, make sure you have an identifying question to show the cross-section of respondents.

Sample size is vital if reliance is to be placed on survey data. How to calculate the appropriate sample size is explained in Chapter 11 in the section headed 'Survey sample size'.

Testing the market

The ultimate form of market research is to find some real customers to buy and use your product or service before you spend too much time and money in setting up. The ideal way to do this is to sell into a limited area or a small section of your market. In that way, if things don't quite work out as you expect, you won't have upset too many people.

This may involve buying in a small quantity of product, as you need to fulfil the order in order to fully test your ideas. Once you have found a small number of people who are happy with your product, price, delivery/execution and have paid up, you can proceed with a bit more confidence than if all your ideas are just on paper.

Pick potential customers whose demand is likely to be small and easy to meet. For example, if you are going to run a bookkeeping business, select 5 to 10 small businesses from an area reasonably close to home and make your pitch. The same approach would work with a gardening, baby-sitting or any other service-related venture. It's a little more difficult with products, but you could buy in a small quantity of similar items from a competitor or make up a trial batch yourself.

Organizational behaviour

04

- Structural options
- Line and staff relationships
- Building and leading teams
- Understanding motivation
- Managing people effectively
- Directors' roles
- Handling change

Organizational behaviour, usually shortened to OB, is the whole rather amorphous area that deals with people, why they behave the way they do and how to create and manage an organization that can achieve the goals set for the business. As one cynical CEO summarized the task: 'to get people to do what I want them to do because they want to do it'.

The single most prevalent reason for a strategy failing lies in its implementation; the analysis and planning behind a proposed course of action are rarely the root of the problem. That is more likely to lie in the selection of the people to implement strategy, their management, motivation, rewards and the way in which they are organized and led. Stated like that, it sounds a fairly simple task. Just work your way through those headings and any MBA worth their salt should be able to get the desired results. Unfortunately, people both individually and collectively are rarely malleable and infinitely variable in their likely responses to situations. The famous German military strategist Moltke's statement that 'No campaign plan survives first contact with the enemy' applies here if the word enemy is replaced by organization.

However, by understanding and applying a number of principles and concepts on the typical MBA syllabus you can improve an organization's chances of achieving its objectives.

Strategy vs structure, people and systems

This is the 'which came first' question akin to that of the chicken and the egg. Unless you are starting up an organization on a greenfield site with no people other than yourself and only a pile of cash, every business situation involves some compromise between the ideal and the possible when it comes to people and structures.

The theory is clear. An organization's strategy, itself a product of its business environment, determines the shape of the organization's structure, the sort of people it will employ and how they will be managed, controlled and rewarded. But in the real world the business environment is constantly changing as the economy fluctuates, competitors come and go, and consumer needs, desires and aspirations alter. In any event a business is limited in its freedom of action. However violent and essential a change in strategy, a business will rarely be free to hire and fire staff at will simply to change direction. The exception is in the case of a complete closure or withdrawal from an activity such as that of Marks & Spencer's controversial closure of its French outlets in 2001. This move was considered vital to the survival of the whole business and despite May Day protests in France the company's shares rose 7 per cent on the announcement.

Figure 4.1 is a useful aid to understanding how to approach OB. The concentric circles are a metaphor to remind us of the circular nature of subject. You can't just tackle one area without having an impact on others.

FIGURE 4.1   A framework for understanding organizational behaviour

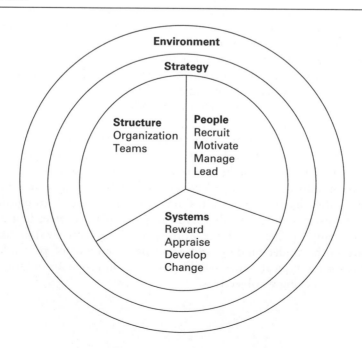

Structures – the options

Just as the skeleton is the structure that holds a body together, a business too has its framework. The goal of any framework is to provide some boundaries while at the same time allowing the whole 'body' flexibility to respond in order to go about its business. While human bodies keep a very similar skeleton to the one they start out with, a business has a number of very different organizational structures to choose from. Also, it is unlikely that any one structure will be appropriate throughout an organization's life.

For an organization a structure has to perform the following functions:

- show who is responsible for what and to whom;
- define roles and responsibilities;
- establish communication and control mechanisms;
- lay out the ground rules for cooperation between all parts of the organization;
- set out the hierarchy of authority, power and decision making.

There are two major building blocks used in shaping an organization's structure beyond the level of the individual: the organizational chart and team composition.

Pictorial methods of describing how organizations work have been around for centuries. Both the Roman and Prussian armies had descriptions of their hierarchical structures and the latter incorporated line and staff relationships. There is also some evidence that the ancient Egyptians documented their methods for organizing and dividing workers on major projects such as the pyramids. However, Daniel C McCallum is generally credited with developing the first systematic set of organizational charts in 1855, to organize railroad building on an efficient basis. The trigger for his innovation was the discovery that the building costs per mile of track did not drop with the length of line being built, contrary to logic. The inefficiencies were being caused by poor organization.

Basic hierarchical organization

This simple structure has every member or part of the organization reporting in to one person (Figure 4.2). It works well when the organization is small, decisions are simple or routine and communications are easy.

This basic structure can be based around one of several groupings, including:

- functions such as marketing or manufacturing;
- geography such as country or region;
- product;
- customer or market segment such as trade, consumers, new accounts or key accounts.

FIGURE 4.2   Basic hierarchical organization chart

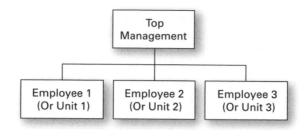

Span of control

The number of people a manager can have reporting to them in a hierarchy is governed by the span of control. Few people reporting and the span of control is termed as narrow, and more as wide.

A narrow span of control means that any one manager has fewer people reporting to them, so communications should be better and control easier. However, as the organization grows, that usually means creating more and more layers of management, so negating any earlier efficiency.

A wide span of control, also known as a flat management structure, involves having many people or units reporting to one person. This usually means having fewer layers of management, but it does call for a greater level of skill from those doing the managing. The nature of the tasks being carried out by subordinates will limit the capacity to run a flat organization. For example, a regional manager responsible for identical units such as branches of a supermarket chain, supported by good and well-developed control systems, may be able to have 10 or more direct reports. But if the organization comprises very different types of unit, for example retail outlets, central bakeries, garages, factories, accounts departments and sales teams, the ability of any one manager to handle that diversity will be limited.

A further factor to take into account is the skill level of both managers and managed. A higher-skilled workforce can operate with a wider span of control as they will need less supervision and a higher-skilled manager can control a greater number of staff.

Line and staff organization

One way to keep an organization structure flat as the enterprise gets bigger and more complex is to introduce staff functions that take over some of the common duties of unit managers. For example, a production manager could probably handle their own recruitment, selection and training of staff while they have a dozen or so people in their domain. Once that expands to hundreds, and if growth is also impacting on other management areas such as sales and marketing, then it may be more efficient to create a specialist HR unit to support the line managers.

Staff positions support line managers by providing knowledge and expertise but the buck ultimately stops with the line manager. Three types of authority are created in a line and staff organization, so alongside some efficiencies lies the possibility for conflict:

- Line authority goes down the chain of command, giving those further up the right and responsibility to instruct those below them to carry out specific tasks.

- Staff authority is the right and responsibility to advise line managers in certain areas. For example, an HR staffer will advise a line manager on redundancy terms, conditions of employment and disciplinary issues.

- Functional authority or limited line authority gives a staff person the ultimate sanction over particular functions such as safety or financial reporting.

There are possibilities for conflict in the relationship between line and staff but these can be minimized in two ways. In the first instance staff people report to their own superiors who have line authority over them. Second, line and staff personnel can be organized into teams with shared goals and objectives (Figure 4.3).

Functional organization

In a functional organization (Figure 4.4) the staff and line managers all re-port to a common senior manager. This places more of a burden on senior management who have a wider span of control and a greater variety of tasks for which to take responsibility. However, this structure concentrates all responsibility in one person and so minimizes the area for conflict. It may also deny an organization the high level of expertise that comes with having a professional staff function. For example, this would leave the onus for being fully conversant with current employment law on a production manager, rather than giving them access to staff advice. They can, of course, read up

FIGURE 4.3 Line and staff organization chart

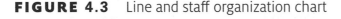

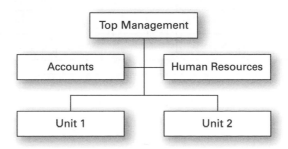

FIGURE 4.4   Functional organization chart

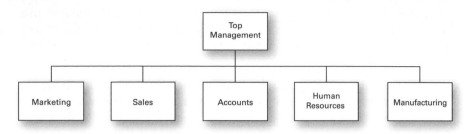

on the law themselves, but that is not quite as good as having it as a part of an everyday skill and experience base.

Matrix organization

A matrix organization gives two people line authority for interlocking areas of responsibility. In Figure 4.5 you can see that a manager is responsible for sales of product group 1 in both Europe and Asia. However, a manager is also responsible for the sales of all product groups within their continent.

The aim of a matrix structure is to ensure that all key areas in an organization have a line manager responsible for championing them. There is still the possibility for conflict of interest. For example, the person responsible for a product group may try to get more attention for their product in a particular market than it really warrants. In theory, the managers in matrix organizations are senior enough to iron out their differences. That is not always the case in practice and in such cases their mutual boss has to resolve the issue.

FIGURE 4.5   Matrix organization chart

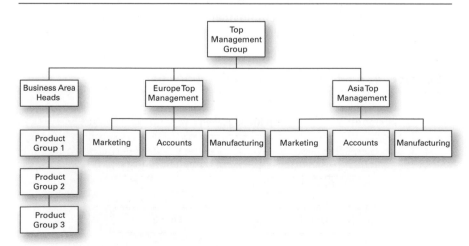

Strategic business unit (SBU)

SBUs (Figure 4.6) are in effect separate enterprises with full responsibility for their own profit or loss. They may themselves be organized in any one of the above structures. If they don't have their own specialist staff function, they may buy it in from the parent company when required. This maintains the concept of full profit accountability.

SBUs are further divided into those that simply have control over current revenue and expenditure and those 'investment centres' that can make capital expenditure decisions such as setting up a new plant, investing in research and development or buying up competitors.

FIGURE 4.6 Strategic business unit organization chart

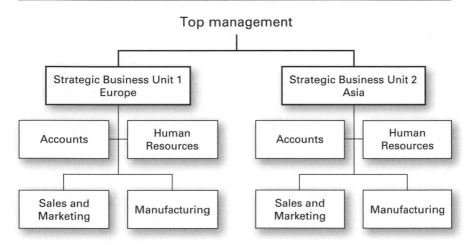

Succession planning

No general would fight a battle without having a reserve force ready to plug gaps that appear in the front line or are caused by casualties in key staff. Perhaps the most spectacular military example was the rapid deployment of Montgomery to head the 8th Army when Churchill's own preferred candidate, 'Strafer' Gott, was killed flying back to Cairo.

For business and other organizations this reserve is usually limited to the process of identifying future potential leaders to fill key positions when staff leave or are themselves promoted. A subsidiary but nonetheless important role of any organization chart is to facilitate this planning.

Elements to consider in this area include:

● broadening existing managers' competences by lateral moves in the organization;

- training and development across a wider skill base than is required for current roles;
- having a database of outsiders who can rapidly be approached by head hunters (specialist recruitment consultants) when the need arises.

Teams

Teams are the component parts of a business's structure and their effective creation and operation are a key way to get exceptional results from an organization. A group of people, even if they work together, are not necessarily a team. Look at Figure 4.7, which compares some of the characteristics of a sports team with those of a random collection of people that meet for a game. You can see immediately what needs to be done to weld people into a team.

FIGURE 4.7   Groups are not the same as teams

Sports team

- Has the right number of players for the game
- Everyone has a clearly defined role
- Concrete and measurable objectives
- An obvious competitor for the team to unite against
- A coach to train and improve players' game
- Right equipment for the game

Sports club

- Just the number of people who turn up
- Positions of players decided on the day
- Often the aims have never been explained and where they have, different people have different aims
- Sometimes the internal competition is more important than winning a game
- Training is ad hoc
- The right equipment is sometimes missing and not all players have the right equipment

Successful teams have certain features in common. They all have strong and effective leadership; clear objectives; appropriate resources; the ability to communicate freely throughout the organization; the authority to act quickly on decisions; a good balance of team members; the ability to work collectively; and a size appropriate to the task.

Team types

Teams can be made up of anything from 5 to 20 people. Anything above 20 is usually too unwieldy and will take up more resources than an organization can afford to devote to one aspect of the business.

Business teams These are a group of people tasked with managing functions and achieving specific results over the longer term. In this example there are three of these, covering sales, administration and warehouse/dispatch. So, for example, the sales team is expected to meet sales targets and the dispatch team to get goods to customers on time. In practice, every firm will have its own definition of business functions.

Project teams These are often cross-functional, made up of people from different areas. These can be assembled for any period of time to look at a particular project. In this example we have assumed that each of these teams has been asked to look at how each function could be made more efficient. The value of having someone from other functions in these teams is to ensure that too parochial a view is not taken.

Taskforce teams This is a short-term body put together quickly to look at one narrow issue or specific problem. For example, if you proposed changing your working hours a taskforce could look at the implications for everyone inside and outside the firm and report back. Then a decision based on the best information, provided by people most affected by the change, can be made.

Team roles

However talented the soloists are in an organization, in the end it is orchestras that make enough 'noise' to make things happen. But teams don't just occur naturally. The presumption that people are going to work together is usually a mistake. Chaos is more likely than teamwork.

Cultures in businesses have very different pedigrees and can pull the organization in very different directions. Take one successful new internet business for example, where people came from financial services, retail and more recently technology. The company's roots were in financial services. Their competitors were banks and brokerage firms and their employees had moved around the sector in search of the ultimate accolade, to become a vice-president. The focus was inwards towards 'hierarchy and title'. Their second cohort of employees came from retailing, the staff of their one-time expanding branch network. For retailers the focus is outwards towards the customer. Their success was measured in the market and the best salespeople had the greatest respect and power. The third group, and the most recent, was the technologists. For these people success was measured by technical expertise. Titles were irrelevant and their main concern was for the completion of the project. Their loyalty was not to the hierarchy but to the principles of the project itself, and to their team.

Putting people with disparate cultures into teams because of their particular professional or job skills may not be effective. If the team is to function effectively, the balance of behavioural styles has to mesh too. These are the key roles identified by Meredith Belbin while a Research Fellow at Cranfield (**www.belbin.com**), which need to be taken if a team is to work effectively (there are other methods of categorizing team roles):

- Chairman/team leader. Stable, dominant, extrovert. Concentrates on objectives. Does not originate ideas. Focuses people on what they do best.
- Plant. Dominant, high IQ, introvert. A 'scatterer of seeds' who originates ideas. Misses out on detail. Thrustful but easily offended.

- Resource investigator. Stable, dominant, extrovert and sociable. Lots of contacts with the outside word. Strong on networks. Salesperson/diplomat/liaison officer. Not an original thinker.

- Shaper. Anxious, dominant, extrovert. Emotional and impulsive. Quick to challenge and to respond to a challenge. Unites ideas, objectives and possibilities. Competitive. Intolerant of woolliness and vagueness.

- Company worker. Stable, controlled. A practical organizer. Can be inflexible but likely to adapt to established systems. Not an innovator.

- Monitor evaluator. High IQ, stable, introvert. Goes in for measured analysis, not innovation. Unambiguous and often lacking enthusiasm. But solid and dependable.

- Team worker. Stable, extrovert, but not really dominant. Much concerned with individuals' needs. Builds on others' ideas. Cools things down when tempers fray.

- Finisher. Anxious introvert. Worries over what could go wrong. Permanent sense of urgency. Preoccupied with order. Concerned with 'following through'.

Building and running a team

These are the five essential elements to establishing and running effective teams.

Balanced team roles

You have to start building a team by recognizing that people are different. Every team member must not only have their 'technical' skills such as being an accountant or salesperson. They must also have a valuable team role. Experts in team behaviour have identified the key team profiles that are essential if a team is to function well. Any one person may perform more than one of these roles. But if too many people are competing to perform one of the roles, or one or more of these roles are neglected, the team will be unbalanced. They will perform in much the same way as a car does when a cylinder misfires.

Shared vision and goal

It is essential that the team has ownership of its own measurable and clearly defined goals. This means involving the team in business planning. It also means keeping the communications channels open as the business grows.

The founding team knew clearly what they were trying to achieve and as they probably shared an office they shared information as they worked. But as the group gets larger and new people join, it will become necessary to help the informal communication systems to work better. Briefing meetings, social events and bulletin boards are all ways to get teams together and keep them facing the right way.

Have a shared language

To be a member of a business team, people have to have a reasonable grasp of the language of business. It's not much use extolling people to improve return on capital employed or reduce debtor days if they have only the haziest notion of what those terms mean, why they matter or how they can influence the results. So you need to develop rounded business skills across all the core team members through continuous training, development and coaching.

Compatible personalities

While having different Belbin team profiles is important, it is equally vital to have a team who can get on with one another. They have to be able to listen to and respect other people's ideas and views. They need to support and trust one another. They need to be able to accept conflict as a healthy reality and work through it to a successful outcome.

Good leadership

First-class leadership is perhaps the most important characteristic that distinguishes winning teams from the also-rans. However good the constituent parts, without leadership a team rapidly disintegrates into a rabble bound by little but a pay cheque. (See later in this chapter for more on leadership.)

The board of directors

One team stands apart from all the others within an organization – the board of directors, usually reduced to the title 'the board'. Directors in major or public companies have a role outside of that of simply heading up a function such as production, sales or marketing, though they may perform one of those functions too. There is often confusion as to where the ultimate power rests in a company; with the directors or the shareholders. In private companies they are often one and the same body but in public companies, even where family ties remain, they are distinct and separate. In law a company is an entity separate from both its shareholders and directors. According to a company's articles of association, some powers are exercised by directors, while certain other powers may be reserved for the shareholders and exercised at a general meeting. If the powers of management are vested in the directors, then they and they alone can exercise these powers. The only way in which shareholders can control the exercise of powers by directors is by altering the articles, or by refusing to re-elect the directors of whose actions they disapprove. Some of a director's duties, responsibilities and potential liabilities are:

- To act in good faith in the interests of the company; this includes carrying out duties diligently and honestly.
- Not to carry on the business of the company with intent to defraud creditors or for any fraudulent purpose.
- Not knowingly to allow the company to trade while insolvent; directors who do so may have to pay for the debts incurred by the company while insolvent.
- Not to deceive shareholders and to appoint auditors to oversee the accounting records.
- To have regard for the interests of employees in general.
- To comply with the requirements of the Companies Acts, such as providing what is needed in accounting records or filing accounts.

Composition of the board

The board is made up of two types of directors, internal and external, and typically the board would exercise major decisions through a number of committees:

- Internal directors: Usually headed up by a chairman who runs board meetings, a CEO (chief executive officer) or managing director who runs the operating business and a number of other directors.
- External directors: Known as non-executive directors, they are usually people of stature and experience who can act as both a source of wise independent advice and a check on any wilder elements on a board. *Financial Times* Non-Executive Directors' Club (**www.non-execs.com**) provides more information on the role of non-executive director, as well as being a potential source of appointments in smaller companies that might appeal to an ambitious, risk-happy MBA.
- Committees: The main board committees are those that oversee remuneration (particularly for directors), auditing, social responsibility (and 'green' matters), mergers and acquisitions, and regulatory affairs.

People

If structures are the skeleton of an organization, people are its blood and guts. Douglas McGregor, a founding faculty member of MIT's Sloan School of Management, began his management classic *The Human Side of Enterprise*, published in 1960, with the question: 'What are your assumptions (implicit as well as explicit) about the most effective way to manage people?' This seemingly simple question led to a fundamental revolution in management thinking. McGregor went on to claim: 'The effectiveness of organizations could be at least doubled if managers could discover how to tap into the unrealized potential present in their workforces.'

Finding the right people, keeping them onside, motivating, managing and rewarding them are the defining distinctions between the most successful organizations and the mediocre. Over the past 30 years or so, organizations have acquired centralized HR (human resources) departments whose purpose is to facilitate people issues, as they often quaintly term their work. McGregor anticipated their arrival with this pithy quote:

> It is one of the favourite pastimes of management to decide, from within their professional ivory tower, what help the field organization needs and then to design and develop programs for meeting these needs. Then it becomes necessary to get the field organization to accept the help provided. This is normally the role of the Change Manager; to implement the change that no-one asked for or wants.

None of this is to suggest that HR departments can't contribute to helping with 'people issues'. It's just that people issues are too important to exclude their immediate superiors from. At the very least, MBA skills include a sound grasp of the key tasks that the HR department is charged with performing.

Recruitment and selection

Taking on new employees is often a more expensive exercise than buying a major item of machinery or a heavy goods vehicle. If that sounds improbable, just check out the figures; the advertising for a middle-ranking executive on a salary of, say, £40,000 may well cost £6,000. If they are taken on using a recruitment consultant you can expect a bill of around a fifth of the first year's pay (£8,000 ($12,500/€9,000)). Three days' interviewing, psychometric testing, preparing a contract of employment, perhaps paying a share of the new employee's removal expenses will bring the total bill up to around £20,000 ($31,700/€22,500). If you get the wrong candidate, and there is a good chance of that happening if you fail with any element of the recruitment process, then you may have to double that figure. Then, of course, there is the cost of not getting the job done that you were recruiting for in the first place.

These are the key stages in the recruitment process.

CASE STUDY Bebo

Michael Birch had what might be seen as six dummy runs before co-founding Bebo. He was a pioneer in the social networking site world, starting up Ringo.com back in 2003, selling it on quickly – with the benefit of hindsight perhaps too quickly. Operating out of a 120 sq ft office in the suburbs of San Francisco, overwhelmed with the initial site traffic and lacking finance, they sold Ringo within six months.

Birch and his wife Xochi met up while studying physics at Imperial College, London. After a six-year slog at Zurich Insurance in computer programming he left, frustrated by the overly bureaucratic environment, a lesson in organizational behaviour that he was to apply to advantage in future ventures. The Birches then started out on their path as serial entrepreneurs. Their first three dotcom start-ups were unsuccessful, but then their luck changed. BirthdayAlarm.com, initially a simple alert service that evolved into an e-cards business, was followed by Ringo, whose sale gave them some cash to roll on to a more substantial venture. Applying everything they had learnt from Ringo and what wasn't working on MySpace, the Birches aimed Bebo squarely at the 30-something age group, but rapidly refocused on teenagers, the site's early adopters.

Within two years of starting, Bebo.com became the most visited social networking site from within the UK, attracting 10.6 million unique visitors, an increase of 63 per cent over the start of the year, ahead of Myspace.com, with just 10.1 million unique visitors. Selling up to AOL in March 2008 left the Birches some £295 ($460/€330) million for their 70 per cent stake and some pointers as to how their next venture will be run. Being able to attract veterans of the internet from companies such as Google, Yahoo! and MSN and fostering their loyalty, Birch claims, is the main 'non-marketing' key to their success.

Writing the job description

Often employers draw up the job description after they have found the candidate. This is a mistake; having it from the outset narrows down your search for suitable candidates, focuses you on specific search methods and gives you a valid reason for declining unwelcome job requests from colleagues and friends. In any event you have to give employees a contract of employment when you take them on and the job description makes this task much easier.

Include the following in a job description:

- the title, such as area sales manager, management accountant or product manager;
- the knowledge, skills and experience you expect them to have or acquire;

- the main duties, responsibilities and measurable outputs expected;
- the work location and general conditions, such as hours to be worked, lunch breaks and paid holiday arrangements;
- the pay structure and rewards;
- who the employee will report to.

Business Link (**www.businesslink.gov.uk** > Employing people > Recruitment and getting started > Recruiting and interviewing) has detailed guidance on writing a job description.

Where you find great employees

There are many ways to find employees; for finding great employees the choices are more limited. Research at Cranfield revealed some alarming statistics. First, nearly two-thirds of all first appointments failed and the employee left within a year, having been unsatisfactory. Second, there were marked differences in the success rate that appear to be dependent on the way in which employees are looked for.

Employing an agency or consultant This is the least popular, most expensive and most successful recruitment method. Only one in fifteen private firms do so for their early appointments, but when they do they are three times more likely to get the right person. The larger the business the more likely they are to take external advice in recruitment. The reasons for success are, in part, the value added by the agency or consultant in helping get the job description and pay package right; and the fact that they have already pre-interviewed prospective employees before they put them forward. These organizations can help here:

- Job Centre Plus (**www.jobcentreplus.gov.uk** > Need to fill a job?) is a free government-funded service to help UK firms fill full- or part-time vacancies at home or overseas. They can offer advice on recruitment and selection methods, local and trade pay rates, training, contracts of employment and, importantly, can offer interview facilities in some of their national network of offices, which can be useful if you are recruiting away from your home base.
- The Recruitment & Employment Confederation (**www.rec.uk.com/ employer** > Choosing an Agency) is the professional association that supports and represents over 8,000 recruitment agencies and 6,000 recruitment professionals. As well as advice on choosing an agent, there is a mass of information on employment law and a directory of members listed by business sector and geographic area.

Advertising in the press You have a large number of options when it comes to press advertising. Local papers are good for generally available skills and where the pay is such that people expect to live close to where they work.

National papers are much more expensive but attract a wider pool of people with a cross-section of skills, including those not necessarily available locally. Trade and specialist papers and magazines are useful if it is essential that your applicant has a specific qualification, say in accountancy or computing.

The goal of a job advertisement is not just to generate responses from suitably qualified applicants, but also to screen out applicants who are clearly unqualified. If you make the job sound more attractive than it really is and are too vague about the sort of person you are looking for, you could end up with hundreds of applicants.

You need to consider the following elements when writing the job advertisement:

- Headline: This is usually the job title, perhaps with some pertinent embellishment. For example, Dynamic sales person required.

- Job information: This is a line or two about the general duties and responsibilities of the job.

- Organization information: Always include something explaining what you do and where you do it.

- Qualifications: Specify any qualifications and experience that are required. You can qualify some aspects of this by saying that a particular skill would be useful but is not essential.

- Response method: Tell applicants how to reply and what information to provide.

Try to include something about your business culture in the advertisement. One firm puts its advertisements sideways on, so applicants have to turn the paper round to read them. They claim that this lets people see that they want people who look at things in unconventional ways to apply and that they are not a run-of-the-mill firm that works like any other firm. Using an active rather than a passive voice will give your advertisement a sense of buzz and enthusiasm.

You can find all the local and national newspapers listed at Newspapers. com (**www.newspapers.com**). From the individual newspaper web link homepage you will find a signpost to 'Advertising' and from there you can find the readership demographics and advertising rate. For example, for the *Metro* (**www.metro.co.uk** > Advertising.metro.co.uk > Who reads us?).

Using the internet Nearly a quarter of all jobs are filled using job boards, a website where employees and employers can get together much along the lines of a dating agency. The internet's advantages are speed, cost and reach. You can get your job offer in front of thousands of candidates in seconds. The fees are usually modest, often less than regional paper job adverts, and in some cases, such as with webrecruit.co.uk (**www.webrecruit.co.uk**), though the fee is a relatively high £595 ($933/€670), they will reimburse you if they can't fill your job. Services through job boards range from passive, where employers and employees just find each other, to the proactive, where online candidate databases are searched and suitable candidates are made aware of your vacancy. Recruiter Solutions (**www.recruitersolutions.co.uk** > Job Boards) is a directory of job board websites and whatjobsite.com (**www. whatjobsite.com** > Jobsite Directory) has a search facility that lets you look for the job boards by country and region and that are most suited to the job on offer and the industry you are in.

Using your network Organizations of every size and shape use contacts and networks when they are recruiting. This route is favoured because it is cheap, informal and can be pursued without the bother of writing a job description, which can in effect be infinitely varied to suit the candidates that may surface. Public sector bodies and many public companies are obliged either by law or convention to advertise vacancies, but that in no way inhibits drawing a potential candidate's attention to the opportunity.

Unfortunately, the statistics indicate that two out of five appointments made in this way fail within six months and the business is back in the recruiting game again. The reasons for this being an unsatisfactory route lie somewhere in the absence of rigour that the approach encourages; only if you can take a thorough approach and be sure of a genuine reason why someone would want to recommend someone to you should you recruit in this way.

Hiring people

Once you have candidates for your vacancy, the next task is to interview, select and appoint. If you have done your homework the chances are that you will have a dozen or more applicants, too many to interview, so this process is somewhat like a funnel, narrowing down until you have your ideal candidate appointed.

Selecting a candidate You need to find at least two and ideally three people who could fill your vacancy to a standard that you would be happy with; this gives you contrast, which is always helpful in clarifying your ideas on the job; and a reserve in case the first candidate drops by the wayside or turns you down. The stages in making your selection are as follows:

- Make a shortlist of the three or four candidates that best suit the criteria set out in your job definition.
- Interview each candidate, ideally on the same day so all the information is fresh in your mind. Plan your questions in advance but be sure to let them do most of the talking. Use your questions to plug any gaps in your knowledge about the candidate. Monster (**www.monster.co.uk** > Employers > Recruitment Centre > Monster Guides > Guide to interview technique) has a useful set of interview questions to ask, with some guidance on how to get the best out of the process.

- Use tests to assess aptitude and knowledge if the job is a senior one such as accountant or sales manager. You can find a test to measure almost any aspect of a candidate's skills, attitude, aptitude and almost anything else you care to name. Thousands of the most successful companies use them and claim to get better candidates and higher staff retention than they would otherwise achieve. Tests cost from £10 a candidate from companies such as Central Test (**www.centraltest.co.uk**); the British Psychological Society (**www.bps.org.uk**) and The Chartered Institute of Personnel and Development (**www.cipd.co.uk**) list various types of test, their purpose and how to use them and interpret results.

Two tests most MBAs will come across both at business school and in job and promotion interviews that can be used in staff selection are the following:

The 16PF (Personality Factor) Questionnaire (**www.16pfworld.com**) Developed in 1949 by Raymond Cattell who set out to measure the whole of human personality using a structure questionnaire assessed against a normative sample reflecting current census statistics on sex, age and race. The scores enable employers, among others, to predict human behaviour.

The 16PF Questionnaire measures levels of: Warmth; Reasoning; Emotional stability; Dominance; Liveliness; Rule consciousness; Social boldness; Sensitivity; Vigilance; Abstractedness; Privateness; Apprehensiveness; Openness to change; Self-reliance; Perfectionism and Tension.

The Myers-Briggs Type Indicator (**www.myersbriggs.org**) This is a personality inventory, based on the psychological types, described by C G Jung, explaining how seemingly random variations in behaviour are actually normal, and due to basic differences in the ways people choose to use their perception and judgement. Developed by Katharine Briggs and her daughter, Isabel Myers, who initially created the indicator during the Second World War to help women working in industry for the first time find the sort of wartime jobs where they would best fit in.

The Indicator uses a battery of questions to identify how a person fits in with the 16 distinctive personality types that result from the interactions among preferences in these four areas:

- The world: Do you prefer to focus on the outer world (Extraversion – E) or on your own inner world (Introversion – I)?

- Information: Do you prefer to focus on the basic information you take in (Sensing – S) or do you prefer to interpret and add meaning (Intuition – N)?

- Decisions: When making decisions, do you prefer to look first at logic and consistency (Thinking – T) or look first at the people and circumstances (Feeling – F)?

- Structure: In dealing with events, do you prefer to get things decided (Judging – J) or do you like to keep an open mind to new information (Perceiving – P)?

The Indicator, once applied, shows a person's propensity towards each of 16 types summarized very briefly below:

- ISTJ: Quiet, serious, dependable, practical, matter-of-fact, realistic, and responsible. Orderly and organized and value traditions and loyalty.
- ISFJ: Quiet, friendly, responsible, and painstakingly accurate. Committed to meeting their obligations.
- INFJ: Want to understand what motivates people and are insightful about others. Committed to serve the common good.
- INTJ: Sceptical and independent, with high standards and original minds. Have great drive for implementing their ideas and achieving their goals.
- ISTP: Tolerant, flexible, patient and quietly analytical but act quickly once they find workable solutions.
- ISFP: Quiet, friendly, sensitive and kind, and dislike disagreements and conflicts. Like their own space and to work at their own pace.
- INFP: Adaptable, flexible, idealistic, loyal to their values and quick to see possibilities. Try to understand people and to help them fulfil their potential.
- INTP: Self-contained, logical, theoretical and abstract, interested more in ideas than in people.
- ESTP: Flexible, pragmatic, and theories bore them – they want to act energetically and spontaneously to solve the problem.
- ESFP: Outgoing, friendly and accepting – they bring both fun and common sense and a realistic approach to their work.
- ENFP: Warmly enthusiastic and imaginative. Need affirmation from others, and readily give appreciation and support.
- ENTP: Quick, ingenious, stimulating, alert, outspoken and bored by routine.
- ESTJ: Practical, realistic, logical and decisive. Good organizer and quick to implement decisions.
- ESFJ: Warm-hearted, conscientious, and cooperative team worker who wants harmony in their environment.
- ENFJ: Warm, empathetic, responsive, and responsible facilitator who wants to help others fulfil their potential.
- ENTJ: Frank, forceful, decisive, assumes leadership readily, likes long-term planning and goal setting.

Making job offers

Having found the ideal candidate, the next step is to get them hired and happy to work for you. However well the interview may have gone, resist making a job offer on the spot. Both you and the candidate need to sleep on it, giving you both the chance to discuss with your partners and consider what has come out of the interviews.

Take up references Always take up references before offering the job. Use both the telephone and a written reference and check that any necessary qualifications are valid. This may take a little time and effort, but is essential as a protection against unsuitable or dishonest applicants.

Put the offer in writing While you may make the job offer on the telephone, face-to-face or in an e-mail, always follow up with a written offer. The offer should contain all the important conditions of the job, salary, location, hours, holiday, work, responsibilities, targets and the all-important start date. This in effect will be the backbone of the contract of employment you will have to provide shortly after they start working for you.

Make them welcome When a new employee joins you, be on hand to meet them, show them the ropes and introduce them to anyone else they are likely to come into contact with. This is crucial if they are going to work in your home alongside you, and these introductions should extend to your spouse, even if they don't work in the business, your children, pets, the postman and neighbours.

They also need to know about the practical aspects of working for you; where they can eat inside and out, coffee making and any equipment they will be working with. If they will be in your home when it is otherwise empty then they need to know where the fuses are and whom to contact if, say, the internet or telephone goes down.

Dealing with unsuccessful candidates

By the very nature of the recruitment task, the person appointed is just the tip of a big iceberg of applicants and interviewees. These people have to be responded to, advising them that they do not have the job. For your first reserve list, those who you may call on if the appointment goes wrong for any reason, it is worth taking particular care with your reply. Here you can emphasize the strength of their application but that the background of another candidate was closer to your needs. You don't have to go into details as to specifically why a particular candidate got the job and they did not.

Aside from exuding professionalism and being plain good manners, the job-hunting world is big and deep and at some stage you and your organization will be fishing there again.

Motivation

As a subject for serious study motivation is a relatively new 'science'. Thomas Hobbes, a 17th-century English philosopher, suggested that human nature could best be understood as self-interested cooperation. He claimed that motivation could be summarized as choices revolving around pain or pleasure. Sigmund Freud was equally frugal in suggesting only two basic needs: the life and the death instinct. These ideas were the first to seriously challenge the time-honoured 'carrot and stick' method of motivation that pervaded every aspect of organizational life, from armies at war to weavers in Britain working through the Industrial Revolution.

The first hint, in the business world, that there might be more to motivation than rewards and redundancy came with Harvard Business School professor Elton Mayo's renowned Hawthorne Studies. These were conducted between 1927 and 1932 at the Western Electric Hawthorne Works in Chicago. Starting out to see what effect illumination had on productivity, Mayo moved on to see how fatigue and monotony fitted into the equation by varying rest breaks, temperature, humidity and work hours, even providing a free meal at one point. Working with a team of six women, Mayo changed every parameter he could think of, including increasing and decreasing working hours and rest breaks; finally he returned to the original conditions. Every change resulted in an improvement in productivity, except when two 10-minute pauses morning and afternoon were expanded to six 5-minute pauses. These frequent work pauses, they felt, upset their work rhythm.

Mayo's conclusion was that showing 'someone upstairs cares', engendering a sense of ownership and responsibility were important motivators that could be harnessed by management. After Mayo came a flurry of theories on motivation. William McDougall in his book *The Energies of Men* (1932, published by Methuen) listed 18 basic needs that he referred to as instincts (eg curiosity, self-assertions, submission). H A Murray, assistant director of the Harvard Psychological Clinic, catalogued 20 core psychological needs, including achievement, affiliation and power.

The motivation theories most studied and applied by business school graduates are those espoused by Maslow (see Chapter 3) and these below.

Theory X and theory Y

Douglas McGregor, an American social psychologist who taught at two top schools, Harvard and the Massachusetts Institute of Technology (MIT), developed these theories to try to explain the assumptions about human behaviour that underlies management action.

Theory 'X' makes the following assumptions:

- The average person has an inherent dislike of work and will avoid it if possible. So management needs to put emphasis on productivity, incentive schemes and the idea of a 'fair day's work'.

- Because of this dislike of work, most people must be coerced, controlled, directed and threatened with punishment to get them to achieve the company's goals.
- People prefer to be directed, want to avoid responsibility, have little ambition and really want a secure life above all.

But, while Theory 'X' does explain some human behaviour, it does not provide a framework for understanding behaviour in the best businesses. McGregor, and others, have proposed an alternative.

Theory 'Y' has as its basis the belief that:

- Physical or mental effort at work is as natural as either rest or play. Under the right conditions, hard work can be a source of great satisfaction. Under the wrong conditions it can be a drudge, which will inspire little effort and less thought from those forced to participate.
- Once committed to a goal, most people at work are capable of a high degree of self-management.
- Job satisfaction and personal recognition are the highest 'rewards' that can be given, and will result in the greatest level of commitment to the task in hand.
- Under the right conditions, most people will accept responsibility and even welcome more of it.
- Few people in business are being 'used' to anything like their capacity. Neither are they contributing creatively towards solving problems.

A typical Theory-X boss is likely to keep away from their employees as much as possible. However small the business, for example, they may make sure that they have an office to themselves, and its door is kept tightly shut. Contact with others will be confined to giving instructions about work and complaining about poor performance. A Theory-Y approach will involve collaborating over decisions rather than issuing orders, and sharing feedback so that everyone can learn from both success and failures, rather than just reprimanding when things go wrong.

Hygiene and motivation theory

Frederick Hertzberg, professor of psychology at Case Western Reserve University in Cleveland, United States, discovered that distinctly separate factors were the cause of job satisfaction and job dissatisfaction. His research revealed that five factors stood out as strong determinants of job satisfaction.

Motivators

- Achievement: People want to succeed, so if you can set goals that people can reach and better, they will be much more satisfied than if they are constantly missing targets.

- Recognition: Everyone likes their hard work to be acknowledged. Not everyone wants that recognition made in the same way, however.

- Responsibility: People like the opportunity to take responsibility for their own work and for the whole task. This helps them grow as individuals.

- Advancement: Promotion or at any rate progress are key motivators. In a small firm, providing career prospects for key staff can be a fundamental reason for growth.

- The attractiveness of work itself (job interest): There is no reason why a job should be dull. You need to make people's jobs interesting and give them a say in how their work is done. That will encourage new ideas on how things can be done better.

When the reasons for dissatisfaction were analysed they were found to be concerned with a different range of factors.

Hygiene factors

- Company policy: Rules, formal and informal, such as start and finish times, meal breaks, dress code.

- Supervision: To what extent are employees allowed to get on with the job, or do people have someone looking over their shoulders all day?

- Administration: Do things work well, or is paperwork in a muddle and supplies always come in late?

- Salary: Are employees getting at least the going rate and benefits comparable with others?

- Working conditions: Are people expected to work in substandard conditions with poor equipment and little job security?

- Interpersonal relationships: Is the atmosphere in work good or are people at daggers drawn?

Hertzberg called these causes of dissatisfaction 'hygiene factors'. He reasoned that the lack of hygiene will cause disease, but the presence of hygienic conditions will not, of itself, produce good health. So the lack of adequate 'job hygiene' will cause dissatisfaction but hygienic conditions alone will not bring about job satisfaction; to do that you have to work on the determinants of job satisfaction.

Other theories of motivation

There are a plethora of theories of how to motivate people at work and elsewhere. (See the partial list below.) As the subject has matured, researchers have segmented the market into ever-smaller sub-topics, for example focusing on certain subgroups, difficult people for example; or special situations such as after a merger or closure of part of a business.

- Achievement motivation theory (Atkinson, 1964)
- Action-outcome expectancy (Heckhausen, 1991)
- Attributional theory of achievement motivation (Weiner, 1972)
- Cognitive dissonance theory (Festinger, 1957)
- Effectance motivation (White, 1959; Harter, 1978a)
- Expectancy times value theory (Vroom, 1964)
- Goal-setting theory (Locke, 1968)
- Intrinsic motivation (Deci, 1975)
- Learned helplessness theory (Seligman, 1975)
- Neuro-linguistic programming – NLP (Bandler and Grinder, 1976)
- Reactance theory (Brehm, 1966)
- Self-efficacy theory (Bandura, 1977)

The guiding principle for all motivation practice is that people respond to a much wider range of stimulations other than life and death, fear and greed or stick and carrot. There is a thumbnail sketch of the 50 or so people whose theories on motivation and organizations have brought them to prominence and that an MBA should have at least an appreciation of at this website (**www.onepine.info/people.htm**).

Leadership

However great the employees are, unless a business has effective leadership nothing of great value can be made to happen. While the boss may have a pretty clear idea of what the business is all about and what makes it special and different, it may not be so clear to those who work further down. Employees often just keep their heads down and get on with the task in hand. While that's a useful trait, it is not sufficient to make a business a great place to work. To make that happen, the boss has to have a precise idea of where the business is heading and use their leadership skills to achieve results.

Tasks

Leaders have three major tasks: to determine the direction, chart the course and set the goals. The direction of a business has a number of components that can be best understood if thought of as being parts of a pyramid. (See Figure 4.8.)

FIGURE 4.8 The purpose pyramid

Start the
planning
process

Mission

Objectives

Key tasks

Action plans

Derive
from the
planning
process

Vision

A vision is about stretching the organization's reach beyond its grasp. Few now can see how the vision can be achieved, but can see that it would be great if it could be done.

Microsoft's vision of a computer in every home, formed when few offices had one, is one example of a vision that has nearly been reached. As a mission statement in 1990 it might have raised a wry smile. After all, it was only a few decades before then that IBM had estimated the entire world demand for its computers as seven!

NASDAQ, the entrepreneurs' stock market, has as its vision: To build the world's first truly global securities market. 'A world-wide market of markets built on a world-wide network of network linking pools of liquidity and connecting investors from all over the world thus assuring the best possible price for securities at the lowest possible costs.' That certainly points to beyond the horizon envisaged by business today.

Having a vision will make it easier to get employees to buy into a long-term commitment to a business – they will see that they could have career opportunities and progression in an organization that knows where it is going.

Mission

A mission is a direction statement, intended to focus your attention on the essentials that encapsulate your specific competence(s) in relation to the market/customers you plan to serve. First, the mission should be narrow enough to give direction and guidance to everyone in the business. This concentration is the key to business success because it is only by focusing on specific needs that a small business can differentiate itself from its larger competitors. Nothing kills off a business faster than trying to do too many different things too soon. Second, the mission should open up a large enough market to allow the business to grow and realize its potential. You can always add a bit on later.

CASE STUDY

Judy Lever and Vivienne Pringle started Blooming Marvellous over 20 years ago when they were both pregnant. After searching for the kind of fashionable clothes they used to wear and drawing a blank, they guessed they had found a gap in the market. They stated their purpose and goals as follows:

> Arising out of our experiences, we intend to design, make and market a range of clothes for mothers-to-be that will make them feel they can still be fashionably dressed. We aim to serve a niche missed out by Mothercare, Marks & Spencer, etc, and so become a significant force in the mail order fashion for the mothers-to-be market.

> We are aiming for a 5 per cent share of this market in the Southeast, and a 25 per cent return on assets employed within three years of starting up. We believe we will need about £25,000 start-up capital to finance stock, a mail order catalogue and an advertising campaign.

They kept on their day jobs and would meet after work every day at Judy's house to answer enquiries, send out leaflets and dispatch products in the post every day. They outsourced work to a pattern cutter, a small factory, some fabric suppliers, and eventually a small distribution centre. After a year or so of modest sales they felt confident enough to set up their first business premises – a 1,200 sq ft warehouse on a business park staffed by four of the women who had been working in their distribution centre.

The company employed 150 people, had 14 shops and had extended its range to include nursery products, toys, themed bedroom accessories and a separate brand called Mini Marvellous catering for children aged 2–8 years, when it sold up to mothercare in 2010. Over a third of sales come directly via their website (**www.bloomingmarvellous.co.uk**).

In summary, the mission statement should explain:

- what business you are in and your purpose;
- what you want to achieve over the next one to three years, ie your strategic goal;
- how, ie your ethics, values and standards.

Above all, mission statements must be realistic, achievable – and brief.

Objectives

The milestones on the way to realizing the vision and mission are measured by the achievement of business objectives. These objectives 'cascade' through the organization from the top, where they are measures of profit, through to measures such as output, quality, reject rates, absenteeism and so forth.

Objective setting is a primary process in which clear performance measures are agreed with every employee. The achievement of specific objectives is the ultimate measure of effective leadership.

Management

Leadership and management are not the same thing, but you need both. A leader challenges the status quo, while a manager accepts it as a constraint. A boss usually has to be both a leader and a manager. Dozens of catchy titles such as bottom-up, top-down, management by objectives and crisis management have been used to describe the many and various theories as to how to manage.

American engineer Frederick Winslow Taylor (circa 1911), who is credited with coining the phrase 'time is money', was one of the pioneers of the search for the 'one best way' to execute such basic managerial functions as selection, promotion, compensation, training and production. Taylor was followed by Henri Fayol (1919), a successful managing director of a mining French company, who developed what he called the 14 Principles of Management, recognizing that his list was neither exhaustive nor universally applicable. He also set out what he saw as the five primary functions of a manager. Nearly a decade later, Luther Gulick, an American, and Lydnall Urwick, a founder of the British management consultancy profession, expanded Fayol's list to seven executive management activities summarized by the acronym POSDCORB:

- Planning: determine objectives in advance and the methods to achieve them.
- Organizing: establish a structure of authority for all work.
- Staffing: recruit, hire and train workers; maintain favourable working conditions.

- Directing: make decisions, issue orders and directives.
- Coordinating: interrelate all sectors of the organization.
- Reporting: inform hierarchy through reports, records and inspections.
- Budgeting: depend on fiscal planning, accounting and control.

By 1973 Canadian academic Henry Mintzberg, now professor of organizations at INSEAD in France, had further expanded the manager's tasks and responsibilities into 10 areas:

1 Figurehead: performs ceremonial and symbolic duties as head of the organization.

2 Leader: fosters a proper work atmosphere and motivates and develops subordinates.

3 Liaison: develops and maintains a network of external contacts to gather information.

4 Monitor: gathers internal and external information relevant to the organization.

5 Disseminator: passes factual and value-based information to subordinates.

6 Spokesperson: communicates to the outside world on performance and policies.

7 Entrepreneur: designs and initiates change in the organization.

8 Disturbance handler: deals with unexpected events and operational breakdowns.

9 Resource allocator: controls and authorizes the use of organizational resources.

10 Negotiator: intermediates with other organizations and individuals.

All of these attempts at formulating an overarching and universal approach to arriving at a single best definition of the role of management foundered on the limitations of the information flow from the front line upwards. Two management theorists, Tom Peters and Nancy Austin, suggest that managers in effective companies get the information they need by getting out of their offices and talking with people – employees, suppliers, other managers, and customers. They coined the approach as 'management by walking around', or 'MBWA' (Peters and Austin, 1985).

Today, the view of the role of a manager is best described as being contingent on the internal and external circumstances they find themselves in. Expanded into the rather grandiose title of 'contingency theory', its exponent Fred Fiedler, a business and management psychologist at the University of Washington, first introduced what he called the contingency modelling of leadership in 1967.

Management styles and processes

Despite the near-universal acceptance that there are no absolutes in management, the search for a tool or technique for helping managers understand and improve on their role as a manager goes on. These are some of the more practical of those attempts.

The Management Grid

Robert R Blake and Jane Srygley Mouton, who worked together at the psychology department of the University of Texas during the 1950s and 1960s, developed the 'Managerial Grid' as a framework for understanding managerial styles. Their grid (see Figure 4.9) had two dimensions, concern for task and concern for people, with management styles being described by their position on the grid:

- Country Club operates on the belief that as long as the people are happy the results will follow.

- Produce or Perish states that we are only here to deliver results. It's an authoritarian style that subjugates people and their concerns to getting tasks performed at all costs. This is very much a Theory X (see above) method of operating.

FIGURE 4.9 The management grid

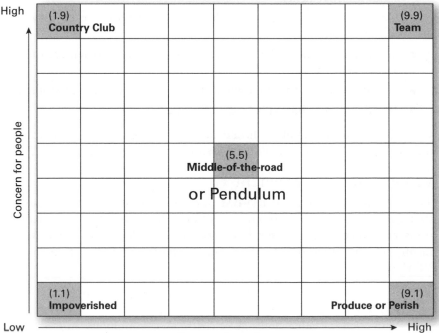

- Impoverished Manager is equally disinterested in both output and people.
- Team Manager has a parallel concern for people and results. This is considered the optimal role.
- Middle of the Road is an attempt to balance the concern for output with a parallel concern for people. In compromising, neither of the competing needs is met satisfactorily. This style can also occur when a manager alternates between putting people first at one stage then if results aren't coming through swinging the other way: this is known as the Pendulum approach to management.

Your position on the grid is arrived at by answering a battery of questions that can be obtained from Chartwell Learning and Development (**www. chartwell-learn.co.uk/teleometrics_instrument/management_leadership_ style**). Alternatively, download a questionnaire from (**www.leadership-and-motivation-training.com/support-files/blake-mouton-questionnaire.pdf**).

Management by objectives

Peter Drucker first described this system in his book, *The Practice of Management* (1954). Drucker's proposition was that managers should side-step what he called the 'activity trap' where managers got involved in the minutiae of day-to-day activities and set them SMART objectives:

- Specific – relate to specific tasks and activities, not general statements about improvements.
- Measurable – it should be possible to assess whether or not they have been achieved.
- Attainable – it should be possible for the employee to achieve the desired outcome.
- Realistic – within the employee's current or planned-for capability.
- Timed – to be achieved by a specific date.

Objectives, Drucker claimed, should cascade throughout the organization, interlocking so that the overall business objectives would be achieved.

Value-based management

The value-based management (VBM) model is the management approach that goes a stage beyond objectives and introduces the idea that organizations are run consistently for long-term shareholder value. That doesn't mean ignoring other stakeholder groups. The three guiding principles of VBM are:

- Creating value: actively seeking ways to increase or generate maximum long-term value.
- Managing for value: colleagues, customers, community and shareholders.

- Measuring value: validating that long-term real value has been created by using appropriate financial techniques such as discounted cash flow (see Chapter 2, 'Investment decisions').

Balanced scorecard

The balanced scorecard (Figure 4.10), developed by Robert Kaplan and David Norton and published in a *Harvard Business Review* article in 1992, is a management process that sets out to align business activities to the vision and strategy of the organization, improve internal and external communications, and monitor organization performance against strategic goals. Its uniqueness was to add non-financial performance measures to traditional financial targets to give managers and directors a more 'balanced' view of organizational performance. Although Kaplan and Norton are credited with coining the phrase, the idea of a balanced scorecard originated with General Electric's work on performance measurement reporting in the 1950s and the work of French process engineers (who created the *Tableau de Bord* – literally, a 'dashboard' of performance measures) in the early part of the 20th century.

Four perspectives are included in the management process, which in effect extends the range of management by objectives and value-based management into areas beyond purely financial target setting. A number of objectives, measures, targets and initiatives can be set to achieve specific key performance indicators (KPIs) for each perspective in terms of:

FIGURE 4.10   The balanced scorecard

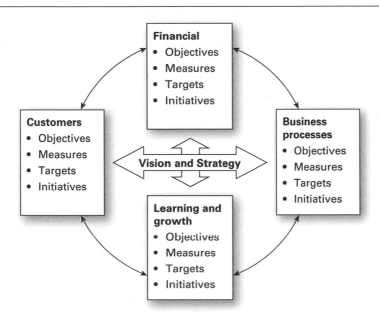

- Financial: These include KPIs for return on investment, cash flow, profit margins and shareholder value.
- Customer: Here the KPIs can be for customer retention rates, satisfaction levels, referrals and complaints.
- Internal business processes: These can include stock turn, accident rates, defects in production, reduction in the number of processes and improvements in communications.
- Learning and growth: Employee turnover, morale levels, training and development achievements and internal promotions vs new recruits are all KPIs to use here.

The four perspectives are linked by a double feedback loop whose purpose is to ensure that KPIs are not in conflict with one another. For example, if customer satisfaction could be achieved by improving delivery times, achieving that by, say, increasing stock levels might conflict with a financial target of improving return on capital employed. (See Chapter 1 for a refresher on financial ratios.)

Delegation: the essential management skill

To be effective an MBA needs to acquire for themselves and engender in their own management team the ability to delegate, also known as the art of getting things done your way by people who are happy to do so. Delegation is the tool that frees up your time for higher tasks – strategic planning, for example. Also, no organization can grow, and from a career perspective no MBA can move up, until someone else is in place to fill their role; delegation is a key tool in developing staff to be ready to take on more responsibility. Done effectively, delegation is also highly motivating. Look back to both the Hawthorne experiment and Hertzberg's hygiene factors described earlier in this chapter to remind yourself why.

The theoretical framework MBAs are most likely to come across that gives guidance on delegation is that espoused by R Tannenbaum and W H Schmidt, published in the *Harvard Business Review* in May/June 1973, in an article entitled 'How to choose a leadership pattern' (Figure 4.11). The thinking behind their ideas was to give managers a way to see how to choose the most appropriate managerial style or use of authority, ranging from boss-centred (task) to subordinate-centred (relationship) dependent on their and their team's capacity for delegation. For example, a manager with weak communication skills, leading an untrained team in an organization with poor or inadequate control systems, will not be able to move far along the continuum.

FIGURE 4.11 The leadership continuum – Tannebaum, Schmidt

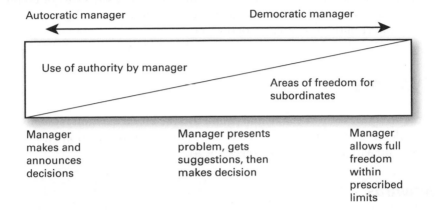

Autocratic manager ← → Democratic manager

Use of authority by manager

Areas of freedom for subordinates

| Manager makes and announces decisions | Manager presents problem, gets suggestions, then makes decision | Manager allows full freedom within prescribed limits |

Eight steps to successful delegation

Delegation is difficult and most people experience a loss of control or a fear that the people they are delegating to are not really capable of doing the task well. These natural fears and concerns have to be understood and managed if delegation is to succeed. These eight steps improve the prospects for success in delegation:

- Decide what tasks to delegate and, equally importantly, what not to: Routine jobs can usually be passed on with little difficulty but other areas may involve training people up. Confidential or disciplinary work, tasks with strategic or legal and regulatory implications, are not likely candidates.

- Don't just select unpopular and tedious tasks to dump on others. Pass on worthwhile work that will genuinely widen experience and skills.

- Choose who to delegate to: Ideally someone with the right skill set, who is not already overloaded and who is likely to stay around long enough for the organization to gain from the experience too.

- Discuss the changes with the person concerned, get their commitment and then let everyone in the relevant part of the organization know about the change in role and why.

- The subordinate concerned must be given the authority to do the job and to make independent decisions.

- Follow up soon and review frequently to make sure the tasks delegated are being done satisfactorily and that no other work is suffering.

- Reward appropriately for a successful delegation.
- Communicate the success to the team to reinforce the value of taking on additional responsibilities, personal development and the opportunities for career progression.

Systems

If the structure is the skeleton and people are the blood and guts, systems are the rules and procedures that enable an organization to function effectively and to prepare itself for the changes ahead.

Rewards

While money is more a hygiene factor than a motivator, people come to work to get paid and if they achieve great results they expect great rewards. There is no single aspect of an employee's life more susceptible to gripes and complaints than pay. So how can you make sure that doesn't happen in your organization?

- First, make sure you are paying at least the going rate for the job in the area. Don't think you are getting a bargain if you get an employee to work for less than that figure; if they do, either they are not good at their job, a poor time keeper or have some other disability that you will find out about later; or they are good and when they find out they will feel cheated and leave. The easiest way to find the going rate is to look at advertisements for similar jobs in your area or visit PayScale (**www.payscale.com** > FOR EMPLOYERS) where you can get accurate real-time information on pay scales.
- Include an element of incentive for achieving measurable goals. This could be commission, perhaps the easiest reward system, but it really only works for those directly involved in selling. Or a bonus for successful performance, usually paid in a lump sum related as closely as possible to the results obtained. The Chartered Institute of Personnel and Development (**www.cipd.co.uk** > Subjects > Pay and reward) gives further guidance on a comprehensive range of reward options.
- Benefits in kind are a form of compensation that is not part of basic pay and that isn't tied directly to their performance. Pension, working conditions, being allowed to wear casual dress, on-site childcare, personal development training, company product discounts, flexible hours, telecommuting and fitness facilities are all on the list of benefits that are on offer in certain jobs today. There may be tax implications on benefits in kind and the Digita Use of employer's assets: benefits in kind calculator (**www.digita.com/**

tiscali/home/calculators/employersassetscalculator/default.asp) will help work out if tax is due and if so how much.

- Team awards can be used to engender better teamwork. Where money is involved it should be spent on things of value to the team. It could be an evening out, or any other social event. It could also be used to buy a business asset that's nice to have but could not really be justified on business grounds, for example a dedicated photocopier.

Appraisals

An appraisal is almost certainly an MBA's first point of contact with an organization's systems and the most likely one to cause dissatisfaction and frustration. Although supposedly not about blame, reward or even praise, that's how it ends up. Its output is a personal development plan to help everyone perform better and be able to achieve career goals.

There are plenty of standard appraisal systems and procedures; many are little more than a tick boxes and rating process; others are built around buzzwords such as '360 degree appraisals', meaning that staff below and above as well as peers have an input into the process.

There are really only four ground rules for successful appraisals:

- The appraisal needs to be seen as an open two-way discussion between people who work together, rather than simply a boss/subordinate relationship, and prepared for in advance. Discussion should be focused on achievements, areas for improvement, overall performance, training and development, and career expectations and not salary (that's for a separate occasion).

- It should be results oriented rather than personality oriented. The appraisal interview starts with a review against objectives and finishes by setting objectives for the next period.

- Appraisals should be regular and timely. At least annually, perhaps more frequent in periods of rapid change. New employees should be appraised in their first three months.

- Sufficient time should be allowed and the appraisal needs to be carried out free from interruptions.

EPIC Training and Consulting Services has a free Workforce Development Toolkit on its website, including a guide on carrying out appraisals and templates for both appraiser and appraisee (**http://workforce.epicltd.com**).

Development

If an organization is only as effective as the people it employs, it follows that the money invested in developing them and improving their skills should translate into improved results for the business as a whole. The statistics support the argument that money spent wisely on development pays dividends, so as a task it forms a major part of the human resources department's workload.

Two acronyms an MBA will find useful to pump-prime any development plan are the following.

KSAs (Knowledge, skills and attitudes)

Development programmes have learning objectives in each of these three areas and all three aspects need to be addressed for development to have the greatest impact:

- Knowledge, described as perception, learning and reasoning. Would it was as simple as that, but the HR and learning gurus have subdivided that into: declarative knowledge or factual information; procedural knowledge, that is, understanding how and when to apply the facts; and strategic knowledge, used in planning and evaluating.

- Skills are concerned with a proficiency level, for example in using a software application such as Excel, making a presentation, operating equipment, closing a sale or negotiating a deal.

- Attitudes are the positive, negative or neutral feelings arising out of opinions and beliefs concerning actions that affect motivation levels, which in turn influence a person's behaviour.

TNA (Training needs analysis)

This process identifies the gap between the skills an organization needs to achieve its strategic and tactical goals and the skills employees currently have. Employee surveys, management observations, customer comments and appraisal are all among the tools used to gather information to identify training needs. (See Figure 4.12.)

Organizations have a wide repertory of tools to apply to ensure that people are developed. Governments have an interest in encouraging training and often provide information on where training programmes are being run

FIGURE 4.12   Training needs analysis worksheet

Development area	Gap identified	Action to be taken to address the gap	Date action to be achieved by
Knowledge			
Skills			
Attitudes			
Learning options			

as well as offering grants to help with the costs. These should be explored at the outset, as any financial assistance can sweeten the budgetary pill. The main options in terms of learning methods are:

- On-the-job coaching and mentoring: This is where people learn from someone more experienced how a job should be done. The advantages are that it is free and involves no time away from work. It should also be directly related to an individual's training needs. However, it is only as good as the coach and if they are untrained you could end up simply replicating poor working standards.

- In-house classroom training: This is the most traditional and familiar form of training. Some, or all, of your employees gather in a 'classroom' either on your premises or in a local hotel. You hire in a trainer or use one of your own experienced staff. This method provides plenty of opportunity for group interaction and the instructor can motivate the class and pay some attention to individual needs. The disadvantages, particularly if it is held away from your premises, are that you incur large costs that are more to do with hospitality than training, it is time consuming and it may be difficult to release a large enough number of employees at the same time to achieve economies of scale.

- Public courses: These are less expensive than running a training programme in a hotel. You can also select different courses for different employees and so tailor the training more precisely to their needs. Most public courses are generic and the other attendees are more likely to come from big business or even the public sector. So, much of what is covered may be of little direct relevance to your business and quality can be patchy.

- Interactive distance learning: This kind of training can be delivered by a combination of traditional training materials, teleconferencing, internet and e-mail discussions. You miss out on the personal contact, but the costs are much lower than traditional training.

- Off-the-shelf training programmes: These come in packaged kits, which may consist of a training manual, video or a CD ROM. Once again the cost is lower than for face-to-face training, but you miss out on a professional trainer's input.

- Universities and colleges: Many universities and business schools now offer programmes tailored for the needs of the organization. Professional instructors who understand the needs of small firms deliver these. They are relatively expensive but can often be very effective.

- Business games, case studies and simulation exercises: A business game is virtually mandatory at some stage while taking an MBA. The game is constructed as a model, usually though not always software based, to simulate an entire company or industry or a particular functional area. They allow trainees working in teams to see how their decisions and actions influence a bigger picture. Outward Bound activities are also popular MBA development tools, using hazardous remote environments to create opportunities for conflict, leadership and the prospects of cohesion. These are also popular as elements in the management selection process.

Preparing for development

To make sure you get the best out of investment in development, follow these guidelines:

- Introduce a routine that ensures all employees attending training are briefed at least a week beforehand on what to expect and what is expected of them.
- Ensure that all employees discuss with their manager or supervisor what they got out of the training programme – in particular, did it meet both their expectations. This should take place no later than a week after the programme.
- Managers should check within a month and then again at regular intervals to see whether skills have been improved, and that those skills are being put into practice.
- Evaluate the costs and benefits of your training and development plans, arriving at financial ratio such as return on investment, and use this information to help set next year's training budget.

Managing change

The story told in business schools to illustrate the dangers of ignoring the need for change is that of the hypothetical frog dropped into a pot of boiling water. The immediate impact of a radically different environment spurs the frog into action, leaping out of the pot. The same frog placed in the same pot, but where the initial temperature is much lower, will happily allow itself to be boiled to death, failing to recognize the danger if the process is slow enough.

The first task of a leader, therefore, is to define an organization's purpose and direction. This inevitably means changing those in response to changing circumstances.

Why change is necessary

The need for change comes from two main directions: either a new impetus from outside or inside the organization; or from the natural evolution of the organization itself.

Impetus-driven change

These are the primary sources of the impetus for change that disturb the equilibrium of an organization:

- New management: This doesn't always trigger change but the temptation to tamper with even the best of organizations is usually too much for a 'new broom'. The person appointed almost invariably will want to put their stamp on strategy and structure; if all was really so hunky-dory, why appoint them in the first place?

- Competitor behaviour: This can be either new entrants or existing players changing the dynamics in your markets by competing with better products, lower prices or smarter operations.

- Technology: Changes here can hit whole business sectors. For example, the advent initially of online DVD services and more recently of broadband delivery has profoundly changed the environment for the retail video rental business.

- Economic, political or legal environment: These include such factors as: business cycles altering demand levels radically; changes of government with consequent shifts in expenditure and taxation; and regulatory changes such as those affecting the tobacco industry and its ability to promote its wares.

Natural evolution

Organizations are in some ways like living organisms and have a natural progression from birth through childhood, adolescence, adulthood, senility and death. Some stages in the process for an organization are easily recognizable. All have a start and finish date and though their life span varies, for businesses at least, the average is around 35 to 38 years. Some last much longer; there is a small club for businesses who have been around for over 250 years. (Japan's 1,400-year-old Kongo Gumi may be the oldest business enterprise, but guns (Beretta), banking (Rothschild) and booze (the Gekkeikan brewery founded in 1627) also feature strongly (see 'Business history').)

The phases of growth

Larry Greiner, a Harvard professor, identified the key phases an organization has to go through in its path to maturity. (See Figure 4.13.) Churchill and Lewis (Churchill, N C and Lewis, V L (1983) 'The Five Stages of Small Business Growth', *Harvard Business Review*, May/June) refined this for small businesses.

Each phase of growth calls for a different approach to managing the organization. Sometimes strong leadership is required; at others a more consultative approach is appropriate. Some phases call for more systems

FIGURE 4.13   The five phases of growth

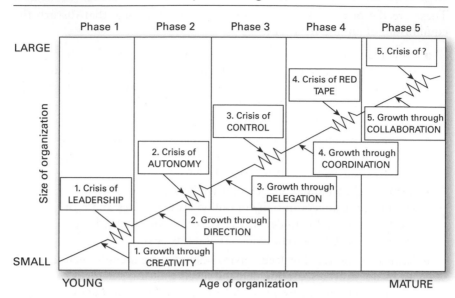

SOURCE: L E Greiner, *Harvard Business Review*, July/August 1972.

and procedures, some for more cooperation between staff. Often leaders believe that taking on another salesperson, a few hundred thousand square metres of space or another bank loan can solve the problems of growing up. This approach is rather like suggesting that the transition from infancy to adulthood could be accomplished by nothing more significant than providing larger clothes.

Managing the process

Because change is inevitable and unpredictable in its consequences doesn't mean that it can't be managed as a process. These are the stages in managing change:

- Tell them why: Change is better accepted when people are given a compelling business reason. Few bankers would question the need for change after the 2008 debacles at Bear Stearns, SocGen and Northern Rock.

- Make it manageable: Even when people accept what needs to be done, the change may just be too big for anyone to handle. Breaking it down into manageable bits can help overcome this.

- Take a shared approach: Involve people early, asking them to join you in managing change, and give key participants some say in shaping the change right from the start. This will reduce the feeling that change is being imposed and more brains will be brought to bear on the problem.

- Reward success early: Flag up successes as quickly as possible. Don't wait for the year-end or the appraisal cycle. This will inspire confidence and keep the change process on track.

- Expect resistance: Kurt Lewin, a German-born professor at the Massachusetts Institute of Technology (MIT), was one of the first researchers to study group dynamics and how change can be best effected in organizations. In 1943 in an article entitled 'Defining the Field at a Given Time' published in the *Psychological Review*, Lewin described what is now known as Force Field Analysis. This is a tool (see Figure 4.14) that you can use to anticipate resistance to change and plan to overcome it.

- Recognize that change takes longer than expected: Three researchers (Adams, J, Hayes, J and Hopson, B) explained in *Transition: Understanding and Managing Personal Change* (1976, Martin Robinson, London) the six stages that people go through when experiencing change and hence the reason the process takes so long. The stages are: immobilization or shock, disbelief, depression, acceptance of reality, testing out the new situation, rationalizing why it's happening and then final acceptance. Most major changes make things worse before they make them better. More often than not, the immediate impact of change is a decrease in productivity as people struggle to cope with new ways of working while they move up their own learning curve. The doubters will gloat and even the change

FIGURE 4.14   Force field analysis template

What is the problem/ change issue?			
Where are we now?			
Where do we want to get to?			
What/who are the main forces at work?	Driving forces	Neutral forces	Resisting forces
What action can we take to help driving forces, encourage neutral forces to help and to overcome resisting forces?			

champions may waver. But the greatest danger now is pulling the plug on the plan and either adopting a new plan or reverting to the status quo. To prevent this 'disappointment' it is vital both to set realistic goals for the change period and to anticipate the time lag between change and results.

Monitoring staff morale

One way both to identify the need for change and to keep track of progress while implementing changes is to carry out regular surveys of employee attitudes, opinions and feelings. HR-Survey (**www.hr-survey.com** > Employee Opinions) and Custom Insight (**www.custominsight.com** > View Samples > Sample employee satisfaction survey) provide fast, simple and easy-to-use software to carry out and analyse Human Resources surveys. They both have a range of examples of surveys that you can see and try before you buy, which, who knows, might just be enough to stimulate your thinking.

Business history

05

- The foundations of contract law
- The first business gurus
- Early accounting (and the death penalty!)
- Stock markets and coffee houses
- Limiting liabilities
- Encouraging innovations
- Banking beginnings
- The world's oldest ventures

'May you live in interesting times' – an expression part curse, part exhortation that might have been coined for the years straddling the first and second decades of the 21st century.

As this era looks eerily similar to the world depression triggered in 1929 the philosopher, George Santayana's quote – 'those who cannot learn from history are doomed to repeat it' – is peculiarly appropriate. Henry Ford, the founder of the car company, famously said: 'History is more or less bunk. It's tradition. We don't want tradition. We want to live in the present and the only history that is worth a tinker's damn is the history we make today.'

There are reasons why an MBA student should acquire a basic appreciation of the milestone events that have led up to the current theories of how organizations, their constituents and their surrounding environments currently operate. The first is much the same reason as why most people learn something of the history of their country, its neighbours, its friends and enemies. Such a study lends interest, context and an appreciation of how we got to where we are today. It is much easier to understand, for example, the enmity between the French and the British with a smattering of information on the Hundred Years' War, the Peninsula War and the smouldering commercial and territorial disputes that ranged around the world from the Americas to India as well as across the African continent.

The second reason is perhaps even more important. Harvard professor Geoffrey Jones, who edited *The Oxford Handbook of Business History* (2008, Oxford Handbooks in Business & Management) with University of Wisconsin-Madison professor Jonathan Zeitlin, claims in his core history text used at Harvard that: 'Over the last few decades, business historians have generated rich empirical data that in some cases confirms and in other cases contradicts many of today's fashionable theories and assumptions by other disciplines. But unless you were a business historian, this data went largely unnoticed, and the consequences were not just academic. This loss of history has resulted in the spread of influential theories based on ill-informed understandings of the past. For example', Jones continues, 'current accepted advice is that wealth and growth will come to countries that open their borders to foreign direct investment. The historical evidence shows clearly that this is an article of faith rather than proven by the historical evidence of the past.'

How business history is studied in business schools

If you had taken your MBA before 2000 you would have been unlikely to find business history on the curriculum anywhere outside of the top dozen or so business schools. The subject, however, is fast becoming mainstream. Even comparative newcomers are embracing the subject. Reading Business School, for example, set up its Centre for International Business History (CIBH) in 1997, Cardiff has established an Accounting and Business History Research Group (ABHRG) and the Copenhagen Business School's Centre for Business History, established in 1999, is undertaking a long-term study into the nature and consequences of banking crises. The past few years should give them plenty of material to work on!

Business history as taught in business schools has no single unified body of knowledge in the manner in which, say, accounting, marketing or organizational behaviour has. It would be impossible to study accounting without covering the principles underpinning the key financial reports and how to interpret financial information. While there may well be some unique content in specialized electives, say on Financial Analysis of Mergers, Acquisitions and Other Complex Corporate Restructurings taught at the London Business School, or Dealing with Financial Crime on offer at Cass Business School, the core accounting syllabus in all business schools is near identical – though the way in which it is taught may not be.

History is taught in school and university in eras or themes: the Tudors, the Renaissance, the European World, for example. In one of the premier

UK university history departments nothing much is covered after 1720, while at Harvard Business School nothing much before 1820 is included in the syllabus! At Copenhagen MBA students may have a thorough grasp of Norwegian, Swedish and Danish banking in the interwar years without even a passing reference to the Industrial Revolution, mercantilism or the development of the great family business dynasties. It is just that the subject is too vast to be covered in a meaningful way except by narrowing down the range. Business history is taught eclectically and MBAs swapping notes on their experiences of Business History may find very little in common.

Here, a broad sweep of the subject is taken, providing snapshots of important milestones on matters of enduring significance to business. The content is divided into three eras that are to some extent homogeneous, though the time periods covered in each are very different. The subject starts from 4000 BC, though the purists would argue that organization and innovation started at least 8,000 years earlier when some communities gave up foraging for farming, adopting fundamentally new tools and techniques for making a living. Unfortunately, little or nothing survives in documented form to make it possible to study such ancient business history. The eras covered range from 3,000 years down to a mere half-century. You are probably aware of the claim that 90 per cent of all the scientists that ever lived are alive today. Well, much the same claim can be made for business innovations. While many important and essential developments occurred many hundreds and even thousands of years ago, the most recent era is the best documented and the most prolific.

The three periods covered are representative samples of some important milestones in business history, selected here as they are the eras least familiar to most students who have at least a passing appreciation of the post Industrial Revolution business world. Although for teaching purposes neat dates are often ascribed to such eras, in practice there is considerable overlap. The Fuggers and the Hanseatic League extended beyond what is commonly regarded as Mediaeval, while patents began their life in that period but didn't have a serious impact until much later.

Babylon and beyond (4000 BC–1000 AD)

Two enduring legacies from the ancient business world are the foundations of commercial law and the first efforts at accounting. Both these areas were subject to bursts of rapid development as new ideas took hold. For example, the introduction of coined money in about 600 BC by the Greeks allowed bankers to keep account books, change and lend money, and even arrange for cash transfers for citizens through affiliate banks in cities thousands of miles away. The Greeks were less interested in accounting as a way to influence business decisions than as a mechanism for citizens to maintain real authority and control over their government's finances. Members of the

Athens Popular Assembly were responsible for controlling receipt and expenditure of public funds and 10 state accountants, chosen by lot, kept them up to the mark.

Although it was not until AD 1080 that the first law school was established, in Bologna, Italy, and incidentally still in business today, contract law governing transactions and protecting consumer rights had already been around for nearly 4,000 years.

One early example of a family-run business is included here to show that the phenomenon is not peculiar to the Middle Ages and beyond.

Accountancy: single-entry bookkeeping

Sometime before 3000 BC the people of Uruk and other sister-cities of Mesopotamia began to use pictographic tablets of clay to record economic transactions. The script for the tablets evolved from symbols and provides evidence of an ancient financial system that was growing to accommodate the needs of the Uruk economy. The Mesopotamian equivalent of today's bookkeeper was the scribe. His duties were similar, but even more extensive. In addition to writing up the transactions, he ensured that the agreements complied with the detailed code requirements for commercial transactions. Temples, palaces and private firms employed hundreds of scribes and, much as with the accounting profession today, it was considered a prestigious profession.

In a typical transaction of the time, the parties might seek out the scribe at the gates to the city. They would describe their agreement to the scribe, who would take from his supply a small quantity of specially prepared clay on which to record the transaction.

Governmental bookkeeping in ancient Egypt developed in a fashion similar to the Mesopotamian. The use of papyrus rather than clay tablets allowed more detailed records to be made more easily. And extensive records were kept, particularly for the network of royal storehouses within which the 'in kind' tax payments such as sheep or cattle were kept, as coinage had not yet been developed.

Egyptian bookkeepers associated with each storehouse kept meticulous records, which were checked by an elaborate internal verification system. These early accountants had good reason to be honest and accurate, because irregularities disclosed by royal audits were punishable by fine, mutilation or death. Although such records were important, ancient Egyptian accounting never progressed beyond simple list making in its thousands of years of existence. Almost one million accounting records in tablet form currently survive in museum collections around the world.

China, during the Chao Dynasty (1122–256 BC), used bookkeeping chiefly as a means of evaluating the efficiency of governmental programmes and the civil servants who administered them. A level of sophistication was achieved which was not surpassed in China until after the introduction of the double-entry system a thousand years later.

Accounts in ancient Rome evolved from records traditionally kept by the heads of families, where daily entry of household receipts and payments were kept in an *adversaria* or daybook, and monthly postings were made to a cashbook known as a *codex accepti et expensi*.

Up to mediaeval times, this single-entry system of bookkeeping, divided into two general parts, Income and Outgo, with a statement at the end showing the balance due to the lord of the manner, prevailed in England, as elsewhere. Although these accounts were fairly basic, they were sufficient to handle the needs of the very simple business structures that prevailed. Businessmen operated for the most part on their own account, or in single-venture partnerships that dissolved at the end of a relatively short period of time. This, incidentally, was still the essence of the structure of Lloyd's insurance market into the 21st century. Judging from the uniformity of the way the single-entry bookkeeping was practised, it seems fairly certain that a model was worked out, written up, and widely adopted.

Law: Hammurabi's Code: 1795–1750 BC

Business needs law to determine property rights, without which no meaningful enterprise can take place, and to govern the behaviour and responsibilities of buyers, sellers and others involved in any transaction. The laws that govern business behaviour have evolved over millions of years. The Hammurabi code of laws is the earliest-known example of an entire body of laws, arranged in orderly groups, so that all might read and know what was required of them. The code was carved on a black stone monument, 8 feet high, and clearly intended to be in public view. The stone was found in the year 1901, not in Babylon, but in a city of the Persian mountains, to which some later conqueror must have carried it in triumph. The original code now resides in the Louvre Museum in Paris, though much of it has been erased by time.

The code regulates in clear and definite strokes the organization of society in general and commercial dealings in particular. One law states that 'if a man builds a house badly, and it falls and kills the owner, the builder is to be slain. If the owner's son was killed, then the builder's son is slain.' Even 4,000 years ago it was considered necessary to protect consumers from shoddy workmanship.

The following laws give evidence of a fairly sophisticated business environment that was well established and prolific enough to require detailed regulation:

- If a merchant entrust money to an agent (broker) for some investment, and the broker suffer a loss in the place to which he goes, he shall make good the capital to the merchant.
- If, while on the journey, an enemy take away from him anything that he had, the broker shall swear by God and be free of obligation. This is a forerunner of the term 'force majeure' which under today's

contract law frees both parties from liabilities and obligations when an extraordinary event beyond their control (war, natural disaster, strike etc) occurs.

- If a merchant give an agent corn, wool, oil, or any other goods to transport, the agent shall give a receipt for the amount, and compensate the merchant therefore. Then he shall obtain a receipt from the merchant for the money that he gives the merchant.

- If the agent is careless, and does not take a receipt for the money which he gave the merchant, he cannot consider the un-receipted money as his own.

- If the agent accept money from the merchant, but have a quarrel with the merchant (denying the receipt), then shall the merchant swear before God and witnesses that he has given this money to the agent, and the agent shall pay him three times the sum.

Hammurabi's code was certainly not the earliest. Preceding sets of laws have disappeared, but several traces of them have been found, and Hammurabi's own code clearly implies their existence. He only claimed to be reorganizing a legal system long established.

Family business: Kongo Gumi: 578 to date

According to an 8th-century chronicle considered to be Japan's oldest written history, the first Kongo came to Japan from what is now South Korea and remained in the country at the request of Emperor Yomei. The first Kongo built Shitennoji, one of Japan's first Buddhist temples, in Osaka and the company still serves as its 'chief carpenter', handling repairs and construction of new buildings almost exclusively.

Just as it did in 578, the firm specializes in building traditional Buddhist temples and Shinto shrines, although it has branched out somewhat into general contracting. There are no textbooks to teach *miyadaiku* (specialists in the construction of shrines and temples) how to construct their complex wooden frameworks. The skills are passed down through an apprenticeship-like system, where younger carpenters 'learn and steal' the trade from the master. The skills are considered an intangible cultural asset, for which they feel a great responsibility and a need to pass it on to younger generations.

The firm has been in profit for as long as employees can remember, racking up sales of 9.4 billion yen (RM304m) in the last business year. It hasn't all been smooth sailing, though. In the late 19th century, business nearly came to a halt owing to an anti-Buddhist movement that led to the destruction of some temples. During the last war, the company managed to survive by building wooden boxes for military use.

Masakazu Kongo, the firm's current boss, has some enduring advice for businesses: 'Everybody may be fretting about the recession, how tough times are, but you shouldn't be overwhelmed by all the gloom. Believe in your business and stick to it.'

Mediaeval merchants (1000–1700)

The next half millennium saw as much development in the business world as had occurred in the whole of recorded history up to that date. The first business advisers hit the road with a message very similar to the one espoused by the *Economist* magazine (9–15 March 2002) nearly a thousand years later: 'Be honest, be frugal, be prepared.' A network of international banks straddled Europe; city and family conglomerates were established, some that survive to this day.

The first 'management consultants'

This is one of the earliest business gurus, an anonymous Norwegian author, offering advice to the international businessmen of the day in a treatise entitled 'The King's Mirror' (circa AD 1260). The treatise is wide ranging, with only part of it dealing with merchants of the day. From this we can see that written expert advice for business people is by no means a recent innovation. We can also deduce that long before Stanford and Harvard launched their MBA programmes, numeracy, networking and corporate responsibility were high on the list of skills needed for success in business. The tips about how to behave on foreign business trips and on forging partnerships are as valid now as they were 800 years ago:

- He should be 'polite and agreeable' but should examine goods before he buys them and in the presence of witnesses. If by chance he has purchased inferior goods, let him resell them for what they are and, taking his losses, deceive no one, as he has been deceived.
- When abroad, the merchant should live well but carefully and with restraint of speech and passion.
- He should study especially the local law books, when he has time. He should master the customs of the place he is trading in.
- He should shun drinking, chess, harlots, quarrelling, and gambling.
- He should study the sky, directions, and the sea so as to be able to navigate. All merchants have great need of arithmetic.
- Let him cultivate the friendship of the officials of the country in which he trades and pay the dues that are required. Let him see to it that none of the government's property gets into his cargo.
- He should sell quickly if he can get suitable prices and then be off, for a quick turnover is the life of trade.
- He should always buy shares in a good ship or in none at all.
- If he acquires wealth rapidly, then he should invest part of his wealth in a partnership trade with others doing the travelling, but he should be cautious in selecting partners.

- If he acquires a great deal of wealth in trade, let him divide it into three parts. Let him invest one-third in partnership with experienced and reliable men who are permanently located in towns. The other two-thirds may then be invested in various business ventures for the sake of the safety that lies in diversity.

Banking and the Knights Templar

Despite being remembered mostly for their military prowess during the crusades, this order of knights became, in part by accident, the first major international banking institution. Their specific forte was in keeping the highways open to allow pilgrims to come to the Holy Land unmolested. This goal inevitably meant that the Templars owned some of the mightiest castles, and because of their awesome reputation as fighting men, their castles served as ideal places to deposit money and other valuables. A French knight, for example, could deposit money or mortgage his chateau through the Templars in Paris and pick up gold coins along the route to Jerusalem, and back again if he survived! The Templars charged a fee both for the transaction and for converting the money into various currencies along the route.

Over the years the business grew and eventually the Templars ran a network of full-service banks stretching across Europe from England to Jerusalem. At their maximum strength the Templars employed about 7,000 people, owned 870 castles and fortified houses and were the principal banker to popes and kings.

Free trade and the Hanseatic League

Following the ravages of the Black Death in Europe, cities began to grow and prosper as trade increased and small-scale manufacturing revived. In the northern German seaports, merchants and traders sought protection for their business transactions and the transport of their goods. The city of Lubeck had made a treaty with the city of Hamburg in 1230, which established free trade between the two and guaranteed that the road linking the North Sea and the Baltic Sea would be guarded. The absence of a strong central government in Germany allowed the cities to make such treaties, and soon other communities asked to join the arrangement. Riga, Danzig, a trade centre in London in 1266, and Novgorod in Russia all became part of the League's network of 85 cities.

At its peak the League maintained an army and a navy, guarded roads from city to city, kept a fortress and a storehouse in each city, waged war and enforced the merchant's laws at the various fairs.

Hansa businessmen created partnerships for single ventures only, sending a ship from one port to another and then dissolving the organization. Their bookkeeping techniques were crude, and they constantly fought over the division of profits and the calculation of losses.

As powerful rulers created nation states in England, France, Russia and Sweden, this loose federation of merchants simply could not succeed as modern nation states emerged. Its last general assembly is said to have been held about 1669, but its power had long since evaporated.

The House of Fugger

Fugger's business was a bridge between the Mediaeval and modern worlds. The dynasty began in 1367 when Hans Fugger moved his family to Augsburg, Bavaria, and started a business weaving fustian, a strong cotton-and-linen fabric. His sons Andreas and Jacob I developed the family textile trade before severing their partnership in 1454. On their own, both branches continued to expand their reach. Andreas and his sons moved into finance, in Antwerp and Venice as well as Augsburg. Jacob's sons evolved from trade in textile goods to cotton and spice, and ultimately into mining and processing silver and copper. The family developed a network of trading posts under Jacob's nephew and successor Anton that by 1525 extended from the Mediterranean to the Baltic.

When Anton's nephew Hans Jacob (1516–75) took over, he kept control of their holdings through regular reports from their worldwide network of agents. These reports were consolidated into 'Fugger Newsletters' and circulated among their associates. This was one of the first uses of the word 'news' to refer to deliberate attempts to gather the latest intelligence. Three branches of descendants survive today; one of them – Prince Carl Fugger-Baben-hausen – re-established the Fugger bank in 1954.

The era of ventures (1700–1900)

Throughout history until the 18th century most businesses were small, self-financed and usually short-lived affairs. True, there were exceptions; The East India Company was a monopoly that all but ran India and the Far East, even having its own military and governmental functions. The Peruzzi Company, one of the largest Florentine business ventures, was 60 per cent financed by seven family members and 40 per cent by ten outsiders as far back as 1300. It was organized as quasi-permanent multiple partnerships. Pacioli's double-entry bookkeeping system (see Chapter 1) had made long-term ventures possible for the Venetian merchant adventurers. But the general rule was that business was either a one-man band or family affair, using their own limited financial resources, and any collaboration with other business people was on a venture-by-venture basis. The Industrial Revolution was about to change all that, but three other trading innovations, though less well recognized, were set to have an equally profound effect on business life.

Intellectual property rights

A patent gives the owner of an invention the right to take legal action against others to prevent the unlicensed manufacture, use, importation or sale of the patented invention. Its purpose is to give inventors the breathing space to develop a business based on the invention, or to license it to someone who can. A patent is in essence a bargain between the state and the inventor. The state offers a short-term monopoly of around 20 years, in return for the inventor making a full description of the invention – known as a specification – public through the Patent Office. In this way, other inventors can readily have access to the latest thinking in practically every area of technology and build on that to make further inventions. That in turn creates wealth and opportunities for the country concerned. The speed with which information now flows and the global nature of enterprise mean that any benefit is more to the general good rather than to any country, but the principle remains.

The origins of patents for invention are obscure and no one country can claim to have been the first in the field with a patent system. In about 1200 Venice granted 10-year monopolies to inventors of silk-making devices, and in 1444 published the text of the oldest patent law in the world, officially announced as 'Inventor Bylaws'. However, Britain can claim to have the longest continuous patent tradition in the world. Its origins can be traced back to the 15th century, when the Crown started making specific grants of privilege to manufacturers and traders.

Such grants were signified by Letters Patent, open letters marked with the king's Great Seal. Henry VI granted the earliest known English patent for invention to Flemish-born John of Utynam in 1449. The patent gave John a 20-year monopoly for a method of making stained glass, required for the windows of Eton College, that had not been previously known in England.

Two important legal conditions were established that apply today:

- The famous patent of Arkwright for spinning machines was not allowed for the lack of an adequate specification in 1785, after it had been in existence for 10 years.

- Watt's 1796 patent for steam engines established the important principles that valid patents could be granted for improvements to an existing patented device.

The Japanese took an interesting approach to the subject. Because at the time there was a tendency to abhor new things, a 'Law for New Items' was proclaimed in year 6 of the Kyoho Era (1721). It was not until 1885 that the Japanese Patent Office was up and running. The first patent applied for was a patent for 'Hotta's Method for Rust Stopping Paint and Painting Method', applied for by Zuishou Hotta. The Chinese Patent Office opened in 1985. The late opening of the communist and former communist patent offices was due to their philosophical reluctance to accede private property rights.

Stock markets

The need for stock exchanges developed out of early trading activities in agricultural and other commodities. During the Middle Ages, traders found it easier to use credit that required supporting documentation of drafts, notes and bills of exchange. The history of the earliest stock exchange, the French stock exchange, goes back to the 12th century when transactions occurred in commercial bills of exchange. To control this budding market, Phillip the Fair of France (1268–1314) created the profession of *couratier de change*, which was the predecessor of the French stockbroker. At about the same time, in Bruges, merchants began gathering in front of the house of the Van Der Buerse family to engage in trading. Soon the name of the family became identified with trading and in time a 'bourse' came to signify a stock exchange. At the same time, stock exchanges began to materialize in other trading centres like the Netherlands (Amsterdam Bourse) and Frankfurt (the Deutsche Stock Exchange, formerly the Börse).

In 1698, when one John Castaing in 'Jonathan's Coffee-house' in Exchange Alley in the City of London began publishing a list of stock and commodity prices called 'The Course of the Exchange and other things', the business of stock exchanges really got under way. By 1761 a group of 150 stockbrokers and jobbers had formed a club at Jonathan's to buy and sell shares. In 1773 the brokers erected their own building in Sweeting's Alley, with a dealing room on the ground floor and a coffee room above. Briefly known as 'New Jonathan's', members soon altered the name to 'The Stock Exchange'.

It was not until 1791 that the United States had its first bourse when the Philadelphia traders organized a stock exchange. The following year, 21 New York traders agreed to deal with each other under a buttonwood tree on Wall Street. By 1794 the market had moved indoors. India's premier stock exchange, Bombay Stock Exchange (BSE), can also trace its origin back as far as 125 years when it started as a voluntary non-profit-making association. In the 1870s, a securities system was introduced in Japan and public bond negotiation began. This resulted in the request for a public trading institution, and the 'Stock Exchange Ordinance' was enacted in May 1878. Based on this ordinance, the 'Tokyo Stock Exchange Co., Ltd' was established on 15 May 1878 and trading began on 1 June.

These early stock exchanges were gentlemen's clubs governed only by a few house rules. Trading rarely started before 10.30 and was over by 15.30. No records were filed, no rules governed the case of a trader who could not deliver what he had sold and nothing prevented prices being manipulated.

Limited liability companies

From the earliest trading times to the present day, the most popular legal structure under which to operate has been as a sole trader, which in effect means every man for himself. In the beginning, a merchant always risked his own money, if he had any to invest: if he travelled, as most did, he risked his life on the journey. The caravan trade of Asia, Asia Minor, and North and Central Africa ploughed their way through the sands that separated distant cities and seaports. The largest caravans comprised thousands of camels and required careful administration. They also stimulated people to band together in partnerships, pooling protection costs and profits to spread the risks. The partnerships would usually last only for the particular journey. Later on, older merchants who had made money from earlier ventures could join such expeditions by putting up money, without the hardship of making the trip themselves. This could be seen as an early form of limited partnership.

As the ventures became more costly and of longer duration, partnership structures of fixed duration between 1, 3 or 5 years became common, with an ever-increasing range of partners with differing shares in the venture. To add to the complications these partners could join and leave, perhaps for no more sinister reason than death, at different times.

The concept of limited liability, where the shareholders are not liable, in the last resort, for the debts of their business, changed the whole nature of business and risk taking. It opened the floodgate, encouraging a new generation of entrepreneurs to undertake much larger-scale ventures without taking on themselves all the consequences of failure. As the name suggests, in this form of business liability is limited to the amount you contribute by way of share capital and, in the event of failure, creditors' claims are restricted to the assets of the company. The shareholders of the business are not normally liable as individuals for the business debts beyond the paid-up value of their shares.

The concept itself can be traced back to the Roman Empire, where it was granted, albeit infrequently, as a special favour to friends for large undertakings by those in power. The idea was resurrected in 1811 when New York State brought in a general limited liability law for manufacturing companies. Most US states followed suit and eventually Britain caught up in 1854. Today, most countries have a legal structure incorporating the concept of limited liability.

Business law

06

- Forms of business
- Employing staff
- Innovation issues
- Tax legalities
- Trading regulations
- Rules on mergers and acquisitions

Some business schools take law very seriously; for example, at Northwestern University's Kellogg School and George Washington University, MBA students can take a joint MBA and JD (juris doctor), the basic professional degree for lawyers. Babson in Wellesley, Massachusetts has law as one of its core subjects. Penn State, on the other hand, offers only an optional module in the second year on 'Business Law for Innovation and Competition'.

Nevertheless, lawyers dominate big businesses in the United States and both Congress and the Senate. In the UK around 12 per cent of MPs are either barristers or solicitors, the largest professional grouping in the House of Commons. Other than very large businesses, it is not usual to have either a qualified lawyer or a legal department in businesses in the UK. Such services are usually bought in on either a contractual or ad hoc basis. Law is an imprecise field. As Henry L Mencken, the American journalist and critic, so succinctly expressed it: 'a judge is a law student who marks his own examination papers'.

The complexity of commercial life means that, sooner or later, you will find yourself taking, or defending yourself against, legal action. It may be a contract dispute with a customer or supplier, or perhaps the lease on your premises turns out to give you far fewer rights than you hoped. A former employee might claim you fired them without reason. Or the Health and Safety Inspector will call and find some aspect of your machinery or working practices less than satisfactory.

Ignorance does not form the basis of a satisfactory defence, so every MBA needs to know enough law to know when they might need legal advice, however high their standard of ethics and social responsibility may be.

Corporate structures

As an MBA it's highly likely that you will be working for a conventional company, private or public (see Chapter 2 for more on public companies). There are, however, a number of distinct forms that a business can take, the choice of which depends on a number of factors: commercial needs, financial risk and the need for outside capital.

In most parts of the world corporate structures are broadly similar despite a variety of exotic sounding names. Sole trader is personaline imone in Lithuania and empresário emnome individual in Portugal; Partnerships are Offene Gesellschaft – OG in Austria and verejná obchodná spoloènos in Slovakia; limited partnerships are Kommanditgesellschaft – KG in Austria and komanditná spoloènos in Slovakia and the limited company is Sabiedriba ar ierobežotu atbildibu in Latvia and Socitatea cu Raspundere Limitata in Romania.

Each of these forms is explained briefly below, together with the procedure to follow on setting them up. You can change your ownership status later as your circumstances change, so while this is an important decision it is not a final one.

Sole trader

Over 80 per cent of businesses start up as sole traders and indeed around 55 per cent of all businesses employing fewer than 50 people still use this legal structure. It has the merit of being relatively formality free and, unless you intend to register for VAT, there are few rules about the records you have to keep. There is no requirement for your accounts to be audited, or for financial information on your business to be filed at Companies House.

As a sole trader there is no legal distinction between you and your business – your business is one of your assets, just as your house or car is. It follows from this that if your business should fail, your creditors have a right not only to the assets of the business, but also to your personal assets, subject only to the provisions of the Bankruptcy Acts. The capital to get the business going must come from you – or from loans. There is no access to equity capital.

Partnerships

Partnerships are effectively collections of sole traders and, as such, share the legal problems attached to personal liability. There are very few restrictions to setting up in business with another person (or persons) in partnership, and several definite advantages. By pooling resources you may have more capital; you will be bringing, hopefully, several sets of skills to the business; and if you are ill the business can still carry on.

There are two serious drawbacks that you should certainly consider. First, if your partner makes a business mistake, perhaps by signing a disastrous contract, without your knowledge or consent, every member of the partnership must shoulder the consequences. Under these circumstances your personal assets could be taken to pay the creditors even though the mistake was no fault of your own.

Second, if your partner goes bankrupt in his or her personal capacity, for whatever reason, his or her share of the partnership can be seized by creditors. As a private individual you are not liable for your partner's private debts, but having to buy him or her out of the partnership at short notice could put you and the business in financial jeopardy. Even death may not release you from partnership obligations and in some circumstances your estate can remain liable. Unless you take 'public' leave of your partnership by notifying your business contacts and legally bringing your partnership to an end, you could remain liable.

The legal regulations governing this field are set out in the Partnership Act 1890, which in essence assumes that competent businesspeople should know what they are doing. The Act merely provides a framework of agreement that applies 'in the absence of agreement to the contrary'. It follows from this that many partnerships are entered into without legal formalities – and sometimes without the parties themselves being aware that they have entered a partnership!

The main provisions of the Partnership Act state:

- All partners contribute capital equally.
- All partners share profits and losses equally.
- No partner shall have interest paid on his capital.
- No partner shall be paid a salary.
- All partners have an equal say in the management of the business.
- Unless you are a member of certain professions (eg law, accountancy, etc) you are restricted to a maximum of 20 partners in any partnership.

It is unlikely that all these provisions will suit you, so you would be well advised to get a 'partnership agreement' drawn up in writing by a solicitor at the outset of your venture.

Limited partnerships

One possibility that can reduce the more painful consequences of entering a partnership is to form a limited partnership combining the best attributes of a partnership and a company.

A limited partnership works like this. There must be one or more general partners with the same basic rights and responsibilities (including unlimited liability) as in any general partnership, and one or more limited partners who are usually passive investors. The big difference between a general partner and a limited partner is that the limited partner isn't personally liable for debts of the partnership. The most a limited partner can lose is the amount that he or she: paid or agreed to pay into the partnership as a capital contribution; received from the partnership after it became insolvent.

To keep this limited liability, a limited partner may not participate in the management of the business, with very few exceptions. A limited partner who does get actively involved in the management of the business risks losing immunity from personal liability and having the same legal exposure as a general partner.

The advantage of a limited partnership as a business structure is that it provides a way for business owners to raise money (from the limited partners) without either having to take in new partners who will be active in the business or having to form a limited company. A general partnership that's been operating for years can also create a limited partnership to finance expansion.

Limited company

Of the 4.5 million businesses trading in the UK, over 1.4 million are limited companies. A similar proportional split applies to the 22 million businesses in the United States. As the name suggests, in this form of business your liability is limited to the amount you state that you will contribute by way of share capital, though you may not actually have to put that money in.

A limited company has a legal identity of its own, separate from the people who own or run it. This means that, in the event of failure, creditors' claims are restricted to the assets of the company. The shareholders of the business are not liable as individuals for the business debts beyond the paid-up value of their shares. This applies even if the shareholders are working directors, unless of course the company has been trading fraudulently. Other advantages include the freedom to raise capital by selling shares.

Disadvantages include the cost involved in setting up the company and the legal requirement in some cases for the company's accounts to be audited by a chartered or certified accountant. Usually it is only businesses with assets approaching £3m that have to be audited but if, for example, you have shareholders who own more than 10 per cent of your firm they can ask for the accounts to be audited. The behaviour of companies and their directors is governed by Companies Acts that have come into effect since 1844, the latest of which came into effect in November 2006.

Public limited company (PLC)

PLCs are companies that can sell shares to the public at large, either through a recognized stock market or by advertising in the press or through intermediaries. They need to fulfil some minimum, not too onerous conditions:

- It must state that it is a PLC in its articles of association.
- It must have an authorized share capital of at least £50,000.
- Before it can trade, £50,000 ($78,400/€56,200) of share capital must be taken up and a quarter of that must be actually paid up.
- Each allotted share must be paid up to at least a quarter of its nominal value.
- There must be at least two shareholders, two directors and a company secretary who meets certain standards in terms of qualifications or experience.

See also Chapter 2 for more on public capital.

Company limited by guarantee

This type of incorporation is used for non-profit organizations that require corporate status as a means of protecting participants. There are no shareholders but its members give an undertaking to contribute a nominal amount towards the winding up of the company in the event of a shortfall when it closes down. It cannot distribute its profits to its members, and is therefore eligible to apply for charitable status if necessary. You may find this type of company being used by a business as a means of isolating part of its activities, such as clubs or sports associations that are not part of its profit-generating business.

Co-operative

A co-operative is an enterprise owned and controlled by the people working in it. Once in danger of becoming extinct, the workers' co-operative is enjoying something of a comeback. There are functioning co-operatives in some 90 countries employing over 800 million people worldwide. The International Co-operative Alliance (**www.ica.coop/ica**) represents agriculture, banking, fisheries, health, housing, industry, insurance, tourism and consumer co-operatives and is the largest non-governmental organization in the world.

Over 4,990 independent co-operatives exist in the United Kingdom, employing some 237,800 people and generating sales of £33.5 billion a year. Co-ops sell bicycles, furniture, camping equipment, appliances, carpeting, clothing, handicrafts and books. Co-operative wholesalers exist like those in the hardware, grocery, and natural foods businesses. Some co-operatives disseminate news, and others are for artists. Co-operative electric and telephone utilities exist, as well as co-operatively managed banks, credit unions, and community development corporations.

Some co-ops provide healthcare, such as health maintenance organizations and community health clinics. Co-operative insurance companies have also been established, as well as co-operative food stores, food-buying clubs, and discount warehouses. You get the idea. Co-ops have been set up in virtually every area of business you can possibly imagine. You can find out everything you need to know about the size, structure and prospects of co-operatives in a free 36-page report that can be downloaded at: **www.uk.coop/resources/documents/uk-co-operative-economy-2010**.

Help and advice on business corporate structure

A Guidance Note entitled 'Business Ownership' is available from Companies House (**www.companieshouse.gov.uk** > Guidance Booklets).

Business Link (**www.businesslink.gov.uk** > Taxes, returns and payroll > Choosing and setting up a legal structure > Legal structure: the basics) has a guide to putting your business on a proper legal footing, explaining the tax and other implications of different ownership structures.

Cooperatives UK (**www.cooperatives-uk.coop** > Services > Co-operative Development) is the central membership organization for co-operative enterprises throughout the UK. This link is to the regional network.

Desktop Lawyer (**www.desktoplawyer.co.uk** > BUSINESS > BUSINESS START-UP > Choosing a business structure > The Partnership) has a summary of the pros and cons of partnerships as well as inexpensive partnership deeds.

Employment law

Trading regulations

Organizations are heavily regulated in almost every sphere of their trading operations. Some types of business require a permit before they can even start trading and all businesses have to comply with certain standards when it comes to advertising, holding information or offering credit. These are the regulations that govern the trading activities of most business ventures.

Getting a licence or permit

Some businesses, such as those working with food or alcohol, employment agencies, mini-cabs and hairdressers, need a licence or permit before they can set up in business at all. Even playing music in public, recorded or live, or putting a table and chairs on a pavement means getting permission from someone. Your local authority planning department can advise you on what rules will apply to your business. You can also use this Business Link website (**www.businesslink.gov.uk** > Your type of business) from which you can use their interactive tool to find out which permits, licences and registrations will apply and where to get more information.

Advertising and descriptive standards

Any advertising or promotion you undertake concerning your business and its products and services, including descriptions on packaging, leaflets and instructions and those given verbally, have to comply with the relevant regulations. You can't just make any claims you believe to be appropriate for your business. Such claims must be decent, honest, truthful and take into account your wider responsibilities to consumers and anyone else likely to be affected; if you say anything that is misleading or fails to meet any of these tests then you could leave yourself open to being sued.

The five bodies concerned with setting the standards and enforcing the rules are:

- The Advertising Authority (**www.asa.org.uk** > Advertising Codes) for printed matter, newspapers, magazines and so forth and the internet.

- Ofcom (**wwwofcom.org.uk** > About Ofcom > Compliance, Accessibility and Diversity) is responsible for ensuring advertisements on television and radio comply with rules on what can and cannot be advertised, including any special conditions such as the timing and content of material aimed at children.

- The Financial Services Authority (**www.fsa.gov.uk** > Being regulated > Financial Promotions) has the responsibility to see that financial promotions are clear, fair and not misleading.

- The Office of Fair Trading (**www.oft.gov.uk** > Advice and resources > Resource base > Approved codes of practice) is responsible for ensuring that advertisements are not misleading or making unfair or exaggerated comparisons with other products and services and to help consumers find businesses that have high standards of customer service.

- Trading Standards (**www.tradingstandards.gov.uk** > For business > guidance leaflets > Trade Descriptions) covers anything such as quantity, size, composition, method of manufacture, strength, performance, place of manufacture, date, brand name, conformity with any recognized standard or history.

Complaints, returns and refunds

Customers buying products are entitled to expect that the goods are 'fit for purpose' in that they can do what they claim, and, if the customer has informed you of a particular need, that they are suitable for that purpose.

The goods also have to be of 'satisfactory quality', that is, durable and without defects that would affect performance or prevent their enjoyment. For services, you must carry out the work with reasonable skill and care and provide it within a reasonable amount of time. The word reasonable is not defined and is applied in relation to each type of service. So, for example, repairing a shoe might reasonably be expected to take a week, while three months would be unreasonable.

If goods or services don't meet these conditions, customers can claim a refund. If they have altered or waited an excessive amount of time before complaining or have indicated in any other way that they have 'accepted', they may not be entitled to a refund, but may still be able to claim some money back for a period of up to six years. Trading Standards (**www.tradingstandards.gov.uk** > For business > guidance leaflets > A Trader's Guide to the Civil Law Relating to the Sale and Supply of Goods and Services) provides a summarized guide to the relevant laws in clear plain English.

Distance selling and online trading

Selling by mail order via the internet, television, radio, telephone, fax or catalogue requires that you comply with some additional rules over and above those concerning the sale of goods and services described above. In summary, you have to provide written information, an order confirmation, and the chance to cancel the contract. During the cooling-off period customers have the unconditional right to cancel within seven working days, provided they have informed you in writing by letter, fax or e-mail.

There are, however, a wide range of exemptions to the right to cancel, including: accommodation, transport, food, newspapers, audio or video recordings and goods made to a customer's specification. The Office of Fair Trading (**www.oft.gov.uk** > Advice and resources > Advice for businesses > Selling at a distance) publishes a guide for business on distance selling.

Protecting customer data

If you hold personal information on a computer on any living person, customer or employee for example, then there is a good chance you need to register under the Data Protection Act. The rules state that the information held must have been obtained fairly, be accurate, held only for as long as necessary and held only for a lawful purpose.

You can check if you are likely to need to register using the interactive tool on the Business Link website (**www.businesslink.gov.uk** > IT & e-commerce > Data protection and your business > Comply with data protection legislation).

Consumer credit licence

If you plan to let your customers buy on credit, or hire out or lease products to private individuals or to businesses, then you will in all probability have to apply to be licensed to provide credit. If you think you may need to be licensed, read the regulations on the website of the Office of Fair Trading (**www.oft.gov.uk** > Advice and resources > Advice for businesses > Offering credit > Do you need a credit licence).

Employment legislation

Employing people full or part time is something of a legal minefield, starting with the job advert and culminating with the point at which you decide to part company. Three comprehensive sources of information on the legal aspects of employment are:

- Acas (**www.acas.org.uk** > Our publications > Rights at work leaflets) is a link to free leaflets provided by the Advisory and Conciliation Service, who should know a thing or two about employment law.
- Business Link (**www.businesslink.gov.uk** > Employing people > Recruitment and getting started).
- TheSite.org (**www.thesite.org** > Work & Study > Working > Workers' Rights) is a site run by YouthNet UK, a charity that helps young people have access to high-quality, impartial information as an aid to making decisions. It covers everything to do with work, including drug testing at work. While the site's centre of gravity is young people, the law as described applies to employers.
- WorldEmploymentLaw.com (**www.worldemploymentlaw.com**) provides up-to-date labour law covering some 14 countries including the United States, China, India, Brazil and Russia.

Advertising the job

As with any advertising, you are governed by the laws on discrimination and equal opportunities. That means that any reference to gender, age, nationality, sexual orientation or religion is not permitted. You can still describe the job and the ideal candidate in terms of their experience, knowledge, attitude and qualifications. For tips on the sentences you can use, visit VizualHR.com (**www.oneclickhr.com** > HR Guide > Recruitment & Selection > Recruitment). The basic information, tips about the applicant, the organization, the job and the job package are free and very adequate; you have to subscribe for fuller information.

Contracts of employment

Employers are required to give employees a contract of employment within two months of their starting work. The contract has to contain all the obvious things such as where the job is to be, what the responsibilities are, pay, holiday entitlement, as well as details on sick pay, pension, period of notice and the grievance and disciplinary procedure.

Business Link (**www.businesslink.gov.uk** > Employing people > Paperwork > Create a written statement of employment) has an interactive tool to create a document of everything you are required by law to give a new employee. The law requires that all workers have a statutory right to at least four weeks' paid annual leave, pro rata for part-timers; that you pay the statutory minimum wage, dependent on the age of the employee; that they work within the working time limits (48 hours a week); and that parents are entitled to periods of paid leave when they have children (up to 52 weeks for women and one or two weeks for men).

Employment records

Employers must maintain records on employees, keeping note of absences, sickness, disputes, disciplinary matters, accidents, training, holidays and any appraisals or performance reviews. If you have an unsatisfactory employee and want to dismiss them, this information will be vital. OyezWaterlow (**www.oyezwaterlow.co.uk** > HR Paper Forms) has a record keeping system priced at £78.95 ($123.76/€88.69).

Software such as that provided by Vizual Management Solutions (**www. vizualms.co.uk** > Personnel Manager) will cost several times that of the paper version and for most small businesses will add little value. If you can write a simple database program using software such as Access then that is worth exploring. If you keep records on a computer you will need to be mindful of the Data Protection Act as it applies to employee records. You can get that from the Information Commissioner's Office (**www.ico.gov.uk** > For organizations > Data protection guide).

Safety at work

Employers have a 'duty of care' to ensure that anyone working for you is working in a safe environment and is not exposed to possible health and safety hazards. You need to make an assessment of risk and working conditions covering everything from fire exits to ensuring that ventilation, temperature, lighting and toilet facilities meet health and safety requirements. The Health and Safety Executive (**www.hse.gov.uk** > Businesses > Small businesses) has ready-made risk assessment forms and a basic guide to health and safety at work.

Unfair dismissal

Although it's the handful of cases usually brought by City workers that grab the headlines, some 53,000 unfair dismissal claims are filed with tribunals each year: in the UK alone just under half of those are won by the employee, with the average claim being settled for £5,000. Employers who have been through the process say that it's the stress and administrative burden rather than the settlement itself that is of greatest concern. You can find a list of

CASE STUDY

Societé Générale, the French bank, reported a trading loss of €4.9 ($6.8/£4.4) billion on 24 January 2008 after liquidating €50 ($69.7/£44.5) billion in what the bank says were unauthorized futures positions taken by a relatively junior trader, Jerome Kerviel. The bank claims that Kerviel forged documents and e-mails to suggest he had hedged his positions. But Kerviel insists that his bosses at SocGen, as the bank is generally known, must have been aware of his massive risk taking, and turned a blind eye as long as he was making money for the bank.

Kerviel plans to file a complaint for unfair dismissal and extract compensation from his employer based around three points of defence. First, Societé Générale appears to have terminated his contract without a face-to-face meeting, as is required by French labour laws.

Second, the bank's losses may only have occurred while unwinding Kerviel's positions in January 2008, during what was an unprecedented period of global stock market turbulence. This situation makes it unclear exactly how much responsibility Kerviel bears for the total losses.

Third, he had no obvious motive and seems to have made no personal profit from his trades. In fact his behaviour has made him a folk hero in France, with over 150 Facebook groups showing an interest in his fate.

His chances of success in an unfair dismissal case look at least fair. In April 2007, Laura Zubulake, 44, won £15.5 ($24.3/€17.4) million from UBS in New York after a male executive said she was fired because she was 'old and ugly and she can't do the job'. Three years earlier, Elizabeth Weston received a £1 ($1.6/€1.12) million settlement from Merrill Lynch over a colleague's 'lewd' comments over a Christmas lunch.

Although Kerviel's actions put him at the top of the 'rogue trader' list, he is unlikely to head the unfair dismissal stakes. That title is likely to go to six women, five female employees in New York and one at the London office of German-owned bank Dresdner Kleinwort Wasserstein (DKW). They are suing for £800 ($1,254/€900) million over allegations that the company refused to promote them and discriminated against them by allowing after-hours trips to strip clubs for male colleagues and humiliating sexual banter in the office.

fair reasons for dismissing an employee on Monster's Employment Law (**www.compactlaw.co.uk/monster/empf9.html**). Also Iambeingfired (**www.iambeingfired.co.uk** > Claim Evaluator) is worth examining as it gives the employee's side of the argument. The Claim Evaluator Tool takes an employee through a series of questions to see if they have a case for unfair dismissal, which could be useful as MBAs are often high on the casualty list during restructuring or after acquisitions. The site also has comprehensive information on all aspects of employment law that impinge on the likelihood of being dismissed.

Intellectual property

The holy grail of competitive business strategy is to have a product or service with sufficient unique advantage to make it stand out from others in the market. It is equally important that such an advantage cannot be easily copied. In other words, there is a barrier to entry preventing others from following the same path to riches. The advantage can be anything – the business name (Body Shop), a catchy slogan (Never knowingly undersold – John Lewis), some technological wizardry (Dolby Noise Reduction), an instantly recognizable logo (Google) or even a jingle such as that used by Microsoft's Windows operating system during start-up.

The generic title covering this area is 'intellectual property', usually shortened by MBAs to IP, and it splits down into a number of distinct areas.

CASE STUDY

When Mark Zucherberg, then aged 20, started Facebook from his college dorm back in 2004 with two fellow students, he could hardly have been aware of how the business would pan out. Facebook is a social networking website on which users have to put their real names and e-mail addresses in order to register; then they can contact current and past friends and colleagues to swap photos, news and gossip. Within three years the company was on track to make $100 (£64/€72) million sales, partly on the back of a big order from Microsoft that appears to have set its sights on Facebook as either a partner or an acquisition target.

Zuckerberg, wearing jeans, Adidas sandals and a fleece, looks a bit like a latter-day Steve Jobs, Apple's founder. He also shares something else in common with Jobs. He has a gigantic intellectual property legal dispute on his hands. For three years he has been dealing with a law suit brought by three fellow Harvard students who claim, in effect, that he stole the Facebook concept from them.

Businesses spend a lot of time and money creating and protecting IP, so you need at least an appreciation of the legal issues involved. The case above is an example of how things can go wrong from the outset. You should also read up about Dyson's 'Patent Nightmare' (**www.dyson.co.uk/about/story/patent.asp**), as graphic a description of a contest between David and Goliath as you are likely to find.

The MBA Information Resource Centre at the end of the book provides world contact points for Intellectual Property matters, as well as the information at the end of this section.

Patents

A patent can be regarded as a contract between an inventor and the state. The state agrees with the inventor that if he or she is prepared to publish details of the invention in a set form and if it appears that he or she has made a real advance, the state will then grant the inventor a 'monopoly' on the invention for 20 years. The inventor uses the monopoly period to manufacture and sell his or her innovation; competitors can read the published specifications and glean ideas for their research, or they can approach the inventor and offer to help to develop the idea under licence.

However, the granting of a patent doesn't mean that the proprietor is automatically free to make, use or sell the invention him- or herself, since to do so might involve infringing an earlier patent that has not yet expired.

A patent really only allows the inventor to stop another person using the particular device that forms the subject of the patent. The state does not guarantee validity of a patent either, so it is not uncommon for patents to be challenged through the courts.

What you can patent

What inventions can you patent? The basic rules are that an invention must be new, must involve an inventive step and must be capable of industrial exploitation.

You can't patent scientific/mathematical theories or mental processes, computer programs or ideas that might encourage offensive, immoral or antisocial behaviour. New medicines are patentable but not medical methods of treatment. Neither can you have just rediscovered a long-forgotten idea (knowingly or unknowingly).

If you want to apply for a patent, it is essential not to disclose your idea in non-confidential circumstances. If you do, your invention is already 'published' in the eyes of the law, and this could well invalidate your application.

Copyright

Copyright gives protection against the unlicensed copying of original artistic and creative works – articles, books, paintings, films, plays, songs, music, engineering drawings. To claim copyright, the item in question should carry this symbol: © (author's name) (date). You can take the further step of recording the date on which the work was completed, for a moderate fee, with the Registrar at Stationers' Hall. This, though, is an unusual precaution to take and probably only necessary if you anticipate an infringement.

Copyright protection in the UK lasts for 70 years after the death of the person who holds the copyright, or 50 years after publication if this is later.

Copyright is infringed only if more than a 'substantial' part of your work is reproduced (ie issued for sale to the public) without your permission, but since there is no formal registration of copyright the question of whether or not your work is protected usually has to be decided in a court of law.

Designs

You can register the shape, design or decorative features of a commercial product if it is new, original, never published before or – if already known – never before applied to the product you have in mind. Protection is intended to apply to industrial articles to be produced in quantities of more than 50. Design registration applies only to features that appeal to the eye – not to the way the article functions.

To register a design, you should apply to the Design Registry and send a specimen or photograph of the design plus a registration fee (currently £90). The specimen or photograph is examined to see whether it is new or original and complies with other registration requirements. If it does, a certification of registration is issued which gives you, the proprietor, the sole right to manufacture, sell or use in business articles of that design.

Protection lasts for a maximum of 25 years. You can handle the design registration yourself, but, again, it might be preferable to let a specialist do it for you. There is no register of design agents, but most patent agents are well versed in design law.

Trademarks and logos

A trademark is the symbol by which the goods or services of a particular manufacturer or trader can be identified. It can be a word, a signature, a monogram, a picture, a logo or a combination of these.

To qualify for registration the trademark must be distinctive, must not be deceptive and must not be capable of confusion with marks already registered. Excluded are misleading marks, national flags, royal crests and insignia of the armed forces. A trademark can apply only to tangible goods, not services (although pressure is mounting for this to be changed).

To register a trademark, you or your agent should first conduct preliminary searches at the trademarks branch of the Patent Office to check there are no conflicting marks already in existence. You then apply for registration on the official trademark form and pay a fee (currently £200). Registration is initially for 10 years. After this, it can be renewed for periods of 10 years at a time, indefinitely.

It isn't mandatory to register a trademark. If an unregistered trademark has been used for some time and could be construed as closely associated with a product by customers, it will have acquired a 'reputation', which will give it some protection legally, but registration makes it much simpler for the owners to have recourse against any person who infringes the mark.

Names

Business and domain names involve a cross-section of IP issues. A good name, in effect, can become a one- or two-word summary of your marketing strategy; Body Shop, Toys 'R' Us, Kwik-Fit Exhausts are good examples. Many companies add a slogan to explain to customers and employees alike 'how they do it'. Cobra Beer's slogan 'Unusual thing, excellence' focuses attention on quality and distinctiveness. The name, slogan and logo combine to be the most visible tip of the iceberg in a corporate communications effort and as such need a special effort to protect.

Business name

When you choose a business name, you are also choosing an identity, so it should reflect:

- who you are;
- what you do;
- how you do it.

Given all the marketing investment you will make in your company name, you should check with a trademark agent whether you can protect your chosen name (descriptive words, surnames and place names are not normally allowed except after long use). Also, check if the name is one of the 90 or so 'controlled' names such as bank, royal or international for which special permission is needed. Limited companies have to submit their choice of name to the Companies Registration Office along with the other documents required for registration. It will be accepted unless there is another company with that name on the register or the Registrar considers the name to be obscene, offensive or illegal.

Registering domains

Internet presence requires a domain name, ideally one that captures the essence of your business neatly so that you will come up readily on search engines and is as close as possible to your business name. Once a business name is registered as a trademark (see earlier in this chapter), you may (as current case law develops) be able to prevent another business from using it as a domain name on the internet.

Registering a domain name is simple, but as hundreds of domain names are registered every day and you must choose a name that has not already been registered, you need to have a selection of domain names to hand in case your first choice is unavailable. These need only be slight variations, for example Cobra Beer could have been listed as Cobra-Beer, CobraBeer or even Cobra Indian Beer, if the original name was not available. These would all have been more or less equally effective in terms of search engine visibility.

Help and advice on intellectual property matters

- UK Intellectual Property Office (**www.ipo.gov.uk**) has all the information needed to patent, trademark, copyright or register a design.
- International intellectual property information at: European Patent Office (**www.epo.org**), US Patent and Trade Mark Office (**www.uspto.gov**) and the World Intellectual Property Association (**www.wipo.int**).
- The Chartered Institute of Patents and Attorneys (**www.cipa.org.uk**) and the Institute of Trade Mark Attorneys (**www.itma.org.uk**), despite their specialized-sounding names, can help with every aspect of IP, including finding you a local adviser.
- The British Library (**www.bl.uk** > Collections > Patents, trade marks & designs > Key patent databases) links to free databases for patent searching to see if someone else has registered your innovation. The library is willing to offer limited advice to enquirers.
- Business Link (**www.businesslink.gov.uk** > IT & e-commerce > E-commerce > Web hosting options) has comprehensive up-to-date information on choosing a domain name and registering and protecting that name.
- Guidance Notes entitled 'Choosing a Company Name' are available from Companies House (**www.companieshouse.gov.uk** > Guidance Booklets).

Principles of taxation

Tax in its various forms can account for up to half of a business's turnover. Taxes constitute the largest single creditor, the most likely event to cause a business to fold and ranks first in the pecking order when it comes to the disposal of assets in such an event. These two judgments against the Inland

Revenue Commissioner gave the spur to the 'inventive' approach taken to the subject of tax by many businesses and their accountants:

- Lord Tomkin – IRC v Duke of Westminster (1936): 'Every man is entitled if he can to order his affairs so as that the tax attaching under the appropriate Acts is less than it otherwise would be. If he succeeds in ordering them so as to secure the result, then, however unappreciative the Commissioners of Inland Revenue or his fellow taxpayer may be of his ingenuity, he cannot be compelled to pay an increased tax.'

- Lord Clyde – Ayrshire Pullman Motor Services and Ritchie v IRC (1929): 'No man in this country is under the smallest obligation, moral or other, so to arrange his legal relations to his business or his property as to enable the Inland Revenue to put the largest possible shovel into his stores.'

For business people the justification for tax minimization is overwhelming. No other activity can enhance net profits so dramatically. Every pound in tax saved drops straight to the bottom line.

Tax evasion, avoidance and mitigation

The opportunities are endless, from the seemingly prudent – Marks & Spencer seeking to obtain group tax relief in respect of losses incurred by certain European subsidiary companies in Belgium, France and Germany – to the plain criminal – stuffing the business with false invoices. (China has the dubious distinction of being the world capital of false invoicing. In 2007/08 police there investigated 3,511 cases involving issuing false or tax-offsetting invoices, arrested 2,979 suspects, confiscated 10,510,000 fake invoices, smashed 101 illegal invoice-printing operations and retrieved 9.2 billion yuan (£640 million) in under-declared taxes.)

The challenge for directors and managers is to recognize the distinction between different types of behaviour when it comes to tax law:

- Tax fraud, often called tax evasion to soften the underlying meaning: This involves the intentional behaviour or actual knowledge of the wrongdoing, for example reducing the tax burden by underreporting income, overstating deductions, or using illegal tax shelters; this is a criminal matter.

- Tax mitigation involves the taxpayer taking advantage of a fiscally attractive option afforded to him by the tax legislation and 'genuinely suffers the economic consequences that Parliament intended to be suffered by those taking advantage of the option', as one Law Lord summed the subject up. So, for example, if a business is allowed to offset the cost of an asset against tax, then so long as it actually buys the asset it is mitigating its tax position.

- Tax avoidance lies in the blurred line between tax mitigation and tax fraud and is usually defined by the test of whether your dominant purpose – or your sole purpose – was to reduce or eliminate tax liability.

Tax types

As a business you are responsible for paying a number of taxes and other dues to the government of the day, both on your own behalf and for any employees you may have as well as being an unpaid tax collector required to account for end consumers' expenditure.

There are penalties for misdemeanours and you are required to keep your accounts for six years so that at any point, should tax authorities become suspicious, they can dig into the past even after they have agreed your figures. In the case of suspected fraud there is no limit to how far back the digging can go.

Corporation tax

Companies pay tax on their profits at varying rates dependent on their size and the amount of profit made. These tax rates can be adjusted each year in the Budget. The current rates are published throughout the world on the Worldwide-Tax website (**www.worldwide-tax.com**). Corporation tax in many other countries is much lower. Bulgaria, for example, at the time of writing charges 10 per cent, the lowest in the EU.

Corporation tax covers the profit made in an accounting period, usually of one-year duration but can be shorter under special circumstances, but never longer. Companies are responsible for working out their own tax liability, paying the tax due and filing their tax return no later than 12 months after the end of the accounting period.

Capital allowances

The purchase of capital items such as plant, machinery and equipment, buildings and any such long-term assets is treated for tax purposes in a particular manner. In the profit and loss account these costs are usually shown as an item of depreciation spread over the working life of the asset(s) concerned. For tax purposes, however, depreciation is not an allowable expense; rather, it is replaced with a 'writing-down allowance', the amount of which varies according to the policies favoured by the government of the day.

Capital gains tax

Any asset a business disposes of, other than the goods it normally trades in, is liable, in the event of there being a profit, to pay capital gains tax (CGT). This tax was once very complex, but has now been simplified greatly.

Capital losses

Many sales of assets, old vehicles, computers and so forth, involve a loss rather than a gain. Subject to offsetting any tax relief already claimed from writing down allowances during the asset's life, such losses are usually offset against gains made on the sale of other assets within a set time period, usually several years.

Pay as you earn (PAYE)

Employers are responsible for deducting income tax from employees' pay and making the relevant payment to HMRC. If you trade as a limited company then, as a director, any salary you receive will be subject to PAYE. You will need to work out the tax due. HM Revenue and Customs (**www.hmrc.gov.uk/ employers/employers-pack.htm**) gives details on PAYE in this Employers Pack. This is a complex area, as no two employees are likely to have the same tax circumstances due to the myriad of tax credits on offer for various circumstances.

Subcontractors Companies often seek to circumvent the complexities of PAYE and employment law by using subcontractors. This is particularly so in industries such as construction, but here there are strict and precise rules. Subcontractors must hold either a Registration Card or a Subcontractors Tax Certificate. Where a subcontractor holds a Registration Card, the 'employer' must make a deduction for the subcontractor's tax and National Insurance contribution (NIC) liability. Where the subcontractor holds a Subcontractors Tax Certificate, the contractor will pay salary gross, leaving the tax to be paid by them. At the end of the day, if tax is not paid there is every likelihood that the employer will be pursued by the tax authorities.

National Insurance (NI)

Almost everyone who works has to pay a separate tax, National Insurance, collected by HMRC that, in theory at least, goes towards the state pension and other benefits. NI is paid at different rates and self-employed people pay Class 4 contributions calculated each year on the self-assessment tax form.

The amount of National Insurance paid depends on a mass of different factors; married women, volunteer development workers, share fishermen, self-employed and small earnings are all factors that attract NI rates of between 1 and 12 per cent. HMRC (**www.hmrc.gov.uk** > Library > Rates & Allowances > National Insurance Contributions) provide tables showing the current contribution rates and elsewhere on the site (**www.hmrc.gov.uk** > employers > National Insurance) you can download an Employers Annual Pack with all the complexities of NI paperwork.

Value added tax (VAT)

VAT, a tax common throughout Europe though charged at different rates, is a tax on consumer spending, collected by businesses. Basically it is a game of pass the parcel, with businesses that are registered for VAT charging each other VAT and deducting VAT charged. At the end of each accounting period the amount of VAT you have paid out is deducted from the amount you have charged out and the balance is paid over to HM Revenue and Customs. In the UK the standard rate is 20 per cent, while some types of business charge lower rates and some are exempt altogether. In the UK, businesses should register for VAT if their sales are expected to reach around £70,000 ($110,000/€78,600).

The way VAT is handled on goods and services sold to and bought from other European countries is subject to another set of rules and procedures. HM Revenue and Customs (**www.hmrc.gov.uk** > Businesses and Corporations > VAT) publishes a series of guides, such as 'Should you be registered for VAT?' and a General Guide.

VAT is a legal minefield with fine judgments being the order of the day, as Marks & Spencer can confirm. For decades it was obliged to pay VAT on its chocolate teacakes as the Revenue categorized them as a biscuit, a luxury rather than 'food' and hence liable to VAT. M&S persuaded the European Advocate General that the Revenue was wrong putting it in line for a £3.5 ($5.5/€3.9) million refund.

Economics

07

- Schools of economic thought
- Market structures and competition
- Managing growth
- Understanding business cycles
- Fiscal and monetary policy considerations
- Assessing economic success

Economics has been something of a backwater subject but the crisis that hit the global economy at the end of the first decade of the 21st century changed all that. There is hardly anyone in business who hasn't heard and felt the clash between the Keynesian view that economies need occasionally to be kick started and that of the Monetarists who claim most problems with economies can be solved with a liberal injection of cash – quantitative easing. In fact, as by 2010/11 it had become evident from the contrasting behaviour of governments around the world all heavily armed with schools of their own economist, there is no conclusive universally applicable strategy for managing economies. Gordon Brown, the British Prime Minister who claimed to have banished boom and bust, was proved decisively wrong. Perhaps the best way to appreciate why economists never agree lies in this quote by Maynard Keynes: 'When the facts change I change my mind.'

The jury is out on who the got the whole subject of economics under way, but two serious contenders are Aristotle (382–322 BC) who, in his work *Topics*, got the subject of human production under way, and Chanakya, whose treatise Arthasastra (economics), written in the period 321–296 BC, laid out a framework for the economic management of India's agriculture, forestry, wildlife, mining, transport and trade.

Alfred Marshall, the dominant figure in British economics until his death in 1924, defined economics in his influential textbook *Principles of Economics* as: 'a study of mankind in the ordinary business of life; it examines that part of individual and social action which is most closely connected with the attainment and with the use of the material requisites of well-being. Thus it is on one side a study of wealth; and on the other, and more important side, a part of the study of man.' Today that definition has been shortened in most textbooks on the subject to: 'Economics is the social science which examines how people choose to use limited or scarce resources in attempting to satisfy their unlimited wants.'

The dismal science, as economics is often referred to, reveals something of the contradictions inherent in the subject itself. Science to most people means a subject comprising fundamental truths that hold good under all conditions and forever. Two and two equals four, or the area of a circle = πr^2, work equally as well as propositions in Mongolia and on the Moon. But put two economists together and you will get three economic theories. Worse still, if you put three together you could end up with six!

Schools of economic thought

Groups of economists who broadly share the same views are collectively known as schools. Thinking of these as places where people are learning about a constantly changing dynamic subject is a more useful concept than considering economics to be a science. With Buddha seeking to eliminate want, Malthus who was sure that human populations grew faster than food production and so charity was self-defeating, Marx and Keynes who for different reasons saw the state's role as central and Adam Smith whose 'Invisible Hand' saw all economic activity as being subject to the law of unintended consequences, there has been and is some scope for diversity.

The two economic theories that every self-respecting MBA must have an appreciation of are:

- Keynesian: A theory of macroeconomics developed by British economist John Maynard Keynes and documented in his book *The General Theory of Employment, Interest and Money*, published in 1936. He argued that low demand is the primary cause of recessions and that government fiscal policies (see below) should be the method employed to create employment, control inflation and stabilize business cycles. This work initiated the modern study of macroeconomics and guided economic thinking, only diminishing in popularity in the 1970s when violent shocks to economies, caused particularly by escalating oil prices, simultaneously led to high unemployment and high inflation rates. This challenged the central implications of Keynesian economics.

- Monetarist: First put forward by the economist Milton Friedman and the Chicago school of economists. Friedman and Anna Schwartz (an economist at the US National Bureau of Economic Research) in their book *A Monetary History of the United States 1867–1960* argued that 'inflation is always and everywhere a monetary phenomenon'. Friedman advocated that a country's central bank should pursue a monetary policy (see below) such as to keep the supply of and demand for money at equilibrium. By 1990 monetarism was being challenged as it could not be reconciled with, among other things, the inability of monetary policy alone to stimulate the economy in the 2001–03 period.

Micro vs macroeconomics

Microeconomics is the study of economics as it affects small units such as individuals, families, firms and industries. Macro is a study of the forces that affect a whole economy. The main concept used in microeconomics, and one that underpins almost the whole subject of economics, is that of the price elasticity of demand. The concept itself is simple enough. The higher the price of a good or service the less of it you are likely to sell. Obviously it's not quite that simple in practice; the number of buyers, their expectations, preference and ability to pay, the availability of substitute products also have an effect. Figure 7.1 is that of a theoretical demand curve.

The figure shows how the volume of sales of a particular good or service will change with changes in price. The elasticity of demand is a measure of the degree to which consumers are sensitive to price. This is calculated by dividing the percentage change in demand by the percentage change in price. If a price is reduced by 50 per cent (eg from $/£/€100 to $/£/€50) and the quantity demanded increased by 100 per cent (eg from 1,000 to 2,000), the elasticity of demand coefficient is 2 (100/50). Here the quantity demanded changes by a bigger percentage than the price change, so demand is considered to be elastic. Were the demand in this case to rise by only 25 per cent, then the elasticity of demand coefficient would be 0.5 (25/100). Here the

FIGURE 7.1   The demand curve

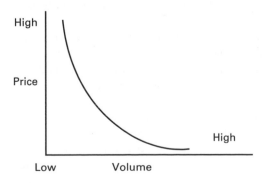

demand is described as being 'inelastic' as the percentage demand change is smaller than that of the price change.

Having a feel for elasticity is important in developing a business's marketing strategy, but there is no perfect scientific way to work out what the demand coefficient is; it has to be assessed by 'feel'. Unfortunately, the price elasticity changes at different price levels. For example, reducing the price of vodka from $/£/€10 to $/£/€5 might double sales, but halving it again may not have such a dramatic effect. In fact it could encourage one group of buyers, those giving it as a present, to feel that giving something that cheap is rather insulting.

Market structures

The whole of the subject of economics as practised in advanced economies is predicated on the belief that market forces are allowed a large degree of freedom. New firms can set up in business, charging the price they see fit, and if their strategy is flawed they will be allowed to fail (see also Chapter 8, Entrepreneurship). Price is allowed to send important signals throughout the economy, apportioning demand and resources accordingly. But perfect competition, where price is allowed such freedom, is only one of four prevailing market structures; although market economies are dominated by near-perfect competition, that is not maintained without a struggle.

The following are the four market structures that are at work in economies.

Monopoly

Monopolies exist where a single supplier dominates the market and so renders normal competitive forces largely redundant. Price, quality and innovation are compromised, so deliver less value to the end consumer than they might otherwise expect. Microsoft has a near-monopolistic grip on the operating system market, as has Pfizer, the pharmaceutical giant, through its patent on the drug Viagra; and British Airports Authority (BAA), which runs Heathrow, Gatwick and Stansted, has a similar hold on London airports' traffic.

Monopolies claim that without being allowed to dominate their market it would be impossible to get sufficient economies of scale to reinvest. That was the argument of the early railway companies and it was BAA's argument in 2008 in defending itself against the prospects of a government-enforced break-up.

In countries where monopolies are seen as being detrimental, bodies exist to regulate the market to prevent them becoming too powerful. The UK has the Competition Commission (**www.competition-commission.org.uk**), the United States the Federal Trade Commission (**www.ftc.gov**) and the EU has

The European Commission (**http://ec.europa.eu/comm/competition/index_ en.html**), all keeping monopolies in check. A duopoly is, as the name would suggest, a particular form of monopoly with only two firms in the market.

Oligopoly

This is where between 3 and 20 large firms dominate a market, or where 4 or 5 firms share more than 40 per cent of the market. The danger for consumers and suppliers alike is that these dominant firms can control the market, to their disadvantage. Supermarket chains in the UK, airlines, oil exploration and refining businesses the world over operate as virtual oligopolies. Frequently the temptation to act in a cartel to fix prices is too great to resist. BA had colluded with Virgin Atlantic on at least six occasions between August 2004 and January 2006, the Office of Fair Trading said.

Between August 2004 and January 2006, British Airways and Virgin Atlantic, the dominant players on the route from London to US cities, colluded with each other to fix the price of fuel surcharges. During that time, surcharges rose from £5 to £60 per ticket. British Airways had to set aside £350 million to deal with fines in the UK and United States.

Perfect competition

This is a utopian environment in which there are many suppliers of identical products or services, with equal access to all the necessary resources such as money, materials, technology and people. There are no barriers to entry, so businesses can enter or leave the market at will and consumers have perfect information on every aspect of the alternative goods on offer.

Competitive markets

Sometimes referred to confusingly as monopolistic competition, this rests between oligopoly and perfect competition, but is closer to perfect competition. Here a large number of relatively small competitors, each with small market shares, compete with differentiated products satisfying diverse consumer wants and needs.

Essential economics

Despite the competing schools of thought on how business and the economy interact, there is at least general agreement on the most important factors. True, there is much disagreement on how important these factors are and even on how they can be influenced, but on the factors themselves there is a measure of agreement. MBAs will need a grasp of these key issues in order to play a full role in shaping the strategy of their organization.

Economic growth

Government's role in economic policy is generally accepted as being to steer a path that ensures long-term growth without leading to a general rise in prices (see Inflation, below). The underlying belief is that growth in goods and services leads to a happier, more satisfied population, while spreading democracy, diversity, social mobility and greater all-round tolerance. Also, the bigger the gross domestic product (GDP) the more guns and bombs a country can afford, both to defend itself and to impose its will on others who are weaker. There is certainly evidence that people judge their well-being by comparing themselves to others, but unfortunately as income goes up, so do expectations.

There have been many attempts at creating a more comprehensive measure of economic health. Gross National Happiness (**www.grossinternational happiness.org/**) and the Genuine Progress Indicator (**www.rprogress.org/ sustainability_indicators/genuine_progress_indicator.htm**) are attempts to include a range of other factors such as life expectancy, crime rates, pollution, long-term environmental damage, resource depletion and income distribution, for example.

GDP is the yardstick taken to measure the economy, even though that doesn't necessarily say much about the level of happiness in a country. There are a number of ways of comparing GDP both between countries and between time periods and, needless to say, economists can't agree which is best.

Gross domestic product

GDP is the total market value of all final goods and services produced in a country in a one-year period. A country's balance sheet, like that for a business, shows the sources and uses of funds. A country's GDP is usually arrived at using the expenditure method, using the equation GDP = consumption (spending by consumers) + gross investment (spending by business) + government spending + (exports − imports). Each component of expenditure plays a part in helping increase GDP and hence economic growth. (See Keynes above.)

The rate of growth of GDP matters greatly. The UK and Europe's long-run GDP growth rate of around 2.5 per cent will lead to a doubling of the countries' wealth in around three decades. China and India, whose growth rate routinely exceeds 8 per cent, will see average wealth double in less than one decade. All other things being equal, companies looking to set up overseas will head for the countries with rapid growth in GDP.

Gross domestic product per person

Measuring a country's total GDP misses an important consideration − the population. If the growth in both GDP and population were uniform there would be no problem, but that is not the case. Britain's country GDP grew at 2.75 per cent between 2003 and 2007, but as the population grew sharply too, GDP per person grew at a rather slower 2.1 per cent. Japan with its shrinking population also grew its GDP per head by 2.1 per cent, matching that of Britain and beating the United States whose growth measured in this way was only 1.9 per cent as opposed to the 2.9 per cent the United States reported for the economy as a whole.

Gross domestic product at purchasing power parity (PPP)

GDP, usually referred to as nominal GDP, is arrived at by the simple process of adding up expenditure and does not reflect differences in the cost of living in different countries or the currency exchange rate prevailing at the time. The same amount of GDP, in other words, can buy a lot more goods and services in one country than another. China's GDP per person is about £1,000 nominal but £3,500 at PPP. Calculating PPP is fraught with problems as people buy very different baskets of goods and services. One way round the imperfections is to produce light-hearted attempts at showing PPP using an external product common to most countries. *The Economist* has published a Big Mac Index (BMI) since 1986, with a few variations such the Tall Latte index and a Coca-Cola map that showed the inverse relationship between the amount of Cola consumed per capita in a country and the general standard of health. In 2007, Commonwealth Securities, an Australian bank, created the iPod Index with much the same aim of calculating a proxy for PPP on a country-by-country basis.

Business cycles

Economies tend to follow a cyclical pattern that moves from boom, when demand is strong, to slump, economists' shorthand for a downturn. The death of the cycle has often been claimed as politicians believe they have become better managers of demand, but the 'this time it's different' school of thinking have been proved wrong time and time again.

The cycle itself is caused by the collective behaviour of billions of people – the unfathomable 'animal spirits' of businesses and households. Maynard Keynes (see above) explained animal spirits as: 'Most, probably, of our decisions to do something positive, the full consequences of which will be drawn out over many days to come, can only be taken as the result of animal spirits – a spontaneous urge to action rather than inaction, and not as the outcome of a weighted average of quantitative benefits multiplied by quantitative probabilities.'

Added to the urge to act is the equally inevitable herd-like behaviour that leads to excessive optimism and pessimism. Charles Mackay (*Extraordinary Popular Delusions and the Madness of Crowds*), Joseph De La Vega (*Confusión de Confusiones*) and the more recent *Irrational Exuberance 2nd edition* (Robert J Shiller) between them provide a comprehensive insight into the capacity for collective overreaction. From the tulip mania in 17th-century Holland and the South Sea Bubble (1711–20) to the internet bubble in 1999 and the collapse in US real estate in 2008, the story behind each bubble has been uncomfortably familiar. Strong market demand for some commodity (gold, copper, oil), currency, property or type of share leads the general public to believe that the trend cannot end. Over-optimism leads the public at large to overextend itself in acquiring the object of the mania, while lenders fall over each other to fan the flames. Finally, either the money runs out or groups of investors become cautious. Fear turns to panic selling, so creating a vicious downward spiral that can take years to recover from.

Categories of cycle

Economics is the science, in so far as it can be considered one, of the indistinctly knowable rather than the exactly predictable. Though all cycles, even the one you are in, are difficult to understand or predict with much accuracy, there are discernible patterns and some distinctive characteristics.

Figure 7.2 shows an elegant curve, which depicts the theoretical textbook cycle.

FIGURE 7.2 Textbook economic cycle

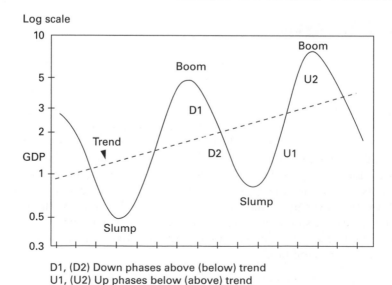

D1, (D2) Down phases above (below) trend
U1, (U2) Up phases below (above) trend

Four phases typically occur in each textbook cycle:

- U1, where demand is picking up and toeing the line of the long-term trend;
- U2, where demand exceeds the long-term trend;
- D1, where demand dips down to hit the long-term trend;
- D2, where demand slumps below the long-term trend.

To make things more complicated, there is not one cycle but at least four that operate, each with different characteristics yet interacting one with the others.

Kondratieff's long waves

Kondratieff (**www.kwaves.com/kond_overview.htm**), a Soviet economist, who fell out with Russia's Marxist leaders and died in one of Stalin's prisons, advanced the theory that the advent of capitalism had created long-wave economic cycles lasting around 50 years. His theories received a boost when the great depression (1929–33) hit world economies and resonated in Britain in 1980–81 when factory closures, high unemployment and crippling inflation devastated the country. The idea of a long wave is supported by evidence that major enabling technologies, from the first printing press to the internet, take 50 years to yield full value, before themselves being overtaken.

Kuznet's cycle

American economist Simon Kuznet, a Nobel Laureate (1971) working in the University of Pennsylvania, made a lifelong study of economic cycles. He identified a cycle of 15–25 years' duration covering the period it takes to acquire land, get the necessary permissions, build property and sell. Also known as the building cycle, this has credibility as so much of economic life is influenced by property and the related purchases of furniture and associated professional charges, for example for lawyers, architects and surveyors.

Juglar cycle

Clement Juglar, a French economist, studied the rise and fall in interest rates and prices in the 1860s, observing boom and bust waves of 9 to 11 years going through four phases in each cycle: prosperity, where investors piled into new and exciting ventures; crisis, when business failures started to rise; liquidation, when investors pull out of markets; and recession, when the consequences of these failures begin to be felt in the wider economy in terms of job losses and reduced consumption.

Kitchin cycle

In 1923, Joseph Kitchin published in the Harvard University Press an article entitled 'Review of Economic Statistics', outlining his discovery of a 40-month cycle resulting from a study of US and UK statistics from 1890 to 1922. He observed a natural cyclical path caused, he believed, by movements in inventories. When demand appears to be stronger than it really is, companies build and carry too much inventory, leading people to overestimate likely future growth. When that higher growth fails to materialize, inventories are reduced, often sharply, so inflicting a 'boom, bust' pressure on the economy.

Monitoring cycles

The National Bureau of Economic Research (**www.nber.org/cycles.htm**) provides a history of all US business cycle expansions and contractions since 1854. The Foundation for the Study of Cycles (**http://foundationforthe studyofcycles.org**), an international research and educational institution established in 1941 by Harvard economist Edward R Dewey, provides a detailed explanation of different cycles. The Centre for Growth and Business Cycle Research based at the School of Social Sciences, The University of Manchester (**www.socialsciences.manchester.ac.uk/cgbcr**), provides details of current research, recent publications and downloadable discussion papers on all aspects of business cycles.

CASE STUDY

Robert Wright, a former commercial pilot, started his first business, Connectair, while on the MBA programme at Cranfield. His aim was to start a small feeder airline bringing passengers into the main UK airport hubs such as Heathrow and Gatwick, where they would connect with the major carriers' flights. He started out at the tail-end of the UK recession in 1982, so to keep costs low, as well as being the MD he was at times the pilot, steward and baggage handler as well as greeting passengers at check-in.

Over the next few years he built the business up to the point where it employed 60 people and made a modest profit. He sold it at the height of the Lawson boom in 1989 to Harry Goodman's International Leisure Group, which collapsed spectacularly in the 1991 economic downturn, leaving crippling debts and thousands of people without jobs.

Wright bought the company back for a nominal £1, financing working capital with backing from 3i, the venture capital firm. Over the next 8 years he and his team built the business up, now renamed City Flyer Express, selling out in 1999, just ahead of the dotcom stock market collapse, to British Airways for £75 million.

Inflation

Inflation is defined as too much money chasing too few goods and if it gets out of control it can devastate an economy. Not all goods and services have to experience price increases. The inflation rate itself is measured by defining a basket of goods and services used by a 'typical' consumer and then keeping track of the cost of that basket using such indices as the retail price index. During the upswing stage of a business cycle there is a tendency to over-shoot, which can lead to the economy 'overheating'. As there is usually a lag while production struggles to catch up with demand, prices rise to 'ration' goods and services. Inflation is generally seen being a problem for a number of reasons:

- 'Inflation makes fools of us all' is a truism about the misleading signals sent by rapid changes in price. Consumers and businesses like certainty, and fluctuating rates of inflation make planning more difficult, which in turns leads to a loss of confidence.

- Inflation redistributes wealth in a haphazard and often unfair manner. For example, savers will find their purchasing power diminish as their fixed sum saved will buy fewer goods and services in the future. Borrowers will benefit as they are effectively paying back a capital sum that is being eroded in value by inflation.

- If the inflation rate is greater than that of other countries, domestic products become less competitive, so exports will be reduced and economic growth will slow.

- High inflation can lead to high wage demands, which can in turn lead to an upward spiral in costs and so feed further inflationary pressures.

Current economic wisdom has it that a modest degree of inflation is healthy provided that everyone knows what it will be and can factor it into their decision making. That is why central banks have as one of their functions monitoring inflation rates and taking action to keep below a certain figure – in the UK this is 2 per cent. Three further aspects of inflation that need to be considered are:

Deflation

The opposite of inflation and occurs when the general level of prices is falling. This can occur after a major bubble collapses and will lead to people putting off purchasing decisions in the expectation of being able to buy later at even lower prices. Japan experienced deflation when its boom in the 1980s turned to a long, wearying bust. Two decades of near zero interest rates have yet to yield anything resembling a dynamic economy. The Nikkei Stock Market Index peaked at 38,916 on 29 December 1989 and at October 2010 was just 9,500 – a measure of the country's economic morass.

Hyperinflation

This is unusually rapid self-feeding inflation; in extreme cases, this can lead to the collapse of a country's monetary system. This occurred in Germany in 1923, when prices rose 2,500% in one month and in Zimbabwe in April 2008 when the annual inflation rate hit 165,000%.

Stagflation

The combination of high economic stagnation with inflation, such as happened in industrialized countries during the 1970s, when OPEC raised oil prices.

Interest rates

Around half the money used to finance businesses is borrowed and private individuals use mortgages, hire purchase and credit cards to fund many of their purchases. Governments too have to use debt through the sale of bonds, when taxes are insufficient to meet their spending plans. The 'price' of borrowed money is the interest paid. Governments can stimulate both business and consumer expenditure by lowering interest rates or choke off demand (see 'Micro vs macroeconomics', above) by raising it. Interest rates are the favourite tool of central banks to control inflation as it can be used to bring supply and demand back into balance.

Interest rates also have a direct bearing on a country's exchange rate. If it is higher than that in other comparable economies it will tend to support the exchange rate at a higher rate, and if lower, the currency will tend to be weaker (see also 'The exchange rate'). There are, however, several different interest rates and governments do not directly control them all:

- Bank Base Rate: This is the interest set by governments, for example by the Bank of England's monetary committee, the US Federal Reserve and the European Central Bank. It is a reference point from which other interest rates are set, but is not the actual interest rate charged by clearing banks to their many and varied clients.

- Libor (London Inter-bank Offered Rate): This is the rate of interest at which banks borrow funds from each other, an essential activity to facilitate global trade and to settle contracts on futures and options exchanges. As such, it is the primary benchmark for short-term interest rates globally. The rate is set by a panel representing around 500 banks and depends on a number of factors, including local interest rates, expectations of future rate movements and the prevailing banking climate. Usually the Libor rate is lower than the rate set by central banks to allow banks a small margin. But if banks lose confidence in their peers' ability to repay then either they stop lending or they charge a premium over the Bank Base Rate. This was the case during the sub-prime crisis in 2007/08. Libor is both sensitive and complex. Rates are set in 10 currencies and for 15 different maturity dates, from an 'overnight' rate maturing tomorrow, a 'spot/next' rate that covers the period to the day after tomorrow, through weeks and months out as far as (but never further than) one year.

- Lending Rate: This is the rate at which banks will lend to businesses and private individuals. It can be anything from a fraction of a percent above either Bank Base Rate or Libor (whichever is the higher) for blue chip firms, a percent or two above for mortgages, and up to 15 per cent above for credit card loans; the higher the perceived risk the higher the rate.

Economic policy and tools

Keeping the economy growing, holding inflation in check and attempting to both anticipate and mitigate the worst effects of downturns in the business cycle are the primary economic goals of government. Dials showing the GDP growth rate and inflation are on every government's economy management dashboard. But these are not the only factors that affect an economy, nor is setting interest rates the only club in a central banker's locker.

Policy options

The UK's 1981 Budget, designed to remove several billion pounds from the economy when the UK was in the depths of recession, provoked an unprecedented letter from 364 economists published in *The Times* stating: 'There is no basis in economic theory or supporting evidence for the government's present policies.' In fact the UK economy recovered and eventually prospered. Even today, no politician, yet alone economist, can agree on whether the 364 economists were right or Lady Thatcher's then Chancellor of the Exchequer, Sir Geoffrey, now Lord, Howe. Although economists disagree on almost everything, they do accept that there are two broad categories of policy: fiscal and monetary.

Monetary policy

Monetarists, as the adherents of this school of thought are known, believe that as the economy runs on money, controlling the supply of the amount of money in circulation is the key to achieving growth without inflation. If the supply of money grows faster than the economy, inflation will rise as too much money will be chasing too few goods; too slow and growth is stifled. There are a number of difficulties in actually executing monetary policies:

- Measuring money: In the first place, agreement has to be reached on what exactly money is. There are at least five different and to some extent overlapping measurements, all attempting to measure the liquid assets at large in an economy. Designated with the prefix M, these measures range from M0, the narrowest definition which includes only the cash held in banks and in circulation, through to M5, the broadest measure which extends to a wide range of other short-term highly liquid financial assets held as a substitute for deposits. Not content with these five measures, some now have letter prefixes to subdivide further the types of liquid assets included. If you can imagine trying to drive a car with several speedometers you will get a feeling for the problem. In the world boom of 1972–73, for example, the UK's M3 and M4 grew at nearly 25 per cent per annum; M5 grew at over 20 per cent, yet M1 grew at only 10 per cent.

- Velocity of circulation: Money's use is as a medium of exchange; we swap it for goods and services, which in turn create the value in an economy that result ultimately in GDP. Over any interval of time, the money one person spends can be used later by the recipients of that money to purchase other goods and services, the suppliers of which can then themselves spend the same cash again. The more times cash circulates each year the higher the velocity and hence the money supply available to fuel GDP. To measure money supply we need to know the velocity of circulation but it is notoriously difficult to do, is different for each of the Ms and can change over time.

Central bankers have three tools to help control the amount of money in circulation:

- Open market operations are where the central bank sells government securities to banks, leaving them with less cash to lend.
- Reserve requirements are the proportion of reserves a bank must keep in relation to the amount of money it can lend. Raising the level of reserves reduces banks' capacity to lend.
- Discount rate is the interest rate the central bank charges banks. Raising that rate reduces the money available to lend.

Fiscal policy

A government's approach to tax and spending is known as its fiscal policy. Cutting taxes and so giving consumers and businesses more money to spend can stimulate an economy. Alternatively, raising taxes can cool an economy down if it looks like overheating. Governments can themselves increase spending, both by using taxes and by borrowing money raised by issuing government securities. The latter approach is termed deficit spending and has been understood and used extensively since popularized by Maynard Keynes in the 1920s. He showed how governments could use this aspect of fiscal policy either to avert a recession or to reduce its effect on unemployment.

The spending multiplier effect

Keynesian economists deduced that government expenditure multiplies through the economy having a far greater ripple effect than the initial sum involved, making such activity more important than the sums themselves may sound. Let's suppose the government decides to embark on a major programme of school building, resulting in $/£/€100 million of salaries for construction workers. The impact of their salaries on the economy depends on their marginal propensity to consume (MPC) – in other words, how much of their salary they will save and how much they will spend. If we suppose that they will save 10 per cent of salary (the approximate 20-year average, though at the time of writing it was less than 6 per cent), then they will spend 90 per cent. That gives an MPC of 0.9, which is 90 per cent expressed as a decimal:

$$\text{The spending multiplier} = \frac{1}{(1 - 0.9)} = 10$$

So the effect of £100 million of government spending on the wider economy is 10 × £100 million, or £1,000 million, because each 90 per cent of a worker's income is spent, which in turn becomes someone else's income of which they spend 90 per cent, and so on.

The tax multiplier

Tax reductions are another way in which governments can affect expenditure by giving or taking money away from consumers, and that too has a multiplier effect. This formula is almost identical to that for the spending multiplier. The only difference is the inclusion of the negative marginal propensity to consume (–MPC). The MPC is negative because an increase in taxes decreases income and hence the ability to consume. If we again assume that 90 per cent of income is spent and 10 per cent saved, we have a marginal propensity to consume of 0.9 and a marginal propensity to save of 0.1. This gives a tax multiplier of –9 (see below), which means that if taxes are raised by £100 million that will result in –9 × £100 million; in other words, £900 million will be taken out of consumption.

$$\text{The tax multiplier} = \frac{-\text{MPC}}{\text{MPS}} = \frac{-0.9}{0.1} = -9$$

The converse is of course true; were taxes reduced by £100 million, consumption would rise by £900 million.

More concerns

Using tools and policies to keep an economy growing and inflation low is certainly a government's primary goal; but they do have some other parallel and interrelated outcomes in mind. These are not so much secondary objectives, but like inflation are more the effect of mismanagement, bad timing or major events in a big economy with which much business is conducted. The most important of these concerns include the following.

Employment vs unemployment

Government's stated goal in this respect is to maintain the economy at full employment. That has the benefit of keeping most citizens happy, while contributing tax to the general good. However, if everyone is in a job the only way a new or growing business can recruit additional staff is to poach from other organizations, usually by offering higher wages. That in turn feeds into inflation, as wage prices, a major component of costs, are rising without there necessarily being an increase in output. Also, high employment can lead to the 'jobs for life' attitude prevalent in Japan for so long that contributed to its market inefficiencies.

In practice, governments actually set their policies to achieve an acceptable level of unemployment. In the UK and United States that is around 5 per cent of the labour force, while in continental Europe between 9 and 10 per cent has become the norm. High unemployment reduces a country's overall GDP through having unproductive workers. If the unemployed also get state welfare, as is the case particularly in continental Europe and to a lesser extent the UK, it increases the cost for the country as a whole.

So maintaining an acceptable rather than full employment is the realistic purpose of economic policy and governments have a number of factors and figures to keep tabs on to achieve that goal:

- Cyclical unemployment: This is the rate of unemployment attributable to a stage in the economic cycle. Typically, during a downturn unemployment will be higher than the normal target rate and lower in the upswing.

- Seasonal unemployment: This occurs at certain times in the year; for example, in winter, construction and casual farm workers are more likely to be laid off.

- Frictional unemployment: This is the result of an economy or geographic area within an economy moving from one type of productive activity to another. The shift from employment in coal and steel mining to other forms of employment, usually in the service sector, is one such shift that Western economies have experienced.

- Structural unemployment: This is caused by workers not having the skills and businesses not having the technology to meet new demands being made on an economy.

- Vacancy rate: This measures the number of unfilled jobs at any one time. A high level of unemployment can be partially offset against lots of vacancies, as people take time to move from one job to another, particularly if that requires moving home.

One further measure a government can take to influence unemployment is to import labour, either through immigration or by accepting seasonal workers from overseas.

The exchange rate

The rate at which different currencies are traded is their exchange rate, with a high rate being viewed as a sign of economic virility. So-called strong rates of exchange mean that citizens and businesses find foreign goods and services relatively cheap. Unfortunately, it also means that foreigners find their goods and services expensive and will buy less and seek new suppliers in countries with more favourable exchange rates.

Most countries have their own currency, but not all governments pursue the same exchange rate policies and each such policy involves different costs and risks:

- Managed and 'not fully convertible' is when the government exercises political and economic control over the exchange rate and the amount of its currency that can be moved in or out of the country. China and India are among many countries that fall into this category. Such constraints can mean that a currency drops sharply in value periodically as the government of the day tries to hold back international pressures.

- Pegged: For the majority of countries which have been anxiously seeking ways to promote economic stability and their own prosperity, the most favourable way has been to peg the local currency to a major convertible currency, such as the euro or US dollar. This means that while the local currency may move up and down against all other world currencies, it will remain or at least attempt to remain stable against the one it is pegged against. In total, 22 states and territories have a national currency that is directly pegged to the euro, including 14 West African countries, 3 French Pacific territories, 2 African island countries and 3 Balkan countries.

- Dollarized: This is a slight misnomer as the term is used to describe a country that abandons its own currency and adopts the exclusive use of the US dollar or another major international currency, such as the euro. The euro, for example, is the official currency in 15 states and territories outside the European Union. In such cases the country in question takes on the risks and costs associated with the 'host' currency. Many of the economies opting for this approach already informally use the foreign currency in private and public transactions.

● Floating and 'fully convertible': These currencies fluctuate as the country in question succeeds or fails. Russia, for example, lifted currency controls in July 2006 as a sign of economic confidence, making the rouble fully convertible. Now it is more attractive to invest in Russia, while Russian businesses can freely, without worry, without any special permit or burden, participate in investments overseas. Barely 8 years earlier the country defaulted on its massive domestic debt, devalued its currency and wiped out Russians' savings. Russia's macroeconomic situation had to become stable to allow this to happen, which has been achieved on the back of large gold reserves, a balanced budget and foreign investment that exceeded capital outflows largely on the basis of oil and gas exploration activity.

Balance of payments

The balance of payments is the difference between all payments coming into a country and those going out. A surplus of payments coming in over those going out is said to be favourable and the opposite is unfavourable. The balance of payments is divided into two accounts: the current account, such as payments for imports, exports, services and transfers of money; and capital account payments for physical and financial assets.

The balance of trade, which is itself a major part of the overall balance of payments, is the difference between the value of goods and services exported out of a country and those imported into the country. When imports exceed exports a country's GDP is reduced by that amount (see GDP earlier in this chapter). Imports and exports are themselves influenced by a country's competitive position, which can be eroded by too high an inflation rate, for example, or by having too strong a currency, which encourages overseas purchases of goods and services, including holidays.

Entrepreneurship 08

- Entrepreneur vs intrapreneur
- Social entrepreneurs
- Creative destruction, the spur
- Why we need entrepreneurs
- Money for business plans

Entrepreneurship is the newest discipline in the business school armoury and in many schools the subject is still not taught. In some it is a topic within economics, which is considered appropriate as J B Say, a French economist in circa 1800, first coined the term entrepreneur, using it to describe 'Someone who shifts resources out of an area of lower and into an area of higher productivity and greater yield'. The most common practice is to reduce the subject to a basic 'start your own business' project culminating in a business plan presentation, with a handful of MBAs going the whole hog and launching a venture.

There is rather more to the subject than just starting a business, though that in itself is a worthy outcome. Governments are fixated with entrepreneurship, secondary schools are teaching it, 1 in 15 people in work runs a business and over half the world work for and report directly to an entrepreneur.

Why entrepreneurship matters

You might be surprised at the number of people and organizations that appear keen to give entrepreneurs a helping hand. *Dragons' Den* panellists, bankers and government ministers all seem eager to lend a helping hand. None of these would-be helpers is particularly altruistic. The primary reasons why entrepreneurs are essential are as follows.

Job creation

Governments need a constant injection of new businesses as they create most of the new jobs in any economy; a fact uncovered by David Birch, a researcher at MIT (Massachusetts Institute of Technology) back in 1979 (*The Job Generation Process*, MIT), and corroborated by dozens of other studies since then. Also, of course, you will pay tax on your profits and become an unpaid tax collector for VAT or Sales Tax on behalf of government agencies.

Another reason governments worry about dampening the effects of economic downturns is the adverse effect they have on business start-ups. In 2010 in the wake of a serious recession the number of new businesses being set up around the world declined by 10 per cent in 20 of the world's richest nations, according to the annual Global Entrepreneurship Monitor (GEM). The decline was the most severe in the United States, where it fell 24 per cent. By contrast the decline was 17 per cent in Denmark, 12 per cent in Spain and Belgium, 9 per cent in Germany and Norway, 7 per cent in Italy and 6 per cent in the United Kingdom. There was no change in France, Iceland, Japan, Netherlands and Slovenia whilst the United Arab Emirates saw start-up activity up by 38 per cent.

Creative destruction and the innovative spur

Creative destruction is a term attributed to Joseph Schumpeter. Born in 1883, he became the youngest professor in the Austrian empire at 26 and finance minister at 36, only to be dismissed after presiding over a period of hyperinflation. A brief spell as president of a small Viennese bank was followed, after its failure, by a return to academia, first in Bonn and then in 1932 at Harvard. He is remembered for two books in particular: *Theory of Economic Development* (1911), where he first outlined his thoughts on entrepreneurship, and *Capitalism, Socialism, and Democracy* (1942), where he detailed how the entrepreneurial process worked and why it mattered. His view was that the fundamental impulse that sets and keeps the capitalist engine in motion comes from 'the new consumers, goods, the new methods of production or transportation, the new markets, the new forms of industrial organization that capitalist enterprise creates'. He pointed out that entrepreneurs innovate and develop new products, services or ways of doing business, and in the process destroy those organizations that can't adapt or have been effectively made redundant. According to the US Department of Commerce statistics new small businesses produce 13 times more patents per employee than large established firms. Schumpeter believed that capitalism has to create short-term losers alongside its short- and long-term winners in order for the economy to grow and prosper: 'Without innovations, no entrepreneurs; without entrepreneurial achievement, no capitalist... propulsion. The atmosphere of industrial revolutions... is the only one in which capitalism can survive.' He went rather further than this by arguing that the more countries tried to mitigate the possibilities of business failing, the worse their economic performance would be. Picking up the pieces through social insurance is fine; propping up failing businesses or declining business sectors is not.

Who makes a good entrepreneur?

There are absolutely no reliable characteristics that predispose people to become entrepreneurs. Despite diligent research, Durham University's General Enterprise Tendency (GET) Test, with 12 questions measuring need for achievement, 12 to assess internal locus of control, 12 to determine creativity, 12 to gauge calculated risk taking and 6 to measure need for autonomy, has failed to gain recognition. Peter Drucker, the international business guru, probably got it right with this description: 'Some are eccentrics, others painfully correct conformists; some are fat and some are lean; some are worriers, some relaxed; some drink quite heavily, others are total abstainers; some are men of great charm and warmth, some have no more personality than a frozen mackerel.' Entrepreneurs do have one distinguishing characteristic in common, however. They put independence and doing their own thing above everything, including getting rich. That doesn't mean they don't want to succeed; it's just that success is not all about money. Research carried out by Simfonec, a science research centre based at Cass Business School (**www.cass.city.ac.uk**), found that 20 per cent of entrepreneurs in their sample (250 entrepreneurs and 250 managers) were dyslexic, whereas managers reflected the UK national dyslexia incidence level of 4 per cent. While it is perhaps comforting to know that dyslexia, or even not completing schooling or university because of it, is no bar to entrepreneurship; it is not something you can do much about.

What can be said with certainty is that there are an awful lot of entrepreneurs everywhere and from every walk of life. Also, it seems likely that entrepreneurs are as likely to be made as born. There are over 4.4 million people running their own business in the UK alone. That is double the number of just two decades or so ago. GEM (**www.gemconsortium.org**), through their Global Entrepreneurship Monitor research programme headed up by Babson College in the United States, collects statistics from 41 countries on business starters and, equally importantly, would-be starters. They rank the UK as being fairly average in terms of numbers. GEM's research indicates that in Europe there are around 30 million owner-managed businesses and five times that figure across the developed world.

Research from various organizations, including Lloyds Bank, NatWest, the Institute for Small Business Enterprise and the US Small Business Association, sheds further light on the small business population and demographics. No section of the public appears to be excluded from the small business world. One in seven businesses are started by people over 50; just over a third of business proprietors are women; 1 in 10 left school early and barely a quarter have a degree; immigrants are as likely to work for themselves as others; and interestingly enough, those who start their business in their teens or early 20s are no more likely to fail than those in the 40s and 50s with a career in big business under their belt. You can search out these and other related data on the Office for National Statistics (**www.statistics.gov.uk**) the US Small Business Association (**www.sba.gov**), the European Small Business Portal (**http://ec.europa.eu** > European Small Business Portal) and The Global Entrepreneurship Monitor (**www.gemconsortiun.org**).

Would you make a good entrepreneur?

All too often, everyone believes themselves to be the right sort of person to set up a business. Unfortunately, the capacity for self-deception is enormous. When a random sample of male adults were asked recently to rank themselves on leadership ability, 70 per cent rated themselves in the top 25 per cent; only 2 per cent felt they were below average as leaders. In an area in which self-deception ought to be difficult, 60 per cent said they were well above average in athletic ability and only 6 per cent said they were below.

A common mistake made in assessing entrepreneurial talent is to assume that success in big business management will automatically guarantee success in a small business.

Rate yourself against the characteristics shown in Table 8.1 and see how you stack up as a potential business starter. A score of over 30 suggests you

TABLE 8.1   Business starter attribute check

Attribute	Score (0–5, where 0 indicates having none of the attribute and 5 rating highly)
Self-confident all rounder	
Ability to bounce back	
Innovative skills	
Results orientated	
Professional risk taker	
Total commitment	
Self-sufficient	
Self-disciplined	

have what it takes and less than 20 should be treated as a warning signal. Get a couple of people who know you well to rate you too, so you get an unbiased opinion.

You can find out more about whether or not entrepreneurship would be right for you by taking one or more of the many online entrepreneurial IQ-type tests. For example:

- Tickle Tests (**http://web.tickle.com/tests/entrepreneurialiq/ ?test=entrepreneurialiqogt**);

- BusMove (**www.busmove.com/other/quiz.htm**);

- Community Futures, a Canadian small business help website, has a 50-question online test to help you rate your entrepreneurial abilities as well as a checklist of desirable traits. See **www.communityfutures.com/cms/Starting_a_Business.159.0.html**.

Entrepreneurial categories

Entrepreneurs are usually associated with successful businesses such as those run by Alan Sugar, Richard Branson, Bill Gates or Roman Abramovich. There are, however, several different types of entrepreneurial ventures, not all associated either with making money or with charismatic leadership. The following are the main subsidiary categories of entrepreneurial organization.

Social entrepreneurs

A social entrepreneur is concerned primarily with achieving sustainable social change, though in many respects the strategies they employ to achieve those goals are similar to those used by other entrepreneurs. The idea of social business is fast becoming mainstream. There is an annual Queen's Award for Industry for Sustainable Development, an ACCA Award for the Best Social Accounts and a School for Social Entrepreneurs (**www.sse.org. uk**) which helps would-be social entrepreneurs to get started. The Schwab Foundation (**www.schwabfound.org**) covers much the same ground in the United States. Columbia Business School's MBA programme has an elective course on Social Entrepreneurship as part of its Research Initiative on Social Entrepreneurship (**www.riseproject.org/cbsprofiles.html**). Students complete projects where they shadow leading social entrepreneurs and social investors for a semester and details of all their case studies are published on their website. Stanford Graduate School of Business (**www.gsb.stanford.edu/ exed/epse**) with its Executive Program in Social Entrepreneurship, Harvard's Strategic Perspectives in Non-profit Management (**www.exed.hbs.edu/ programs/spnm**) and Cardiff Metropolitan University's MBA in Social Entrepreneurship (**www.uwic.ac.uk/courses/business/MBASocialE.asp**) take the subject to the heart of mainstream business education.

According to government statistics, around 55,000 businesses trade with a social or environmental purpose across the UK. They contribute almost £27 billion to the national economy and substantially benefit their local communities by creating employment opportunities, providing ethical products and services, and reinvesting surpluses into society. The primary motivation for social entrepreneurs is to build an ethical venture that is of benefit to the wider community. As one social entrepreneur put it, 'I am trying to build a little part of the world in which I would like to live.' Money is important, but getting rich is not.

Oneworld Health (**www.oneworldhealth.org**), established by Victoria Hale, a social entrepreneur and pharmacologist based in San Francisco, is as different from mainstream drug companies as it is possible to be. It has as its vision to 'serve as a positive agent for change by saving lives, improving health, and fulfilling the promise of medicine for those most in need' and for its values 'Integrity, Courage, Collaboration'. Oneworld assembles experienced and dedicated teams of pharmaceutical scientists; identifies the most promising drugs and vaccine candidates; and develops them into safe, effective and affordable medicines. It partners with companies, non-profit hospitals and organizations in the developing world to conduct medical research on new cures. Then it manufactures and distributes newly approved therapies such as those that tackle malaria, the cause of 300–500 million acute illnesses and over one million deaths annually.

The company scours the shelves of big pharmaceutical companies looking for drugs that for some reason failed to get to market, perhaps because the market proved too small, the benefits too few or that in some other way won't meet the needs of an affluent Western market. Hale even persuaded The University of California, Santa Barbara to donate a patent for a discovery involving the novel use of calcium channel blockers to control the schistosomiasis parasite. Hale and her team believe that that there are huge inefficiencies in the way Western world drugs are currently devised and produced, and with $140 million from the Bill and Melinda Gates Foundation they intend to improve on that situation.

Intrapreneur

The Economist of 25 December 1976 carried a survey called 'The coming entrepreneurial revolution' in which Norman Macrae, the magazine's deputy editor and considered by many as one of the world's best economic forecasters, contended that methods of operation in business were going to change radically in the next few decades. The world, Macrae argued, was probably drawing to the end of the era of big business corporations; it would soon be nonsense to have hierarchical managements sitting in skyscrapers trying to arrange how brainworkers (who in future would be most workers) could best use their imaginations. The main increases in employment would henceforth come either in small firms or in those bigger firms that managed to split themselves into smaller and smaller profit centres that in turn would need to become more and more entrepreneurial.

Two years later, in an article headed 'Intra-Corporate Entrepreneurship – Some Thoughts Stirred Up by Attending Robert Schwartz's School for Entrepreneurs', Gifford Pinchot III and his wife Elizabeth S Pinchot began the process that would lead to their coining the word 'intrapreneuring'. Their organization, Pinchot & Company (**www.pinchot.com**), based around the proposition that you don't have to leave the corporation to become an entrepreneur, advanced the idea that the way for big business to adapt was to create an environment where managers could behave as though they were entrepreneurs, but within the business, using its resources. By 1992 the term intrapreneur had been added to the third edition of *The American Dictionary of the English Language*. 3M's Post-It Note, a product of an entrepreneurial team 'bootlegging' company resources, is an example from one of Pinochet's list of Fortune 500 clients. Others include Apple, DuPont, Cable & Wireless, Nabisco and Proctor & Gamble.

Intrapreneurs, unlike entrepreneurs, don't have 'doing their own thing' at the top of their list of motivators. They feel happier in the comfort zone afforded by a corporate structure and the resources and respectability that provides.

Corporate venturing entrepreneur

Sinclair Beecham and Julian Metcalfe, who started with a £17,000 loan and a name borrowed from a boarded-up shop and founded Prêt à Manger, were not entrepreneurs content with doing their own thing. They had global ambitions and it was only by cutting in McDonald's, the burger giant, that they could see any realistic way to dominate the world. They sold a 33 per cent stake for £25 million in 2001 to McDonald's Ventures, LLC, a wholly owned subsidiary of McDonald's Corporation, the arm of McDonald's that looks after its corporate venturing activities. They joined forces with the corporate venturing arm of a big firm. They could also have considered Cisco, Apple Computers, IBM and Microsoft, who also all have corporate venturing arms. Other corporate venturers include Deutsche Bank, which set up DB eVentures to get a window on the 'Digital Revolution', Reuters Greenhouse, which has stakes in 85 companies, and even the late and un-lamented Enron had venture investments (totalling $110m). For an entrepreneur this approach can provide a 'friendly customer' and help open doors. For the 'parent' it provides a privileged ringside seat as a business grows and so be able to decide if the area is worth plunging into more deeply, or at the least provides valuable insights into new technologies or business processes.

Recent research into corporate venturing by Ashridge (**www.ashridge. org.uk** > Research and Faculty) Business School concluded that less than 5 per cent of corporate venturing units created new businesses that were taken up by the parent company. Moreover, many failed to make any positive contribution whatsoever. There are some success stories, however. McDonald's offloaded its Prêt stake to Bridgepoint, a private equity firm. Bridgepoint bought a majority stake in 2008, including McDonald's 33 per cent shareholding, for £345m. That would suggest that McDonald's at least quadrupled the value of its initial stake. Nokia Venture Partners (NVP), which makes significant minority investments in start-ups in the wireless internet space, had as its biggest success to date the initial public offering of PayPal, in 2002. At a conference in July 1999, they and Deutsche Bank used Paypal's (then called Confinnity) encryption technology to send founders Peter Thiel and Max Levchin $3 million in venture capital as their initial stake, via a Palm Pilot.

Corporate venturing entrepreneurs think big and are happy to cut others with cash in on the deal, if it will help make them rich. Independence for independence's sake is not a high priority.

Entrepreneurship in practice

Business schools usually teach entrepreneurship using the 'Action Learning' approach. This generally takes the form of having a handful of inspiring alumni entrepreneurs back to talk about how they got started. At Cranfield the stars would include a couple of big hitters, Karan (now Lord) Billimoria of Cobra Beer fame, for example. Cass wheels out Stelios Haji-Iannou, founder of easyJet, and London Business School has Tony Wheeler who graduated in 1972 and together with his wife Maureen founded Lonely Planet Publications. Then they will invite a cross-section of those entrepreneurs who have interesting stories to tell, say about raising money, hiring and firing or selling up; or who are recent leavers that switched career paths from, say, big corporate lives to small business. At IMD, in Lausanne on Lake Geneva in Switzerland, the emphasis is on family businesses, and Warren Buffett, whose son looks set to take over at Berkshire Hathaway, is typical of the speakers there.

The spirit of the teaching is around preparing a business plan to be presented to a panel along the lines of *Dragons' Den*, often with similar outcomes in that the business gets funding. It would be incorrect to suggest that droves of MBAs rush off to found ventures straight off, but perhaps three or four in a hundred do. Within a decade that will have risen to around 40 per cent according to research carried out for Top MBA (**www.topmba.com**).

Aside from getting funding and marks towards their MBA grade, the most successful business plans are usually entered into one of a number of Business Plan Competitions. These offer prizes such as Nano Challenge (**www.nanochallenge.com**) offering two prizes of €300,000, promoted by Veneto Nanotech, the company managing the Italian Cluster for Nanotechnologies and PriceWaterhouse Coopers. Usually more modest awards of cash, consulting and investment are on offer. Small Business Notes (**www.smallbusinessnotes.com/planning/competitions.html**) has a business plan directory with around 100 competitions around the world.

You don't have to be in a business school to enter most of these competitions, though you may find it hard to find out about them if you are not and you will almost certainly be up against a business school team. Oxford Saïd Business School (**www.sbs.ox.ac.uk/21challenge**) will take entries from individuals, teams, new companies, existing companies creating spin-offs, students, scientists, academics and entrepreneurs. Regional, national and international participation is encouraged.

Ethics and social responsibility

- Owners vs directors
- Stakeholder groupings
- Ethical and responsible strategies
- Whistle-blowing
- Green pays off

Actions for which a person or group of people can be held accountable and so commended or blamed, disciplined or rewarded, are said to lie within their sphere of responsibility. Anything that lies outside our control also lies beyond the scope of our responsibilities. Ethics, known in academic circles as moral philosophy, is concerned with classifying, defending, and proposing concepts of right and wrong behaviour in the way in which we discharge our responsibilities. While many responsibilities lie within the scope of the law, shareholders' protection, discrimination at work, misleading advertising and so forth (see Chapter 6 for more on business law), both in those areas and in the grey area that surrounds them lies the province of ethics and social responsibility. Right and wrong in themselves are often not too difficult to separate out. The problem usually stems from competing 'rights' – giving shareholders a better return vs saving the planet, for example, and the inherent selfishness of humans. Many, if not all, of our actions are triggered by self-interest. In fact, much of the justification for capitalism's attraction lies in the 'invisible hand' theory advanced by Adam Smith in his defining book, *The Wealth of Nations* (1776):

> Every individual... generally, indeed, neither intends to promote the public interest, nor knows how much he is promoting it. By preferring the support of domestic to that of foreign industry he intends only his own security; and by directing that industry in such a manner as its produce may be of the greatest value, he intends only his own gain, and he is in this, as in many other cases, led by an invisible hand to promote an end which was no part of his intention.

Unfortunately, the invisible hand suggests only that businesses and consumers, in being selfish, may by accident do good, not that their actions are made ethical in the process. Many purely selfish actions, say by operating a cartel to rip off consumers, or adopting a polluting production process purely to boost the bottom line, fall firmly into the unethical bracket. Even overtly ethical actions, for example when a business gives to charity or supports a 'not for profit' event, such as Coca-Cola's sponsorship of the Olympic Games over an 80-year period, can prove ethically questionable. In the first place Coca-Cola, McDonald's, Samsung and the other Olympics' sponsors hope for a share of the huge marketing benefits that accrue from such association. Secondly, supporting the Games may be the 'right' thing to do, but supporting the 2008 host country, China, a regime with a questionable human rights track record, may well be 'wrong'.

Business ethics defines the categories of duty for which we are morally responsible. Lists of moral duties and rights can be lengthy and overlapping. The duty-based theory advanced by a British philosopher, W D Ross (1877–1971), provides a short list of duties that he believed reflects our actual moral convictions:

- Fidelity: the duty to keep promises.
- Reparation: the duty to compensate others when we harm them.
- Gratitude: the duty to thank those who help us.
- Justice: the duty to recognize merit.
- Beneficence: the duty to improve the conditions of others.
- Self-improvement: the duty to improve our virtue and intelligence.
- Non-maleficence: the duty to not injure others.

Ross recognized that there will be occasions when we must choose between two conflicting duties. For example, should your business be involved in any way with products that facilitate abortions? On one side of that moral argument lies beneficence in improving the conditions of women and, on the other, non-maleficence in not doing injury to the unborn child. You can find out more about the theoretical aspects of ethics on The Internet Encyclopedia of Philosophy (**www.iep.utm.edu/e/ethics.htm**) and on related business issues on the Free Management Library website (**www.managementhelp.org/ethics/ethxgde.htm**).

Teaching ethics and social responsibility in business schools

This subject is perhaps the most controversial and disputed in terms of the teaching methodology and content used in business schools. A recent survey on Corporate Social Responsibility Education in Europe found that while most business schools had some content in this area, only a quarter had a specific topic, module or elective covering the ground. In 2008, courses in corporate social responsibility (CSR), ethics, sustainability or business and society are now a requirement for 58 per cent of MBAs, up from 45 per cent in 2003 and 34 per cent in 2001. Most had the subject embedded in various other subject areas, for example under titles such as a combination of 'Accounting, Corporate Governance, Law and Public Governance' or 'Stakeholder Management'. Others had ethics and social responsibility covered in the context of specific disciplines – ethical accounting systems or marketing and ethics. Georgia Tech College of Management's MBA set as a business ethics paper the task 'Analyze Sarbannes–Oxley from both conceptual and implementation perspectives', which is largely a single issue of directors' responsibilities to investors.

There is widespread use of practitioner speakers from business or non-governmental organizations (NGOs) as well as case studies from industry, and these methods dwarf the more academic methods (lectures, tutorials) used in other subject areas. Tuck School of Business at Dartmouth, for example, teaches a 'brief mini-course' based on discussions of ethical issues encountered by its faculty in cases involving their experience 'particularly on the functional areas of business as exercised in both the US and the global marketplace, where different local practices and cultural norms seem to muddy the ethical water'. The academics, however, are on the march! Nottingham University Business School has an International Centre for Corporate Social Responsibility and a Professor of CSR (Corporate Social Responsibility). INSEAD has a chaired professor of Business Ethics and Corporate Responsibility, though the focus there appears to be very much around ethical consumerism, deception in marketing and marketing ethics. But the University of Chicago Graduate School of Business leads the field in raising the bar on teaching in this field. It's the only business school anywhere to have a Nobel laureate – Robert Fogel, winner of the 1993 Nobel Prize in economics – teaching 'A Guide to Business Ethics'.

Owners vs directors: the start of the ethical tug of war

Directors are appointed by the owners of a business to control a business and look after their interests in their absence. When enterprises were small and local this was an expediency rarely invoked, as owners more often than not were the directors and where they were not it was usual to ensure at least some family oversight. Now, where nearly two-thirds of all business activity is conducted by giant global enterprises, this separation of ownership from control has become both necessary and commonplace. Also, such businesses have replaced 'owners' with 'shareholders'. The difference is subtle but it is the key to understanding the requirement for including business ethics and social responsibility on the business school curriculum.

Shareholders only rarely own more than a small fraction of any one business, they have no special reason to identify with the founders' vision or code of behaviour and they are preoccupied with relatively simple outcomes such as growth in earnings per share. If they become unhappy in that respect they just swap their holding in that business for a similar stake in another. In fact, even if such shareholders are satisfied with financial performance when a sector is out of 'favour', say, as retailers may be during a recession, they may well sell their holding in any event. The main holders of large shareholdings in businesses now are fund managers and pension funds and arguably these have an even greater imperative to focus their attention on earnings. True, they exert pressure from time to time but that is usually when they see too much control moving into the hands of one director, say when there is an attempt to combine the roles of chairman and chief executive. Also, when directors are trying to pay themselves more than they may be worth or are trying to improve their lot in some other way at the expense of shareholders, a fund manager may step in. Fund managers are not always honest brokers with regard to looking after shareholder interest. For example, during a takeover there is a good chance that a fund manager will find themselves with holdings in both buyer and seller.

The board of directors has in effect replaced the 'owner' as the custodian of the moral tone and in setting standards of behaviour towards everyone the business has dealings with. They are in some ways encouraged by legal constraints placed on them to take a narrow view of those responsibilities. They are required 'to act in good faith in the interests of the company'; 'not to deceive shareholders and to appoint auditors to oversee the accounting records'; 'not to carry on the business of the company with intent to defraud creditors or for any fraudulent purpose'; and 'to have regard for the interests of employees in general'. (See Chapter 4 for more on the responsibilities of directors.)

Directors and managers also have responsibilities to protect their customers when using their products or services or when visiting company premises and to follow rules inhibiting pollution in the operating processes. But it is only relatively recently that companies have been required to take a wider view of their responsibilities to other 'stakeholder' groups. Enlightened managers, or those that are particularly astute, depending on your level of cynicism, have often taken on broader responsibilities, sponsoring charities, funding social amenities such as play areas or providing low-cost housing. These initiatives are often spurred on by enlightened self-interest, say to help with recruiting and retaining employees; with getting favourable PR; or in the case of low-cost housing, providing amenities is a usual requirement in getting planning consent for a property development or a site for, say, a supermarket.

CASE STUDY Unilever – embedding ethics

In 1887, William Hesketh Lever, already a highly successful soap manufacturer, was looking for a new site for his factory to allow him to expand. The site also needed to be near a river for importing raw materials, and near a railway line for transporting the finished products. The 56 acres of unused marshy land at the site that became Port Sunlight, named after his soap, was far more than he needed simply for manufacturing purposes. Lever had something more all-embracing in mind. His stated aims were to create an environment that allowed his workers 'to socialize and Christianize business relations and get back to that close family brotherhood that existed in the good old days of hand labour'. His intention was to extend his responsibilities beyond making money for himself and to share that, albeit on his own terms, with everyone who worked for him. Between 1899 and 1914 Lever built some 800 houses, taking an active part himself in the design. The community's population of 3,500 shared allotments, public buildings, including the Lady Lever Art Gallery, schools, a concert hall, open air swimming pool, church, and a temperance hotel. His cottage hospital, built in 1907, continued until the introduction of the National Health Service in 1948. He also introduced schemes for welfare, education and the entertainment of his workers, and encouraged recreation and organizations which promoted art, literature, science or music.

Unilever, as the company is now known, has carried the Lever values and vision on into corporate life. The company's behaviour in all affairs is governed by a set of clear, stated and communicated guidelines. Starting with its core value, 'As a multi-local multinational we aim to play our part in addressing global environmental and social concerns through our own actions, and working in partnership with stakeholders at local, national and international levels', the company has developed a comprehensive set of principles to guide its behaviour in all aspects of its work. The guidelines it expects employees to work to include always working with integrity with 'the highest standards of corporate behaviour towards everyone we work with, the communities we touch, and the environment on which we have an impact'. The full value statement can be seen on its website at this link (**www.unilever.com/ourvalues**).

Understanding stakeholders

So we can see that directors and by extension the managers of an organization first saw that their primary, often their only, responsibility was to look after the shareholders' interests. Measures were, and still are, taken to attempt to ally their interests, for example linking bonuses to share price or profits. For the most part these attempts have failed, as the case of Enron showed, where shareholders were systematically deceived. Also, in the whole sub-prime debacle bankers were rewarded for systematically repackaging toxic loans and spreading them in near-undetectable layers around the globe, to the eventual detriment of their shareholders and the taxpaying public at large who had to pick up the bill. But even where it is possible to ally directors' interests with those of shareholders, that leaves a myriad of other interested parties effectively disenfranchised, except in so far as they are expressly protected by laws.

The idea that businesses had a responsibility other than to shareholders was brought to popular attention in Howard R Bowen's book *Social Responsibilities of the Businessman* (1953, New York: Harper and Brothers), but it was a decade later before the term 'stakeholder' was coined in an internal memorandum at the Stanford Research Institute in 1963. Over the next two decades the term stakeholder was debated and defined until Edward Freeman, a professor at the Darden School of Business (**www.darden.virginia.edu**), University of Virginia, in his book *Strategic Management: A Stakeholder Approach* (1984, United States: Pitman Bowen), set out simple guidelines that anyone in an organization could understand and follow. Freeman's stakeholders were defined as 'any group or individual who can affect or is affected by the achievement of the organization's objectives'.

Mapping out the stakeholders

Freeman (see above) divided stakeholders into six distinct categories, owners, employees, customers, suppliers, communities and governments, with which an organization has varying responsibilities or 'social contracts'. The first step in the process of developing an ethical strategy is to identify all the people, institutions and agencies that your organization is likely to impinge on in the normal course of its activities.

Figure 9.1 gives an example of a stakeholder map. It shows how stakeholders move outwards from the individual at the centre, to internal groups including their immediate work environment, colleagues, team and peers, and on to external groups, suppliers, customers, shareholders and eventually on to ever-distant publics and organizations.

Assessing obligations

Not all stakeholders will be affected by any one particular strategy or course of action, nor will those that are affected be affected to the same degree. So the next step in the process is to see which stakeholders will be affected and to what degree. This can be done using a Stakeholder Relevance Matrix, as in Figure 9.2. This shows which stakeholder groups will be affected by the decision to relocate a production unit to a new lower-cost country.

FIGURE 9.1   Stakeholder mapping

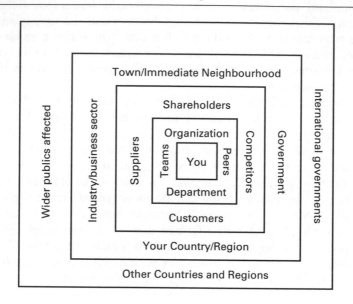

FIGURE 9.2   Stakeholder relevance matrix

Proposed strategy Move production to lower-cost country	Positively affected	Adversely affected
Directly affected	Employment created in new country New community in new country	Existing workforce Existing community in existing country Local subcontractors will lose work
Indirectly affected	Shareholder returns improved	Home government gets less tax Management will have to travel more

The next step in the process is to analyse the specific interests/expectations and rights/responsibilities of each affected stakeholder group. Following through with the example of relocating a factory, we can see in Figure 9.3 the different expectations and rights of the three stakeholder groups seen to be most relevant to this decision.

FIGURE 9.3   Stakeholder rights and expectations grid

Stakeholders			
	Customers	Shareholders	Employees
Rights	Be given information on all factors concerning new production source	To be informed in the annual report and accounts or sooner if the implications will cause public discussion	To statutory redundancy payments
Expectations	Any change should be seamlessly implemented	That the company will treat employees properly That the move is in the long-term best interest of the organization	To be consulted and given help with job search

Stakeholder strategies

Having identified the stakeholders and weighed up their rights and expectations, an organization has basically three possible ethical stances it can take:

- Immoral business: Make decisions that are clearly unethical to large groups of stakeholders. The Mafia and organized crime in general certainly fit into this category, as in many respects do the sex industry, large tracts of the gambling industry and arguably the tobacco and drinks industry too. These last three are accepted as being a customer's inalienable right to free choice, aided by being major employers and taxpayers.

- Amoral business: Make decisions without considering their ethical implications either through carelessness, indifference or the mistaken belief that business is there to make profit only. Such businesses see governments and their laws as the only ethical or moral constraint they need concern themselves with.

- Moral business: All decisions are made considering what is ethical, fair and just.

Implementing ethical and responsible strategies

Ethics and values play a central role in shaping a company's identity and reputation, building its brands, and earning the trust of customers, suppliers or other business partners. While honesty, fairness and responsibility are crucial for building a good reputation, an organization that is looking for pre-eminence in its field needs to go beyond just meeting stakeholders' needs. It has to emphasize the message that it is attractive as a business partner and as a good corporate citizen. To achieve this status the following steps need to be pursued:

- Acknowledge and monitor all stakeholders with a valid claim on your attentions.
- Communicate regularly with stakeholders, listening to their interests and concerns.
- Actively cooperate with stakeholders to minimize risks.
- Always avoid actions that endanger lives.
- Use processes that are sensitive to stakeholders' needs.
- Recognize the danger that managers' convenience and the needs of most other stakeholder groups will almost always be in conflict.
- Resolve stakeholder conflicts speedily and fairly.

Resolving conflict

Unfortunately, however ethical and socially responsible an organization is, it will at some stage, perhaps even frequently, find itself pursuing a strategy that upsets other stakeholder groups. A recent example of one such conflict was Shell's decision, announced in April 2008, to pull out of the London Array wind farm. This £2 billion project for 341 turbines capable of producing 1,000 megawatts of power was a key part of the UK government's strategy to produce 15 per cent of UK energy needs from renewable sources by 2015, with an aspiration to raise that to 20 per cent by 2020. Given that in 2008 renewable energy accounted for only 2 per cent of output in the UK, the London Array was seen as important, perhaps vital, to achieving those goals. But Shell had to weigh up the consequences of upsetting the UK government, Friends of the Earth and its other German and Dutch partners in the project, with other concerns. Shell's view was that the cost of wind farms was simply spiralling out of control, with steel prices rising with increased world demand from such countries as China and India. In any event, world turbine production was booked up years in advance. Shell already had stakes in 11 wind farms producing over 1,100 megawatts and reckoned that as a company it could make the same contribution to the environment at a much lower cost to its shareholders, but probably on another continent and in another technology.

Resolving stakeholder conflicts calls for tact and communications and the recognition that while you can't please everyone, you can still be ethical. About 1 per cent of Shell's investments are in green projects. For example, a company subsidiary, Shell Solar, has played a major role in the development of first-generation CIS (copper indium diselenide) thin-film technology. This it believes to be the most commercially viable form of photovoltaic solar technology to generate electricity from the sun's energy. Together with its joint venture partner in this project, Saint Gobain, it has a pilot plant under construction in Saxony, Germany that will produce sufficient solar panels to save 14,000 tonnes of CO_2 per year. So stakeholders such as the UK government and Denmark's DONG Energy in the London Array project had to be weighed up against Saint Gobain, with the German government being party to both strategies through the participation of that country's energy giant, E.ON. All the while, Shell was under pressure to match its historic profit growth. Authenticity Consulting (**www.authenticityconsulting.com/misc/long.pdf**) has a useful checklist to help with decisions about resolving stakeholder conflict.

Whistle-blowers – an ethical longstop

Not surprisingly, the people most likely to know about unethical or socially irresponsible behaviour are those working in the organization itself. Governments around the world have adopted measures to encourage a flow of information on ethical problems and fraud from whistle-blowers – that is, anyone employed or recently employed by a public body, business organization or charity who reveals evidence of wrongdoing. Whistle-blowers have also been given a measure of legal protection. In the United States the Lloyd–La Follette Act of 1912 started the ball rolling, giving federal employees the right to provide Congress with information, to be followed by a patchwork of laws covering such fields as water pollution, the environment, the Sarbanes–Oxley Act (2002) to deal with corporate fraud and the Whistleblower Protection Enhancement Act (2007). In the UK the Public Interest Disclosure Act (1998) and various laws enacted by the European Union and other governments provide a framework of legal protection for individuals who disclose information.

Many firms too have established ways to attract information on frauds being committed against them, including 24-hour hotlines and corporate ethics offices. For example, Vodafone's (**www.vodafone.com/start/responsibility/supply_chain/whistle-blowing.html**) 'Speak Up' programme – launched in 2006/07 – provides suppliers and employees working in its supply chain with a means of reporting any ethical concerns. Fewer than 10 incidents were reported in 2006/07. That low figure may be less to do with the absence of ethical problems and more to do with the deeply ingrained biases against whistle-blowing and a distrust of assurances that retribution will not follow, especially in areas far removed from the watchful eyes of a corporate ethics office.

These organizations can provide further background on the subject:

- The National Whistleblowers Centre (**www.whistleblowers.org**): Focuses on exposing government and corporate misconduct, promoting ethical standards and protecting the jobs and careers of whistle-blowers.

- Spinwatch (**www.spinwatch.org**): Monitors the role of public relations and spin in contemporary society and has worked with whistle-blowers, anonymously, on some of the most contentious issues: Northern Ireland, the role of the media, genetic engineering, the oil industry, tobacco smuggling, food and farming, and the war in Iraq, for example.

- Whistleblower (**www.whistleblower.co.uk**): Run by journalists and set up to allow people to sell stories to the media confidentially. It has had a measure of success, breaking the story on how the Richard and Judy Show's 'You Say, We Pay' competition was ripping off viewers.

- The Chartered Institute of Personnel and Development (CIPD) has a factsheet on whistle-blowing at this weblink: **www.cipd.co.uk/hr-resources/factsheets/whistleblowing.aspx**.

Does being ethical pay off?

There is plenty of anecdotal evidence that ethical and socially responsible organizations are better places to work. At the very least, being ethical provides an organization with an insurance policy limiting its exposure to a range of legal liabilities for faulty products, misleading advertising, price fixing and discrimination at work, for example. But evidence on whether being ethical helps a business organization to become and stay more profitable is less clear. Corpedia (**http://welcome.corpedia.com**), a compliance and ethics training company with clients in 60 countries, including RadioShack, EMC, Xerox and PepsiCo, produces an index of companies deemed ethical. Companies such as Intel, Starbucks, The Timberland Company and Whole Foods Market are in its index, which it claims has outperformed the S&P 500 by more than 370 per cent over 5 years. The rather more scientific and comprehensive FTSE4Good Index Series (**www.ftse.com/Indices/ FTSE4Good_Index_Series/Performance_Analysis.jsp**) also shows the ethical companies to be ahead, though by a rather smaller margin. Over the 5 years to May 2008, the 400 companies in the FTSE4Good Index were about 15 per cent ahead of the general index.

But that still begs the question of what constitutes 'good'. The FTSE4Good Index sets out to measure the performance of companies that meet globally recognized corporate responsibility standards. For inclusion a company must be:

- working towards environmental sustainability;
- developing positive relationships with stakeholders;

- upholding and supporting universal human rights;
- ensuring good supply chain labour standards;
- countering bribery.

It also excludes companies that have been identified as having business interests in these industries:

- tobacco producers;
- companies manufacturing either whole, strategic parts, or platforms for nuclear weapon systems;
- companies manufacturing whole weapons systems;
- owners or operators of nuclear power stations;
- companies involved in the extraction or processing of uranium.

This only serves to highlight the problem of deciding what is ethical and what is not. For example, is mining uranium for nuclear power really more harmful than, say, switching to biofuels which, aside from probably releasing between two and nine times more carbon gases over the next 30 years than fossil fuels, will almost certainly cause food prices to stay high, particularly in the developing world? Or is the motor industry, whose products kill more people every year than the armaments industry, a more ethical and socially responsible sector?

However, a small but growing band of business schools believe that there is enough mileage in social responsibility and ethics to launch 'green' MBA programmes that emphasize a triple bottom line, also known as 'TBL' or '3BL' – profit, people, planet. Antioch University (**www.antiochne.edu/om/mba**), New England, Dominican University (**www.greenmba.com**), California and Duquesne University (**http://mba.sustainability.duq.edu**) in Pittsburgh are among those offering such programmes.

10 Operations management

- Outsourcing
- Production methods
- Controlling operations
- Maintaining quality
- Information systems

To stay ahead, companies need to generate innovation, organize production, collaborate with other companies and manage the performance of activities, processes, resources and control systems used to deliver goods and services. Operations management is the catch-all title used to hold all these disparate fields together. Often in business schools the subject is afforded a distinct syllabus of its own, as for example is the case at Cranfield School of Management, Warwick and Bocconi, in Milan, Italy. At Cardiff Business School, Logistics and Operations Management are bundled together with a strong emphasis on 'Lean Thinking' and in Barcelona's Esade Business School 'Innovation' is the partner subject.

However the subject is taught, the foundations if not the content started out with the work of Frederick W Taylor. Usually referred to as the 'father of scientific management', he studied and measured the way people worked, searching out ways to improve productivity. His book, *The Principles of Scientific Management* (1911, Harper and Row, New York), showed how science could replace apprenticeship as the way to transfer knowledge about how tasks should be done. Though much misunderstood and misapplied – the Soviet Union adopted his methods as the foundation for its five-year plans – Taylorism, as his work became known, was the spur to the many variants and extensions that are today bundled under operations management.

The next big boost to the discipline took place with the introduction of mathematical models used during the Second World War to make maximum use of scarce resources. Fairly mundane tasks, such as removing bottlenecks in tank production, led to dramatic increases in output. More esoterically, operations research, as this branch of the subject became known, was used to work out the optimum size of convoy to evade destruction by German U-boats as well as the depth at which explosives would be most effective against the submarines themselves.

MBAs, unless they have a strong background in mathematics, are unlikely to be able to apply any of the techniques and tools described below without expert help. But they do need to be aware that such methods are on hand and so can recommend their application when the opportunity or relevant problem arises.

Outsourcing and the value chain

The classic opening question in any business analysis that MBAs will find themselves addressing with increasing frequency is: what business are we in? Later in that analysis will come a more fundamental and challenging question: what business should we be in? These are strategic boundary questions that will be explored in more detail in Chapter 12, Strategy. The answers are also key to deciding what operations a business should and should not undertake itself, and the answer will not always be the same, as business competence and market opportunities change.

FIGURE 10.1   Maternity clothes value chain

Creative design → Purchase of materials → Make up garments →
Package and distribute → Retail through own outlets → Consumers

The business example shown in Figure 10.1 doesn't have to do all the activities, from creative design, through manufacture, to selling out from its own retail outlets. It is highly likely that there are other businesses better at certain elements of the process. For example, most businesses don't retail the products they manufacture, and even within the same industry different approaches are taken. Dell only sells direct via the internet, Apple sells via the internet, through a small number of company-owned outlets and through other retailers. IBM, having virtually created the personal computer industry in 1981, sold its PC division to the Chinese company Lenovo on 1 May 2005 for $655 million in cash and $600 million in Lenovo stock, moving away from personal consumers to concentrate on businesses.

Outsourcing is the activity of contracting out the elements that are not considered core or central to the business. There are obvious advantages to outsourcing: the best people can do what they are best at. But the approach can get out of hand, if left unmanaged. In 2008, IBM completed a major overhaul of its value chain and for the first time in its century-long history created an integrated supply chain (ISC) – a centralized worldwide approach to deciding what to do itself, what to buy in and where to buy in from. Suppliers were halved from 66,000 to 33,000; support locations from 300 to 3 global centres, in Bangalore, Budapest and Shanghai. Manufacturing sites reduced from 15 to 9, all 'globally enabled' in that they can make almost any of IBM's products at each plant and deliver them anywhere in the world. In the process IBM has lowered operating costs by more than $4 billion a year.

Quality control is one strategic issue when it comes to outsourcing, and an emerging danger with the arrival of the 'socially minded customer' is that people are looking more closely at companies and their products before buying from them. Getting garments made cheaply by child labour is very much an issue on consumers' radar. So while outsourcing plays a vital role in operations, it still has to be managed and to conform with corporate ethical standards.

Production methods and control

Manufacturing has come a long way since Adam Smith's observation in his book, *An Inquiry into the Nature And Causes of the Wealth of Nations* (1776), that:

> The greatest improvement in the productive powers of labour, and the greater part of the skill, dexterity, and judgment with which it is anywhere directed, or applied, seem to have been the effects of the division of labour.... I have seen a small manufactory of this kind where ten men only were employed, and where some of them consequently performed two or three distinct operations. But though they were very poor, and therefore but indifferently accommodated with the necessary machinery, they could, when they exerted themselves, make among them about twelve pounds of pins in a day. There are in a pound upwards of four thousand pins of a middling size. Those ten persons, therefore, could make among them upwards of forty-eight thousand pins in a day. But if they had all wrought separately and independently, and without any of them having been educated to this peculiar business, they certainly could not each of them have made twenty.

By Smith's calculations, organizing production efficiently increased output by 2,400 times, leaving the market itself as the primary limiting factor. Since then the hunt has been on for ever more efficiencies in the methods of production. The main production methods employed today are:

- One-off production is when a single product is made to the individual needs of a customer, for example a designer dress. This is very much the pre-Smith way in which everything was made, often without the use of any machinery.

- Batch production involves the making of a number of identical products at the same time, then moving on to make a different product later. For example, a small food processing factory could make sausage rolls in the morning and pizzas in the afternoon. This approach requires some basic machinery and Smith would probably recognize this process were he alive today.

- Mass production is used for larger-scale production using machinery, often many different machines, for much of the work where individual tasks are carried out repetitively. This is an efficient and low-cost method of production for small and medium-sized businesses.

- Continuous-flow production produces the high volumes required by larger companies. These are highly automated and their cost usually requires them to be run 24/7. By reducing the workforce needed this eliminates one of the blockages that Smith saw: 'the improvement of the dexterity of the workman necessarily increases the quantity of the work he can perform'.

- Computer-aided manufacture (CAM) is a continuous-flow production method controlled by computers, such as used in the motor industry.

- Lean manufacturing is an approach ascribed to Toyota, where they sought to eliminate or continuously reduce waste that is anything that doesn't add value. Waste in the production process taking the 'lean' approach is categorized under such headings as:

  - Transport: Keep process close to each other to minimize movement.

  - Inventory: Carrying high inventory levels costs money and, if too low, orders can be lost. 'Just in time' (JIT) manufacturing should be aimed for.

  - Motion: Improve workplace ergonomics so as to maximize labour productivity.

  - Waiting: Aim for a smooth, even flow so that staff and machines are working optimally, reducing downtime to a minimum.

  - Defects: Aim for zero defects as that directly reduces the amount of waste.

Production scheduling

Production scheduling is the process used to get the optimum amount of output at the lowest cost. Its success is measured by being able to meet delivery promises while hitting profit margin objectives. It achieves this by identifying possible resource conflicts; directing sufficient labour and machinery to tasks on time; accommodating downtime and preventative maintenance schedules; and minimizing stock and work in progress levels. A production schedule also gives the production team explicit targets so that supervisors and managers can measure their performance.

The techniques used to facilitate scheduling which an MBA should understand include the following.

Gantt Charts

Henry Gantt, a mechanical engineer, management consultant and associate of Frederick Taylor, showed how an entire process could be described in terms of both tasks and the time required to carry them out. He developed what became known as the Gantt chart, to help with major infrastructure projects, including the Hoover Dam and US Interstate highway system, around 1910. By laying out the information on a grid with tasks on one axis and their time sequence along the other it was possible to see at a glance an entire production plan as well as highlight potential bottlenecks. Gantt charts can be used for any task, not just production scheduling, as Figure 10.2, giving an example of how a website design project could be planned, demonstrates.

FIGURE 10.2 Gantt chart showing weekly tasks for a website design project

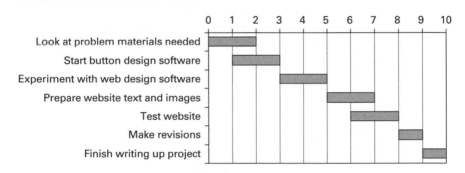

Critical path method (CPM)

A more sophisticated way to schedule operations was developed in the late 1950s. DuPont, the US chemical company, first used CPM to help with shutting down plants for maintenance. Later, the US Navy adapted it and improved it for use on the Polaris project. CPM uses a chart (see Figure 10.3) showing all the tasks to be carried out to complete a scheduled activity, the sequence in which they have to be carried out and how long each event, as tasks are known, will take to be completed. The critical path is the route through the network that will take the longest amount of time. The significance of the critical path is that any delays in carrying out events on this path will delay the whole project. Tasks not on the critical path have more leeway, and may be slipped without affecting the end date of the project. This is called slack or float.

FIGURE 10.3　Critical path method applied

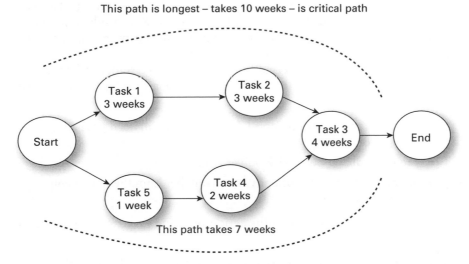

This path is longest – takes 10 weeks – is critical path

Tasks 4 or 5 could between them start or finish up to 3 days
late without delaying completion – so critical path has 3 days slack in it

The steps in the critical planning method process are:

- Identify the events.
- Decide on the sequence in which they must be carried out.
- Draw the network.
- Calculate the completion time for each event.
- Identify the longest and hence critical path.
- Keep the chart updated as events unwind.

Programme evaluation and review technique (PERT) and an activity network, also known as an 'activity-on-node diagram', are more sophisticated forms of CPM that allow for a degree of randomness in activity start and completion times.

Linear programming

In 1947, George Dantzig, an American mathematician, developed an algorithm (a mathematical technique) that could help resolve problems involving operational constraints. His algorithm could, for example, help with situations where several products could be produced, but materials, labour or machine capacity is insufficient to make all that's demanded – the challenge in that last case being to decide what mix of products can be produced that will make the maximum profit and then plan accordingly. Unfortunately, the iterative nature of producing solutions using Dantzig's algorithm proved so tedious that until cheap computers arrived it remained an academic idea of interest only to mathematics students.

The Dantzig algorithm comprises an objective, the quantity to be optimized, for example profit, nutrient content, water flow or production of one particular product out of several, any variables and constraints on them, for example a certain minimum amount of water must flow.

Excel incorporates a Solver add-in feature to solve standard linear programming problems. It is not usually installed when Excel is first loaded so to add this facility:

- Select the menu option Tools | Add_Ins (you will need your original installation disk).
- From the dialog box check Solver Add-In.
- Access to the Solver option is now available from the new menu option Tools | Solver

These websites provide more information on using linear programming in operations:

- Economics Network (**www.economicsnetwork.ac.uk/cheer/ch9_3/ch9_3p07.htm**) provides a detailed explanation and Excel worked example.
- IBM (**www-128.ibm.com/developerworks/linux/library/l-glpk1**) has a worked example.

Queuing theory

Agner Krarup Erlang, a Danish engineer who worked for the Copenhagen Telephone Exchange, had the problem of estimating how many circuits were needed to provide an acceptable telephone service. He found out by empirical observation that the relationship between the number of circuits and the number of telephone customers who could be provided with an acceptable level of service was not as obvious as it at first seemed. For example, in his experiments where one circuit was provided on a network, adding just one more could reduce waiting time by over 90 per cent, rather than just halving it as simple logic might suggest. He published the first paper on queuing theory in 1909 and this new operation scheduling technique was born.

Queuing theory can help answer operational questions such as these for a service business such as a restaurant, bank or call centre: Given the present resources:

- How long will a customer have to wait before they are served?
- How long will it take for the service to be completed?
- How big a waiting area will be needed for the queue?
- What is the probability of a customer having to wait longer than a given time interval before they are served – the classic service

standard problem calling for, say, 'all telephone calls to be answered within 10 rings'?

- What is the average number of people in the queue?
- What is the probability that the queue will exceed a certain length? This can cause congestion, say in a bank or supermarket.
- What time period will the server be fully occupied for and how much idle time are they likely to have, bearing in mind this is a cost to be minimized?

The technique can be used for any operational problem where efficiency is determined by calculating the optimal number of channels required to meet a level of demand. J E Beasley, formerly of the Tanaka Business School (Imperial College) and currently Professor of Operational Research at Brunel University, provides helpful notes on the subject at this web link (**http://people.brunel.ac.uk/~mastjjb/jeb/or/queue.html**).

Inventory management

High inventory levels are popular with marketing departments, as having them makes satisfying customers an easier task; they are less popular with production departments who have to carry inventory costs in their budgets. Finance departments insist on having the lowest possible stock levels, as high stock pushes working capital levels up and return on investment down. (Look back to Financial ratios in Chapter 1 on accounting to see how this works.) This tussle between departments is a strategic issue that has to be resolved by top management. The birth of Waterstone's, the bookshop business founded by Tim Waterstone, fortuitously a marketing visionary, qualified accountant and the company's managing director, provides an interesting illustration of the dimension of the stock control issue. Until the advent of Waterstone's the convention had been to store books spine out on shelves, in alphabetical order, under major subject headings – Computing, Sport, Travel. This had the added advantage of making it easy to see what books needed reordering and stock counts were a simple process. Waterstone, however, knew that 'browsers', the majority (60 per cent, according to his research) of people who go into bookshops to look around, had no idea what book they wanted, so didn't know where to start looking. His differentiating strategy was that as well as following the conventional model of having books on shelves, he scattered the books in piles around the store using a variety of methods: new books in one pile, special offers in another. Sales and profits soared, sufficient to more than compensate for the near doubling of book stock.

Inventory categories

There are three different categories of inventory that a business needs to have and keep track of:

- Finished goods: These are products ready to ship out to customers. For Apple these would be computers, iPods and so forth, for General Motors vehicles and for a baker loaves of bread.

- Work in progress (WIP): These are products in the process of being completed. They have used up some raw materials and had workers paid to start the manufacturing process, so the cost will reflect those inputs. For General Motors WIP would include vehicles awaiting paint or a pre-delivery inspection.

- Raw materials: These are the basic materials from which the end product is made. For General Motors this would include metal and paint, but it could also include a complete bought-in engine for the vehicles in which they use third-party power units.

Economic order quantity (EOQ)

Businesses have to carry a certain minimum amount of stock to ensure that the production pipeline works efficiently and likely demand is met. So the costs associated with ordering large quantities infrequently and so reducing the order cost but increasing the cost of holding stock has to be balanced with placing frequent orders, so pushing the costs in placing orders up, but reducing stock holding costs. EOQ is basically an accounting formula that calculates the point at which the combination of order costs and inventory carrying costs are the least and so arriving at the most cost-effective quantity to order.

The formula for EOQ is:

$$\text{Economic order quantity} = \frac{\sqrt{2 \times R \times O}}{C}$$

Where: R = Annual demand in units; O = Cost of placing an order; C = Cost of carrying a unit of inventory for the year.

InventoryOps.com, a website created and run by Dave Piasecki to support his book *Inventory Accuracy: People, Processes, & Technology* (2003, Ops Publishing), provides a useful starting point in your quest for information on all aspects of inventory management and warehouse operations. At this link (**www.inventoryops.com/economic_order_quantity.htm**), you will find a full explanation of how to use EOQ.

Quality

As well as using efficient operation and control procedures an organization has to deliver a quality product or service. Quality in operations does not carry quite the same meaning as it does in, say, marketing, where it signifies something of a high standard. In operations, quality means that something meets a set of prescribed standards and performs as expected. In other words, promises are made and kept. But quality is also part of the efficiency equation too. Quality below standard can lead to high waste, disrupted schedules and lost orders.

Toyota, an early adopter of 'Lean Manufacturing' and 'Just in Time Production', both cost-reduction strategies, hit the buffers in January 2010 when they had to announce a recall of up to 1.8 million cars across Europe, including about 220,000 in the United Kingdom, following an accelerator problem. The company share price sagged by US $25 (£15.9/€18) billion when the news broke. Akio Toyoda, the company's president appeared before a US Senate hearing to apologize, where he explained that the company's quality problems had been caused by its growth outstripping the speed with which it could develop the appropriate technical expertise. He went on to say that the company's priorities, traditionally ranked as safety, quality and volume, had become confused, with the last moving to a higher position.

The ideas, concepts and techniques that drive thinking on quality come from these management ideas.

Inspection

Frederick W Taylor (see above) in his book *The Principles of Scientific Management* stated that one of the clearly defined tasks of management was to ensure that no faulty product left the factory or workshop. This led to a focus on the detection of problems in the product, testing every item to ensure that it complied with product specifications. The task was carried out at the end of the production process using specially trained inspectors. The 'big idea' emerging from this approach was defect prevention as the means to ensure quality control. Inspection still plays a part in modern quality practices, but less as an answer and more as one tool in the toolkit.

Philosophy

W Edwards Deming (**www.deming.org**), an American statistician and member of the faculty at the New York University Graduate School of Business and Columbia University, where he taught up until 10 days before his death in 1993, is considered as the founder of modern quality management. He took the inspection aspect of quality control a stage further with the introduction of statistical probability techniques. His view was that quality should be designed into products and processes and that mass inspection was redundant as statistical sampling using control charts will signal when a process is out of control.

Deming is remembered most for his 14-point 'System of Profound Knowledge'. In this he explains that becoming a quality-driven organization requires everyone, starting with top management, 'to fully embrace a new way of thinking that involves seeking the greater good for everyone involved and implementing continuous improvement'. He wanted slogans, targets and numerical targets removed and emphasized to all employees in the company that if change is to be made and processes are to be continuously improved then it's down to them to achieve it. Deming's ideas were adopted enthusiastically by the Japanese whose economy, having been crippled by the war (WW2), was ready to embrace radical change. It was not until the Japanese motor industry was cutting deep into its home market that US industry woke up to Deming's message on quality. Total Quality Management, Quality Circles and Six Sigma have become buzzwords for variations and extensions of Deming and other pioneers' work on quality. The latter term was in use in the 1920s where mathematicians used it as the symbol for a unit of measurement in product quality variation. But it was not until the mid-1980s that engineers in the US company Motorola used 'Six Sigma' first as an informal name – later as a brand – for their initiative aimed at reducing defects in production processes. The name Six Sigma was chosen because mathematically it represents 3.4 parts – or defects – per million, an extremely high level of quality.

Information technology

Information technology is universally seen as important by all major business schools, but taught differently and with a different level of emphasis by all. At London Business School the course is relatively short, entitled 'IT for Business Value', and has two intended outputs: to enhance students' confidence in choosing the right technology for meeting business needs; and to examine issues involved in managing the implementation of business systems. At Wharton the Management Information Systems (MIS) course on the MBA programme covers 'the practice of using computer and communication systems to solve problems in organizations and provide the essential skills and technology-based insights needed in order to manage effective problem solving with information technologies and systems (IT&S), and to extract the most value from an actual or potential information system'. The course itself is organized around several 'hands on' cases or projects, through which student teams become familiar with important information technologies, including databases and the internet. MBAs will be expected to have some appreciation of these key issues, though they will usually expect to be able to rely on professional expertise either from within the organization or outside.

Data protection

Holding data on customers, employees and indeed on any living person requires an organization to register with the Information Commissioner's Office (**www.ico.gov.uk** > For organizations > Data protection guide) and to comply with the Data Protection Act's eight principles, which make sure that personal information is:

- fairly and lawfully processed;
- processed for limited purposes;
- adequate, relevant and not excessive;
- accurate and up to date;
- not kept for longer than is necessary;
- processed in line with your rights;
- secure;
- not transferred to other countries without adequate protection.

Website operations

MBAs need a good grasp of how the internet is currently affecting the business operations. Everything from books and DVDs, through computers, medicines and financial services, on to vehicles and real estate is being sold or having a major part of the selling process transacted online. Not only are products and services being sold online, they are being supported both technically and commercially and to an increasing extent being fulfilled online too. Software, films and books are just three 'tangible' product categories for which more or less every business operation can be and is being delivered via the internet. Holidays, airline tickets, software, training and even university degrees are bundled in with the mass of conventional retailers such as Tesco who fight for a share of the ever-growing online market. The online gaming market alone has over 217 million users.

The value of web transactions in the United States in 2007/08 was over $450bn and in the UK alone was £55.5bn, up from £19bn in 2002; the value of sales to households as opposed to businesses over the same period doubled to £14bn; £78 in every £100 spent in 2007/08 on the internet was used to buy physical goods. In the United States 16 million people visited jewellery websites, 35 million hit flower and gift sites and 42 million looked for travel-related products and services.

Not all business sectors are penetrated to the same extent by the internet; according to Forrester (**www.forrester.com**), the internet research company, although sales of clothing and footwear online is a multi-billion business it accounts for only 8 per cent of total sales. Contrast that with computers where 41 per cent of sales occur online.

According to eMarketer (**www.emarketer.com**), 88 per cent of shoppers prefer online to conventional shopping because they can shop at any time; 66 per cent like being able to shop for more than one product and in many outlets at the same time; 54 per cent claim that there are products that they can only find online; 53 per cent like not having to deal with salespeople; 44 per cent reckon product information is better online; and perhaps the most revealing statistic of all, only 40 per cent preferred online to offline because they expected to find lower prices.

Information systems (IS)

If the internet is the external operations powerhouse, IS systems are the mirror image, handling all the data needed to run a 21st-century organization. Every part of a business collects data; production monitors output efficiencies, stock levels and quality; finance gets the accounts, marketing gets figures on customer demand and competitor market share; HR keeps track of pay, training, accidents at work and sickness. But none of this data is much use unless there is an integrated system that can integrate, collate, analyse and disseminate this information in a timely manner and in a format that can be understood and used by operating management.

To be effective, IS needs an appropriate amount of hardware and software, as firms that effectively exploit the power computer information systems can deliver can outperform others. It can play a major role in opening new distribution channels, streamlining supply chains and providing efficient electronic markets. Mainframe/legacy systems, PCs, workstations, intranets and the internet, as well as local area networks (LANs) and wide area networks (WANs), customer relationship management (CRM) and the ubiquitous Moore's Law stating that processing power doubles every 18 months while costs halve, are all vital elements in an MBA's IS vocabulary.

Quantitative and qualitative research and analysis

11

- Decision-making tools
- Statistical methods
- Making forecasts
- Assessing cause and effect
- Soft studies
- Carrying out surveys

Finance, marketing, operations and HRM (human resource management) collect an inordinate amount of data and the IT (information technology) department processes it. However, it falls to the application of analysis techniques to interpret the data and explain its significance or otherwise. Bald information on its own is rarely of much use. If staff turnover goes up, customers start complaining and bad debts are on the rise, these facts on their own may tell you very little. Are these figures close to average, or should it be the mean or the weighted average that will reveal their true importance? Even if the figures are bad, you need to know if they are outside the range you might reasonably expect to occur in any event.

Generally, managers prefer to rely on quantitative methods for analysis and there are always plenty of numbers to be obtained. Figures are efficient, easy to manipulate and you should use them whenever you can. But there is also a rich seam of qualitative methods to get valuable information that you cannot obtain well with quantitative methods. These qualitative methods can be used to study human behaviour and more importantly changes in behaviour. Complex feelings and opinions, such as why employee morale is low, customers are complaining or shareholders dissatisfied, cannot be comprehensively captured by quantitative techniques. Using qualitative methods it is possible to study the variations of complex, human behaviour in context. By connecting quantitative data to behaviour using qualitative methods, a process known as triangulation, you can add an extra dimension to your analysis with people's descriptions, feelings and actions.

In business schools these two methods of analysis are rarely taught together and are even less likely to be taught in the same department, though some marketing professors will manage joined-up analysis in areas such as surveys. At Rotterdam School of Management, Erasmus University (**www.rsm.nl**), for example, in 'Quantitative Platform for Business' students investigate the qualitative as well as the quantitative methods available for problem solving within an organization. But EM Lyon (**www.em-lyon.com/english**) confines its teaching to 'Business Statistics' covering 'the essential quantitative skills that will be required of you throughout the programme'. MIT Sloan School of Management (**http://mitsloan.mit.edu/mba/program/firstsem.php**) has a teaching module, 'Data, Models, and Decision', in its first semester that 'Introduces students to the basic tools in using data to make informed management decisions'. That seems heavy on quantitative analysis, covering probability, decision analysis, basic statistics, regression, simulation, linear and nonlinear optimization, and discrete optimization, but devoid of much qualitative teaching matter. But MIT does uses cases, and examples drawn from marketing, finance, operations management, and other management functions, in teaching this subject.

Quantitative research and analysis

The purpose of quantitative research and analysis is to provide managers with the analytical tools necessary for making better management decisions. The subject, while not rocket science, requires a reasonable grasp of mathematical concepts. It is certainly one area that many attending business school find challenging. But as figures on their own are often of little help in either understanding the underlying facts or choosing between alternatives, some appreciation of probability, forecasting and statistical concepts is essential. It is an area where, with a modicum of application, an MBA can demonstrate skills that will make them stand out from the crowd.

Decision theory

Blaise Pascal (1623–62), the French mathematician and philosopher who with others laid the foundations for the theory of probability, is credited with inaugurating decision theory, or decision making under conditions of uncertainty. Until Pascal's time, the outcomes of events were considered to bc largcly in thc hands of thc gods, but he instigated a method for using mathematical analysis to evaluate the cost and residual value of various alternatives so as to be able to choose the best decision when all the relevant information is not available.

Decision trees

Decision trees are a visual as well as valuable way to organize data so as to help make a choice between several options with different chances of occurring and different results if they do occur. Trees (see Figure 11.1) were first used in business in the 1960s but became seriously popular from 1970 onwards when algorithms were devised to generate decision trees and automatically reduce them to a manageable size.

Making a decision tree requires these steps to be carried out initially, from which the diagram can be drawn:

- Establish all the alternatives.
- Estimate the financial consequences of each alternative.
- Assign the risk in terms of uncertainty allied with each alternative.

Figure 11.1 shows an example decision tree. The convention is that squares represent decisions and circles represent uncertain outcomes. In this example, the problem being decided on is whether to launch a new product or revamp an existing one. The uncertain outcomes are whether the result of the decision will be successful ($/£/€10 million profit), just ok ($/£/€5 million profit)

FIGURE 11.1 Example decision tree

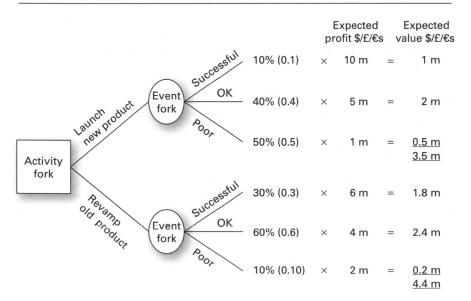

or poor ($/£/€1 million). In the case of launching a new product there is, in the management's best estimate, a 10 per cent (0.1 in decimals) chance of success, a 40 per cent chance it will be ok and a 50 per cent chance it will result in poor sales. Multiplying the expected profit arising from each possible outcome by the probability of its occurring gives what is termed an 'expected value'. Adding up the expected values of all the possible outcomes for each decision suggests, in this case, that revamping an old product will produce the most profit.

The example is a very simple one and in practice decisions are much more complex. We may have intermediate decisions to make, such as should we invest heavily and bring the new product to market quickly, or should we spend money on test marketing. This will introduce more decisions and more uncertain outcomes represented by a growing number of 'nodes', the points at which new branches in the tree are formed.

If the outcomes of the decision under consideration are spread over several years, you should combine this analysis with the net present value of the monetary values concerned. (See Discounted Cash Flow in Chapter 2, Finance.)

Statistics

Statistics is the set of tools that we use to help us assess the truth or otherwise of something we observe. For example, if the last 10 phone calls a company received were all cancelling orders, does that signal that a business has a problem, or is that event within the bounds of possibility? If it is within the bounds of possibility, what are the odds that we could still be wrong and really have a problem? A further issue is that usually we can't easily examine the entire population, so we have to make inferences from samples and, unless those samples are representative of the population we are interested in and of sufficient size, we could still be very wrong in our interpretation of the evidence. At the time of writing, there was much debate as to how much of a surveillance society Britain had become. The figure of 4.2 million cameras, one for every 14 people, was the accepted statistic. However, a diligent journalist tracked down the evidence to find that extrapolating a survey of a single street in a single town arrived at that figure!

Central tendency

The most common way statistics are considered is around a single figure that purports in some way to be representative of a population at large. There are three principal ways of measuring tendency and these are the most often confused and frequently misrepresented set of numbers in the whole field of statistics.

To analyse anything in statistics you first need a 'data set' such as that in Table 11.1.

TABLE 11.1   The selling prices of companies' products

Product	Selling price $/£/€s
1	30
2	40
3	10
4	15
5	10

The mean (or average)

This is the most common tendency measure and is used as a rough and ready check for many types of data. In the example above, adding up the prices – $/£/€105 and dividing by the number of products – 5, you arrive at a mean, or average, selling price of $/£/€21.

The median

The median is the value occurring at the centre of a data set. Recasting the figures in Table 11.1 puts product 4's selling price of $/£/€15 in that position, with two higher and two lower prices. The median comes into its own in situations where the outlying values in a data set are extreme, as they are in our example, where in fact most of the products sell for well below $/£/€21. In this case the median would be a better measure of the central tendency. You should always use the median when the distribution is skewed. You can use either the mean or the median when the population is symmetrical as they will give very similar results.

The mode

The mode is the observation in a data set appearing the most often; in this example it is $/£/€10. So if we were surveying a sample of the customers of the company in this example, we would expect more of them to say they were paying $/£/€10 for their products, though, as we know, the average price is $/£/€21.

Variability

As well as measuring how values cluster around a central value, to make full use of the data set we need to establish how much those values could vary. The two most common methods employed are the following.

Range

The range is calculated as the maximum figure minus the minimum figure. In the example being used here, that is $/£/€40 – $/£/€10 = $/£/€30. This figure gives us an idea of how dispersed the data is and so how meaningful, say, the average figure alone might be.

Standard deviation from the mean

This is a rather more complicated concept as you need first to grasp the central limit theorem, which states that the mean of a sample of a large population will approach 'normal' as the sample gets bigger. The most valuable feature here is that even quite small samples are normal. The bell curve, also called the Gaussian distribution, named after Johann Carl Friedrich Gauss (1777–1855), a German mathematician and scientist, shows how far values are distributed around a mean. The distribution, referred to as the standard deviation, is what makes it possible to state how accurate a sample is likely to be. When you hear that the results of opinion polls predicting elections based on samples as small as 1,000 are usually reliable within four percentage points, 19 times out of 20, you have a measure of how important. (You can get free tutorials on this and other aspects of statistics at Web Interface for Statistics Education (**http://wise.cgu.edu**).)

Figure 11.2 is a normal distribution that shows that 68.2 per cent of the observations of a normal population will be found within 1 standard deviation of the mean, 95.4 per cent within 2 standard deviations, and 99.6 per cent within 3 standard deviations. So almost 100 per cent of the observations will be observed in a span of six standard deviations, three below the mean

FIGURE 11.2   Normal distribution curve (bell) showing standard deviation

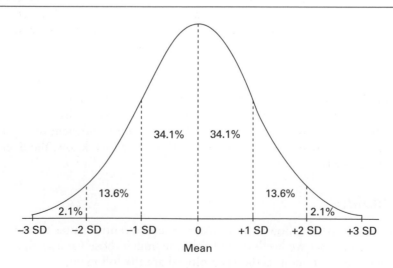

and three above the mean. The standard deviation is an amount calculated from the values in the sample. Use this calculator (**www.easycalculation.com/statistics/standard-deviation.php**) to work out the standard deviation by entering the numbers in your sample.

Forecasting

Sales drive much of a business's activities; it determines cash flow, stock levels, production capacity and ultimately how profitable or otherwise a business will be, so, unsurprisingly, much effort goes into attempting to predict future sales. A sales forecast is not the same as a sales objective. An objective is what you want to achieve and will shape a strategy to do so. A forecast is the most likely future outcome given what has happened in the past and the momentum that provides for the business.

The components of any forecast are made up of three components and to get an accurate forecast you need to decompose the historic data to better understand the impact of each on the end result:

- Underlying trend: This is the general direction, up, flat or down, over the longer term, showing the rate of change.

- Cyclical factors: These are the short-term influences that regularly superimpose themselves on the trend. For example, in the summer months you would expect sales of certain products, swimwear, ice creams and suntan lotion, for example, to be higher than, say, in the winter. Ski equipment would probably follow a reverse pattern.

- Random movements: These are irregular, random spikes up, or down, caused by unusual and unexplained factors.

Using averages

The simplest forecasting method is to assume that the future will be more or less the same as the recent past. The two most common techniques that use this approach are:

- Moving average: This takes a series of data from the past, say the last six months' sales, adds them up, divides by the number of months and uses that figure as being the most likely forecast of what will happen in month 7. This method works well in a static, mature marketplace where change happens slowly, if at all.

- Weighted moving average: This method gives the most recent data more significance than the earlier data since it gives a better representation of current business conditions. So before adding up the series of data each figure is weighted by multiplying it by an increasingly higher factor as you get closer to the most recent data.

Exponential smoothing and advanced forecasting techniques

Exponential smoothing is a sophisticated averaging technique that gives exponentially decreasing weights as the data gets older and conversely more recent data is given relatively more weight in making the forecasting. Double and triple exponential smoothing can be used to help with different types of trend. More sophisticated still are Holt's and Brown's linear exponential smoothing and Box-Jenkins, named after two statisticians of those names, which applies autoregressive moving average models to find the best fit of a time series.

Fortunately, all an MBA needs to know is that these and other statistical forecasting methods exist. The choice of which is the best forecasting technique to use is usually down to trial and error. Various software programs will calculate the best-fitting forecast by applying each technique to the historic data you enter. Then wait and see what actually happens and use the technique that's forecast as closest to the actual outcome. Professor Hossein Arsham of the University of Baltimore (**http://home.ubalt.edu/ntsbarsh/Business-stat/otherapplets/ForecaSmo.htm#rmenu**) provides a useful tool that allows you to enter data and see how different forecasting techniques perform. Duke University's Fuqua School of Business, consistently ranked among the top 10 US business schools in every single functional area, provides this helpful link (**www.duke.edu/~rnau/411home.htm**) to all its lecture material on forecasting.

Causal relationships

Often, when looking at data sets it will be apparent that there is a relationship between certain factors. Look at Figure 11.3. It is a chart showing the monthly sales of barbeques and the average temperature in the preceding month for the past eight months.

It's not too hard to see that there appears to be, as we might expect, a relationship between temperature and sales, in this case. By drawing the line that most accurately represents the slope, called the line of best fit, we can have a useful tool for estimating what sales might be next month, given the temperature that occurred this month (Figure 11.4).

The example used is a simple one and the relationship obvious and strong. In real life there is likely to be much more data and it will be harder to see if there is a relationship between the 'independent variable', in this case temperature, and the 'dependent variable', sales volume. Fortunately, there is an algebraic formula known as 'linear regression' that will calculate the line of best fit for you.

There are then a couple of calculations needed to test if the relationship is strong (it can be strongly positive or even if strongly negative it will still be useful for predictive purposes) and significant. The tests are known as

FIGURE 11.3   Scatter diagram example

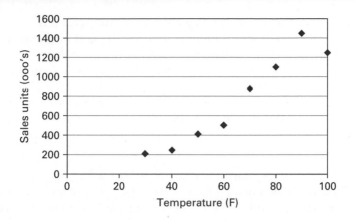

FIGURE 11.4   Scatter diagram – the line of best fit

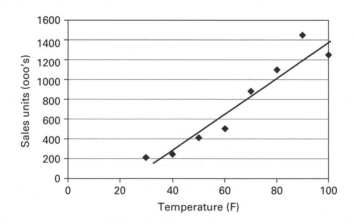

R-squared and the Students *t*-test, and all an MBA needs to know is that they exist and you can probably find the software to calculate them on your computer already. Otherwise you can use Web-Enabled Scientific Services & Applications (**www.wessa.net/slr.wasp**) software, which covers almost every type of statistical calculation. The software is free online and provided through a joint research project with K.U.Leuven Association, a network of 13 institutions of higher education in Flanders.

For help in understanding these statistical techniques, read *The Little Handbook of Statistical Practice* by Gerard E Dallal of Tufts, available free online (**www.tufts.edu/~gdallal/LHSP.HTM**). At Princeton's website (**http://dss.princeton.edu/online_help/analysis/interpreting_regression.htm**) you can find a tutorial and lecture notes on the subject as taught to its Master of International Business students.

Qualitative research and analysis

Qualitative research is a well-entrenched academic tradition in sociology, history, geography and anthropology; it is widely used in the medical and political fields. It has made much less of a mark in business, perhaps because of its image as a softer, more ethereal discipline. That situation is changing with the growing realization that while quantitative research can reveal what issues are important and even where they lie, it is of rather less use in understanding why they have come about or what to do about them. Qualitative research comes into its own particularly when these are important factors:

- Complex issues: Quantitative methods are useful for separating out and measuring individual factors, say what percentage of customers are dissatisfied with a product or service and how many will defect. Qualitative methods can help get an understanding of the linkages between these factors and the competing tensions they arouse.

- Stakeholders' differences: Not everyone involved in an organization sees matters from the same perspective. Often the aggregation nature of quantitative methods makes it difficult to fully appreciate the position of less powerful stakeholders. Qualitative research gives individuals a voice in the analytical process.

- Significant recommendations: When the consequences of research are likely to result in recommendations with significant consequences, for example changing work patterns, shutting down a unit or altering pay and conditions, qualitative research allows attitudes and feelings towards potential courses of action to be explored, leading hopefully to a less contentious outcome.

Researchers used to quantitative analysis frequently dismiss qualitative research as 'unscientific' and 'anecdotal'. It certainly doesn't have to succumb to such criticism, as the array of tools used in qualitative research is large and the tools have a well-documented and rigorous methodology for their application.

Observation

The power of observation as a method of gathering data lies in the inconsistency between what people will say in an interview, or on a questionnaire, and what they actually do. It's not that people are necessarily lying, it's just that their capacity for self-deception is often high. Customers may feel foolish admitting they have difficulty finding their way around a shop and so would not record that fact. That doesn't mean that they don't have a problem and that a company would not gain valuable information from finding out about it.

So observations can give valuable insights into how things look from an outsider such as a customer, supplier or prospective employee. But such insights will only be representative of the time the researcher was observing and may not be indicative of the general level of service. They are often used to provide contextual information alongside some other research method.

Observations themselves generally come in one of two forms:

- Participating observation: This is where the observer takes part in at least some aspect of what is being assessed in order to get a better understanding of insider views and experiences. This, for example, could involve going through the whole procedure of making a purchase or using a service, rather than standing on the sidelines watching others. This is the methodology used in mystery shopping.

- Pure observation: Here the observer stays aloof from the situation under assessment so as not to influence it and so perhaps bias the findings.

The great difficulty in carrying out this type of research is being able to record observations accurately. Taking notes can be conspicuous and will almost certainly put those being observed on their guard.

Interviews

Talking and listening to people is the most basic and the most used method of conducting qualitative research. Qualitative interviews can take several forms and can be incorporated into triangulation methods (see below). These are the main interview types:

- Open-ended ad hoc conversations allowing interviewees to drive the discussion with minimum intervention by the interviewer; for example users of a product or service could be asked to give their feelings without being steered towards questions concerning satisfaction or dissatisfaction. This approach can throw up issues that have not been explored by the researcher.

- Open-ended interviews where the broad issues to be covered are stated, but the course of conversation is allowed to decide the order or ways in which questions are asked.

- Semi-structured interviews where the questions are largely planned in advance, with time left for issues that arise mainly as a result of the conversation itself.

- Qualitative questions built into structured surveys and questionnaires, where the main thrust is to gather quantitative data. For example, in an interview carried out to measure staff morale, questions such as 'how do you feel about the new pay scale?' could be interspersed with questions that gather quantitative data such as 'do you now feel: 10% better off; the same; 10% worse off?'.

- Cognitive interviews: These are used to test respondents' understanding of the meaning of questions or statements and are eventually to be used in questionnaires, user instructions and manuals, for example.

Qualitative interviews differ from surveys, for example in that they adhere less to a fixed set of questions but continually probe and cross-check information, building cumulatively on the knowledge gained from earlier answers. Nevertheless, interviewers at some point have to ask the questions that give them the specific data they need. Good interpersonal skills, sensitivity to the respondent, conducting the interviews at an appropriate time and place, using trained interviewers as well as having an appropriate sample are all vital to successful interviewing.

Focus groups

Focus groups are a form of multiple interview, with small groups of around 8 to 10 people selected with specific key attributes in mind: specific knowledge, experience or socioeconomic characteristics, for example. Participants are invited to attend informal discussion sessions of no more than two hours' duration on a particular topic, facilitated by someone knowledgeable about the issues involved, but tactful and firm enough to keep the group in order and on task. Often an incentive is offered for people to attend. The advantages of using a focus group over interviews include efficiency, as you can get 10 opinions in around twice the time it takes to conduct an interview; and by listening to other people's comments, often more ideas, opinions and experiences and insights can be gained. It is also easier to take notes of the discussion as this is expected and less threatening in a group situation. But, as with interviews, it relies on the views of a small sample and so is not truly representative of any body of opinion.

Three variations on focus groups are:

- Neighbourhood forum: These are structured, regular local meetings for local people to consult about issues of local importance. The term local can mean any characteristic that binds people together – young mothers, pensioners, train users.
- Citizens' juries: These involve a small sample of the public spending perhaps a day or two, at most, debating an issue in a quasi-judicial setting. They hear experts present the various sides to an argument, much as in court they would take evidence from witnesses. This approach is used by local government and police forces, but is also used by major local employers to gain insights into local community issues that they might impinge on.
- Brainstorming sessions: These are group meetings designed to stimulate creative thinking to solve a particular problem or address a single issue. There are three steps to brainstorming. Initially the

group should try to generate as many ideas as possible, without criticism, welcoming unusual and even apparently impractical or impossible propositions. Next, the propositions should be reviewed briefly to either eliminate the ones universally agreed to be unworkable or to combine ideas to form better solutions. Finally, the handful of feasible solutions are discussed and ranked. All that is needed by way of materials are a flip chart, marker pens and Blu-tack to fix the ideas that have been generated visibly onto walls.

Case studies

A case study is a comprehensive and systematic study of a specific organization, event or subject. They can be written, on film or computer and are usually used where wide-ranging, complex questions have to be addressed and the findings used either as a focus for further discussion, for illustrative purposes or for training. The case study needs an underlying question – how did the company go about closing down a particular unit, for example. It doesn't answer the question, rather it provides the 'reader' with information from interviews, company and public documents, observations and such sources, from which they can debate and form an opinion.

Triangulation

This is the rather pretentious name given to the combination of qualitative and quantitative research methods; a sensible process that allows researchers to get the best of both worlds. In fact the disciplines already overlap. Quantitative research produces numbers – the number of people questioned, for example, or how many times a particular feeling or opinion was mentioned in an interview. Qualitative methodology can be used to shed light on qualitative issues, such as how strongly people feel about a certain issue. Triangulation strengthens qualitative and quantitative analyses by combining insights from both.

Surveys

The most common research method that combines quantitative and qualitative processes is the survey. This is a near-ubiquitous tool used in organizations to get a handle on almost every aspect from measuring employee morale or assessing customer satisfaction to getting the views of almost any stakeholder group on almost any issue. MBAs will certainly have to know how to get surveys done and, if working in a small organization, they may well have to do it themselves.

Around half of all surveys are conducted face to face, considered best for tackling consumer markets. Next in popularity come telephone, e-mail and web surveys, which work well with companies and organizations. Postal surveys, once very popular, now account for less than 10 per cent of survey work.

Chapter 3 provides the guidelines for interviewing and questionnaire design.

Survey sample size

The size of the survey undertaken is also important. You frequently hear of political opinion polls taken on samples of 1,500–2,000 voters. This is because the accuracy of your survey clearly increases with the size of sample, as the following table shows:

With random sample of ...	95% of surveys are right within ... percentage points
250	6.2
500	4.4
750	3.6
1,000	3.1
2,000	2.2
6,000	1.2

So, if on a sample size of 600 your survey showed that 40 per cent of women in the town drove cars, the true proportion would probably lie between 36 and 44 per cent. For small businesses, we usually recommend a minimum sample of 250 completed replies.

Andrews University in the United States has a free set of lecture notes explaining the subject of sample size comprehensively (**www.andrews.edu/ ~calkins/math/webtexts/prod12.htm**). At (**www.auditnet.org/docs/statsamp. xls**) you can find some great Excel spreadsheets that do the boring maths of calculating sample size and accuracy for you. ResearchInfo.com (**www. researchinfo.com/docs/websurveys/index.cfm**) gives the basics of writing a program in order for you to use your own questionnaire on the internet.

Strategy

12

- Devising strategies
- Differentiation, cost leadership, focus
- First to market, first to fail
- Tools and techniques for shaping strategy
- Implementing business plans

Joseph Lampel, Professor of Strategy at Cass Business School and author of *Strategy Bites Back* (Financial Times Prentice Hall, 2005), tells the story of when he received an urgent request from one of his MBA students: 'Could I please provide a clear and easy-to-use definition of strategy?' 'My career', wrote the student, 'may depend on it', and 'besides I would like to start the course with a better idea of what I am supposed to be looking out for.' Lampel goes on to explain that he was less surprised by the request than by the fact that it came before the course had even begun. He was used to being approached at the end of the course by students confessing that they still did not know exactly what strategy is.

Strategy, though a core subject in every business school, is less an academic discipline than an ever-shifting appraisal of how an organization should position itself to best meet the challenges it faces. Rather like the quote attributed to one Governor of the Bank of England who said that the true meaning of Christmas would not be apparent until Easter, when it comes to estimating retail sales, successful strategies are really only recognizable after the event. The case below gives a flavour of the dimensions of how strategy is shaped: part marketing, part money, part people, part culture, and mostly an appreciation of an ever-shifting and developing world.

Strategy has three dimensions: the intellectual analytical and thinking aspect used to devise broad strategic direction; the development and shaping of specific actions in pursuit of those strategies; and the implementation of strategy through the execution of business plans. If an organization gets it wrong in any of these areas the results it is aiming for may not be achieved,

CASE STUDY

Michael Dell, gazing around his empire in October 2010, had plenty to be pleased about. Dell's latest product, the Inspiron Duo, scheduled for a pre-Christmas launch, looked like capturing a slice of the tablet market created by Apple with its iPad. He had certainly come a long way since founding his business from his dorm at the University of Texas nearly quarter of a century earlier, aged just 19. He had turned his $1,000 initial stake into a business generating over $60 billion a year in revenues making nearly 16 per cent of PCs sold globally. It was only in 1980 that he had acquired his first computer, the Apple II, and on founding his company, PC Limited, had as his goal to beat IBM. His first product, The Turbo PC, was supported by a no-quibble returns policy and a unique home support service. The IPO in 1988 valued his $1,000 business, founded four years earlier, at $85 million. From the outset Dell had three golden rules: disdain inventory, always listen to the customer and cut out middlemen.

An internet pioneer, the company launched a static online ordering page in 1994, and by 1997 Dell.Com claimed to be the first company to record a million dollars in online sales.

Dell, since its early beginnings, has focused on fundamentally different strategies from its competitors. Unlike Apple, it has never tried to design sexy devices or to build a global network of retail outlets. Dell's strategy was to create the leanest possible supply chain direct to the end user while allowing them to choose the features they wanted. It extended that successful strategy across to related products such as servers, printers and storage devices to build a business shipping 140,000 systems a day worldwide – more than one every second – ranking 34 in the Fortune 500 listing of companies and one of the world's leading brands.

But just as Dell looked to be in an unchallengeable position the company lost its position as the world's biggest maker of personal computers to Hewlett-Packard (HP), a company founded back in 1939 in a Palo Alto garage. No stranger to setbacks, HP had seen that growth in the PC world had crossed from corporate markets to consumers and from developed economies to emerging markets where people had less access to the internet and were both more wary and less able to shop online. In addition, the competition was hotting up on a new front brought about by past success and galloping innovation, with auction sites like eBay and uBid enjoying flourishing growth rates in PC sales. Dell saw that it had to develop new strategies for the new environment. As well as beefing up its website and launching 'IdeaStorm', a blog that has already pulled in 9,000 customer suggestions for improvements, the company's products are now in 10,000 outlets worldwide. It has set up a bulk supply chain alongside its lean customized one and started to design products to hanker after rather than just highly specified black boxes. Dell has also bought up several firms in the IT systems management sector as it sees the shift from product- to service-driven growth as an important factor in the future of its business sector. Dell has had to cut $3 billion of expenses, lay off 8,800 employees and change the mindset of its engineers and designers to reposition it to execute its new strategy.

it may fall behind others in the market or in the worst case fail altogether. Getting all three areas right can be more of an art than a science, rather like a short-sighted person trying to thread several needles, held in parallel by different people, in one swift movement.

Devising strategy – the overview

Credit for devising the most succinct and usable way to get a handle on the big picture has to be given to Michael E Porter, who trained as an economist at Princeton, taking an MBA (1971) and PhD (1973) at Harvard Business School where he is now a professor. His book, *Competitive Strategy: Techniques for Analyzing Industries and Competitors* (1980, Free Press, Old Tappan, New Jersey, United States), which is in its 63rd printing and has been translated into 19 languages, sets out the now accepted methodology for devising strategy. As well as being essential reading in most business schools, courses based on Porter's work are taught in partnership with more than 80 other universities around the world, using curriculum, video content and instructor support developed at Harvard.

The three generic strategies

Porter's first observation was that two factors above all influenced a business's chances of making superior profits. First, there was the attractiveness or otherwise of the industry in which it primarily operated. Second, and in terms of an organization's sphere of influence more important, was how the business positioned itself within that industry. In that respect a business could only have a cost advantage in that it could make product or deliver service for less than others. Or it could be different in a way that mattered to consumers, so that its offers would be unique, or at least relatively so. He added a further twist to his prescription. Businesses could follow either a cost advantage path or a differentiation path industry wide, or they could take a third path – they could concentrate on a narrow specific segment (see Chapter 3 for more on market segments), either with cost advantage or with differentiation. This he termed 'focus' strategy.

Cost leadership

Low cost should not be confused with low price. A business with low costs may or may not pass those savings on to customers. Alternatively, it could use that position alongside tight cost controls and low margins to create an effective barrier to others considering either entering or extending their penetration of that market. Low-cost strategies are most likely to be achievable in large markets, requiring large-scale capital investment, where production or service volumes are high and economies of scale can be achieved from long runs.

Low costs are not a lucky accident; they can be achieved through these main activities:

- Operating efficiencies: New processes, methods of working or less costly ways of working. Ryanair and easyJet are examples where analysing every component of the business made it possible to strip out major elements of cost, meals, free baggage and allocated seating, for example, while leaving the essential proposition – we will fly you from A to B – intact.

- Product redesign: This involves rethinking a product or service proposition fundamentally, to look for more efficient ways to work or cheaper substitute materials to work with. The motor industry has adopted this approach with 'platform sharing', where major players including Citroen, Peugeot and Toyota have rethought their entry car models to share major components; this has become commonplace in the industry.

- Product standardization: A wide range of product and service offers claiming to extend customer choice invariably leads to higher costs. The challenge is to be sure that proliferation gives real choice and adds value. In 2008 the UK railway network took a long, hard look at its dozens of different fare structures and scores of names, often for identical price structures, which had remained largely unchanged since the 1960s, and reduced them to three basic product propositions. Adopting this and other common standards across the rail network they estimate will substantially reduce the currently excessive £½ ($0.8/€0.56) billion transaction cost of selling £5 ($8/€5.6) billion worth of tickets.

- Economies of scale: This can be achieved only by being big or bold. The same head office, warehousing network and distribution chain can support Tesco's 3,263 stores as well it can, say, the 997 that Somerfield had prior to being bought out by the Co-op. The former will have a lower cost base by virtue of having more outlets to spread its costs over, as well as having more purchasing power.

Even young innovative companies have to keep the pressure on cost reduction if they are to maintain their growth rates as they mature. Google, see the case below, shows there is no exception to this rule.

The experience (or learning) curve

The fact that costs declined as the output volume of a product or service increased, though well known earlier, was first developed as a usable

CASE STUDY Google discovers cost cutting

In October 2010, whilst most technology companies were reporting almost static profits and the motor and banking industries barely breaking even, Google managed to report that sales for the third quarter of the year were up 23 per cent compared with the previous quarter. Profit margins held steady at 35 per cent, significantly better than the 31 per cent achieved three years earlier. Their success was not attributed to increased revenues from new products. True Gmail, Google Docs, Google Calendar and other web applications had all played a part in lifting sales revenue by around 3 per cent, but that left the lion's share of profit growth to keeping a tight lid on costs.

Out went bottled water and a host of other perks. Programmes were instituted throughout the company to ensure cost effectiveness. For example, their food service team closely examined café usage, food consumption and labour costs to find areas where efficiency could be improved without compromising food quality and nutrition. Cafeteria opening hours were trimmed back and the practice of those working late taking the dinners provided in the office to eat at home later was discouraged. Afternoon tea on Tuesdays for all and sundry was to be suspended, though to keep morale up, the company stated that there may be occasional surprise 'snack attacks' in the future. Capital expenditure was slashed by 80 per cent and due to natural wastage the company ended the quarter with fewer employees.

TABLE 12.1 Google's sales and profit performance – 2007–Q3 2010

Year	2007	2008	2009	2010 Q1	2010 Q2	2010 Q3
Sales revenue	16,594	21,796	23,651	6,775	6,820	7,286
Y/Y growth rate	56%	31%	9%	23%	24%	23%
Income/profit	5,084	6,632	8,312	2,488	2,365	2,547
As % of revenues	31%	30%	35%	37%	35%	35%

accounting process by T P Wright, an American aeronautical engineer, in 1936. His process became known as the cumulative average model or Wright's model. Subsequently, models were developed by a team of researchers at Stanford, known as the unit time model or Crawford's model, and the Boston Consulting Group (BCG) popularized the process with its experience curve, showing that each time the cumulative volume of doing something – either making a product or delivering a service – doubled, the unit cost dropped by a constant and predictable amount. The reasons for the cost drop include:

- Repetition makes people more familiar with tasks and consequently faster.
- More efficient materials and equipment become available from suppliers themselves as their costs go down through the experience curve effect.
- Organization, management and control procedures improve.
- Engineering and production problems are solved.

BCG itself was founded in 1963 by Bruce D Henderson, a former Bible salesman and engineering graduate from Vanderbilt University, who left the Harvard Business School 90 days before graduation to work for Westinghouse Corporation. From there he went on to head Arthur D Little's management services unit before joining the Boston Safe Deposit and Trust Company to start a consulting arm for the bank. Naming this the experience curve, it was the strategy tool that put BCG on the path to success and has served it well ever since (Figure 12.1).

The value of the experience curve as a strategic process is that it helps a business predict future unit costs and gives a signal when costs fail to drop at the historic rate, both vital pieces of information for firms pursuing a cost leadership strategy. Every industry has a different experience curve that itself varies over time. You can find out more about how to calculate the curve for your industry on the Management And Accounting Web (**http://maaw.info/LearningCurveSummary.htm**), and the National Aeronautics and Space Agency (**http://cost.jsc.nasa.gov/learn.html**) provides a Learning Curve Calculator.

FIGURE 12.1   The experience curve

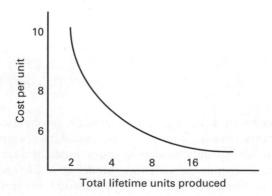

Total lifetime units produced

Differentiation

The key to differentiation is a deep understanding of what customers really want and need and, more importantly, what they are prepared to pay more for. Apple's opening strategy was based around a 'fun' operating system based on icons, rather than the dull MS-DOS. This belief was based on its understanding that computer users were mostly young and wanted an intuitive command system, and the 'graphical user interface' delivered just that. Apple has continued its differentiation strategy, but has added design and fashion to ease of control in order to increase the ways in which it delivers extra value. Sony and BMW are also examples of differentiators. Both have distinctive and desirable differences in their products and neither they nor Apple offers the lowest price in their respective industries; customers are willing to pay extra for the idiosyncratic and prized differences embedded in their products.

Differentiation doesn't have to be confined to just the marketing arena, nor does it always lead to success if the subject of that differentiation goes out of fashion without much warning. Northern Rock, the failed bank that had to be nationalized to stay in business, thought its strategy of raising most of the money it lent out in mortgages through the money markets was a sure winner. It allowed the bank to grow faster than its competitors, who placed more reliance on depositors for their funds. As long as interest rates were low and the money market functioned smoothly, it worked. But once the differentiators that fuelled its growth were reversed, its business model failed.

Focus

Focused strategy involves concentrating on serving a particular market or a defined geographic region. IKEA, for example, targets young, white-collar workers as its prime customer segment, selling through 235 stores in more than 30 countries. Ingvar Kamprad, an entrepreneur from the Småland province in southern Sweden, who founded the business in the late 1940s, offers home furnishing products of good function and design at prices young people can afford. He achieves this by using simple cost-cutting solutions that do not affect the quality of products.

Warren Buffett, the world's richest man, who knows a thing or two about focus, combined with Mars to buy US chewing gum manufacturer Wrigley for $23bn (£11.6bn) in May 2008. Chicago-based Wrigley, which launched its Spearmint and Juicy Fruit gums in the 1890s, has specialized in chewing gum ever since and consistently outperformed its more diversified competitors. Wrigley is the only major consumer products company to grow comfortably faster than the population in its markets and above the rate of inflation. Over the past decade or so, for example, other consumer products companies have diversified. Gillette moved into batteries, used to drive many of its products, by acquiring Duracell. Nestlé bought Ralston Purina, Dreyer's, Ice Cream Partners and Chef America. Both have trailed Wrigley's performance.

Businesses often lose their focus over time and periodically have to rediscover their core strategic purpose. Procter & Gamble is an example of a business that had to refocus to cure weak growth. In 2000, the company was losing share in seven of its top nine categories, and had lowered earnings expectations four times in two quarters. This prompted the company to restructure and refocus on its core business: big brands, big customers and big countries. They sold off non-core businesses, establishing five global business units with a closely focused product portfolio.

First-to-market fallacy

Gaining 'first mover advantage' are words used like a mantra to justify high expenditure and a headlong rush into new strategic areas. This concept is one of the most enduring in business theory and practice. Entrepreneurs and established giants are always in a race to be first. Research from the 1980s that shows that market pioneers have enduring advantages in distribution, product-line breadth, product quality and, especially, market share underscores this principle.

Beguiling though the theory of first mover advantage is, it is probably wrong. Gerard Tellis, of the University of Southern California, and Peter Golder, of New York University's Stern Business School, argued in their book *Will and Vision: How Latecomers Grow to Dominate Markets* (2001, McGraw-Hill Inc., United States) and subsequent research that previous studies on the subject were deeply flawed. In the first instance, earlier studies were based on surveys of surviving companies and brands, excluding all the pioneers that failed. This helps some companies to look as though they were first to market even when they were not. Procter & Gamble (P&G) boasts that it created America's disposable-nappy (diaper) business. In fact a company called Chux launched its product a quarter of a century before P&G entered the market in 1961. Also, the questions used to gather much of the data in earlier research were at best ambiguous, and perhaps dangerously so. For example, the term, 'one of the pioneers in first developing such products or services,' was used as a proxy for 'first to market'. The authors emphasize their point by listing popular misconceptions of who were the real pioneers across the 66 markets they analysed. Online book sales, Amazon (wrong), Books.com (right) – Copiers, Xerox (wrong), IBM (right) – PCs, IBM/Apple (both wrong); Micro Instrumentation Telemetry Systems (MITS) introduced its PC the Altair, a $400 kit, in 1974, followed by Tandy Corporation (Radio Shack) in 1977.

In fact the most compelling evidence from all the research was that nearly half of all firms pursuing a first-to-market strategy were fated to fail, while those following fairly close behind were three times as likely to succeed. Tellis and Golder claim that the best strategy is to enter the market 19 years after pioneers, learn from their mistakes, benefit from their product and market development and be more certain about customer preferences.

Industry analysis

Aside from articulating the generic approach to business strategy, Porter's other major contribution to the field was what has become known as the Five Forces theory of industry structure (Figure 12.2). Porter postulated that the five forces that drive competition in an industry have to be understood as part of the process of choosing which of the three generic strategies to pursue. The forces he identified are:

- Threat of substitution: Can customers buy something else instead of your product? For example, Apple, and to a lesser extent Sony, have laptop computers that are distinctive enough to make substitution difficult. Dell, on the other hand, faces intense competition from dozens of other suppliers with near-identical products competing mostly on price alone.

- Threat of new entrants: If it is easy to enter your market, start-up costs are low and there are no barriers to entry such as IP (intellectual property) protection, then the threat is high.

- Supplier power: The fewer the suppliers, usually the more powerful they are. Oil is a classic example, where less than a dozen countries supply the whole market and consequently can set prices.

- Buyer power: In the food market, for example, with just a few, powerful supermarket buyers being supplied by thousands of much smaller businesses, they are often able to dictate terms.

- Industry competition: The number and capability of competitors is one determinant of a business's power. Few competitors with relatively less attractive products or services lower the intensity of rivalry in a sector. Often these sectors slip into oligopolistic (see also Chapter 7, Economics) behaviour, preferring to collude rather than compete.

You can see a video clip of Professor Porter discussing the Five Forces model on the Harvard Business School website (**http://harvardbusinessonline. hbsp.harvard.edu/hbrol/en/archive/archive.jhtml** > Strategy and Execution > By Author P > The Five Competitive Forces that Shape Competition).

FIGURE 12.2   Five Forces theory of industry analysis (after Porter)

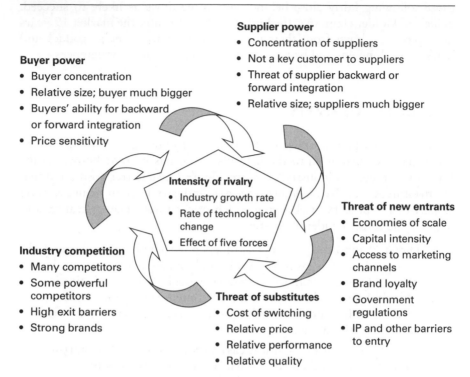

Buyer power
- Buyer concentration
- Relative size; buyer much bigger
- Buyers' ability for backward or forward integration
- Price sensitivity

Supplier power
- Concentration of suppliers
- Not a key customer to suppliers
- Threat of supplier backward or forward integration
- Relative size; suppliers much bigger

Intensity of rivalry
- Industry growth rate
- Rate of technological change
- Effect of five forces

Threat of new entrants
- Economies of scale
- Capital intensity
- Access to marketing channels
- Brand loyalty
- Government regulations
- IP and other barriers to entry

Industry competition
- Many competitors
- Some powerful competitors
- High exit barriers
- Strong brands

Threat of substitutes
- Cost of switching
- Relative price
- Relative performance
- Relative quality

Shaping strategy – tools and techniques

While Porter's Five Forces approach to strategy formulation is, as far as business schools are concerned at least, the standard starting point, there are a number of other tools that an MBA needs to be familiar with. Some pre-date Porter, some overlap, while others home in on specific issues. Like many such tools, they overlap with those used in marketing and in this book you will find SWOT (strengths, weaknesses, opportunities and threats) and perceptual mapping covered in Chapter 3, Marketing.

These are the main tools and techniques an MBA will be expected to know and understand.

Ansoff's Growth Matrix

Igor Ansoff, while Professor of Industrial Administration in the Graduate School at Carnegie Mellon University, published his landmark book, *Corporate Strategy* (1965), where he explained a way of categorizing strategies as an aid to understanding the nature of the risks involved. He invited

FIGURE 12.3 Ansoff's Growth Matrix

	Existing products	New products
Existing markets	Market penetration	Product development
New markets	Market development	Diversification Horlzontal Vertical Concentric Conglomerate

his students to consider growth options as a square matrix divided into four segments. The axes are labelled with products and services running along the 'x' axis, starting with 'present' and 'new'; and markets up the 'y' axis similarly labelled (Figure 12.3).

Ansoff then went on to assign titles to each type of strategy, in an ascending scale of risk (you can find out more about the matrix at **www. strategyvectormodel.com** > Theories > Ansoff Matrix):

- Market penetration, which involves selling more of your existing products and services to existing customers – the lowest-risk strategy.
- Product/service development, which involves creating extensions to your existing products or new products to sell to your existing customer base. This is more risky than market penetration, but less risky than entering a new market where you will face new competitors and may not understand the customers as well as you do your current ones.
- Market development involves entering new market segments or completely new markets either in your home country or abroad.
- Diversification is selling new products into new markets, the riskiest strategy as both are relative unknowns. Avoid, unless all other strategies have been exhausted. Diversification can be further subdivided into four categories of increasing risk profile:
  - Horizontal diversification (entirely new product into current market).
  - Vertical diversification (move backwards into firms supplier's or forward into customer's business).
  - Concentric diversification (new product closely related to current products either in terms of technology or marketing presence but into a new market).
  - Conglomerate diversification (completely new product into a new market).

FIGURE 12.4   The Boston Matrix

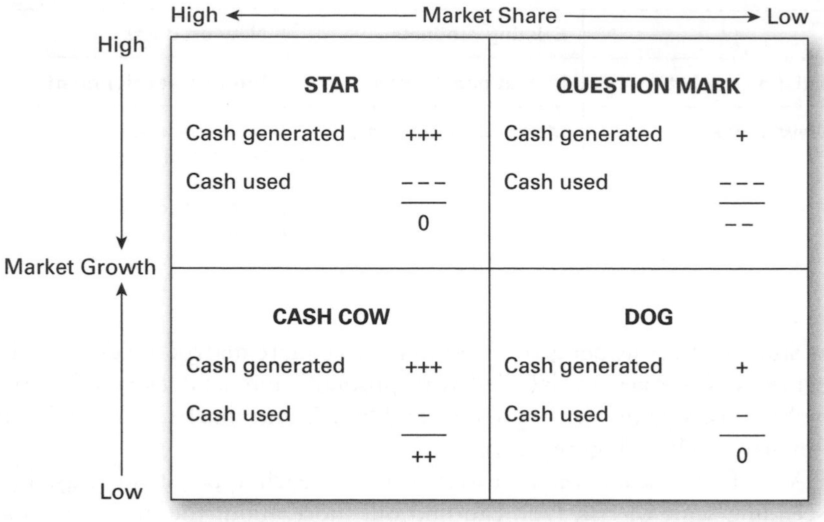

High ◄————————— Market Share —————————► Low

	STAR		QUESTION MARK	
High				
	Cash generated	+++	Cash generated	+
	Cash used	– – –	Cash used	– – –
		0		– –

Market Growth

	CASH COW		DOG	
	Cash generated	+++	Cash generated	+
	Cash used	–	Cash used	–
		++		0
Low				

Boston Matrix

Developed in 1969 by the Boston Consulting Group (see above), this tool can be used in conjunction with the life-cycle concept (see Chapter 3, Product/Service Life Cycle) to plan a portfolio of product/service offers. The thinking behind the matrix is that a company's products and services should be classified according to their cash generating or consumption ability against two dimensions: the market growth rate and the company's market share (Figure 12.4). Cash is used as the measure rather than profit, as that is the real resource used to invest in new offers. The objective then is to use the positive cash flow generated from 'cash cows', usually mature products that no longer need heavy marketing support budgets, to invest in 'stars', that is, fast-growing, usually newer products, positioned in markets in which the company already has a high market share – usually newer markets. 'Dogs' should be disinvested and 'question marks' limited in number and watched carefully to see if they are more likely to become stars or dogs.

The GE–McKinsey Directional Policy Matrix

General Electric was much taken by the visual aspect of the Boston Matrix and was using it to enhance its own performance using another consulting firm, McKinsey and Company, to help. Between them, in 1971 they came up with a variant and in some ways an improvement by substituting business strength and industry attractiveness for market share and market growth rate. The logic being that although these are subjective measures, they are

FIGURE 12.5 The GE–McKinsey directional policy matrix

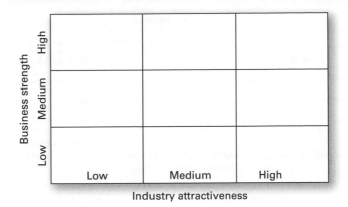

more accessible than market growth and share, as these are hard to establish and in any event the figures are themselves largely subjective suppositions based largely on opinions (Figure 12.5).

Other matrix variations

A dozen or so other similar matrices are in use, each with their own strengths and weaknesses. Arthur D Little Inc, a management consultancy founded in 1886, based in Cambridge, Massachusetts, came up with its own matrix in the late 1970s, using competitive position and industry maturity as the directions. Two business school professors, Gary Hamel (London Business School) and C K Prahalad (University of Michigan), developed a matrix in 1994 as an aid in setting specific acquisition and deployment goals. Other academics, in the United States (Charles W Hofer and Dan Schendel) and in the UK (Cranfield colleagues Malcolm McDonald and Cliff Bowman) as well as companies such as Shell have all added twists to the basic matrix strategy tool.

Cipher Systems (**www.cipher-sys.com/analysis.htm**), a US consultancy firm, provides a collection of strategic analysis tutorials on these and other matrices.

The long-run return pyramid

Another helpful strategy tool is the long-run return pyramid, which is in effect a checklist of growth options. None of the options are mutually exclusive and the tool does not provide for any form of evaluation. Nevertheless, it can be a valuable aide-mémoire to ensure that no stone has been left unturned during the strategic review process. The pyramid's pedigree is

FIGURE 12.6   The long-run return pyramid

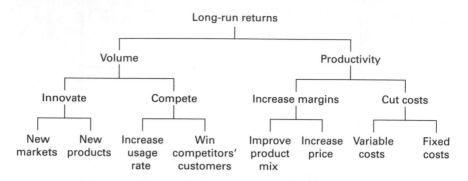

unknown, but it is loosely based on the DuPont's Return on Investment Pyramid, used to trace all the performance ratios that influenced return on investment. The pyramid in the form shown in Figure 12.6 is attributed to Robert Brown, a senior academic at Cranfield School of Management.

PEST (political, economic, social and technological)

This is a framework predating Porter's five forces approach that categorizes the external factors that influence strategy under headings such as political, economic, social and technological forces. Often two additional factors, environmental and legal, are added, changing the acronym to PESTEL analysis (Figure 12.7).

FIGURE 12.7   PESTEL analysis framework

Factor	Event	Impact	Timing	Proposed response
Political				
Economic				
Social				
Technological				
Environmental				
Legal				

Implementing strategy – business plans

All the thinking that goes into devising and shaping strategy has to be set out in a form that will ensure it can be successfully implemented. That form is a business plan setting out in detail the role each part of the organization has to play for the next three to five years. That period is needed as recognizing an opportunity, developing a product or service to exploit that opportunity and bringing that product to market all take time and the plan has to encompass all these stages to be of any value. The dichotomy here is that while strategy takes time for the results to show, the world in which the business is implementing its plans is changing. As one military strategist succinctly put it – all plans disintegrate on contact with the enemy. So three- to five-year business plans need to be reviewed fundamentally each year and progress monitored at least quarterly.

Preparing business plans is a task that MBAs are invariably expected to be able to carry out. It calls for the broad level of understanding of all aspects of the business – cash flow, profit margins, funding issues, marketing and selling, staffing and structures, production, operations, research and development, supply chain etc – that few others in the organization are likely to have. It is an opportunity for an MBA to broaden and deepen their relationships with all key executives as well as the board of directors. So often tedious and always time consuming, the task of preparing business plans should be welcomed as a career progression opportunity par excellence.

Structure of the business plan

The plan is in essence the route map from where the business is to where it wants to get and how it will go about getting to its destination – the roles and responsibilities of key players, the resources required in terms of money, people and materials and so forth. While there is much debate about exactly what should go into the business plan and how it should be laid out, there is no doubt that it is the essential tool for ensuring that a well-thought-out strategy is executed successfully too.

This is the suggested general layout for a business plan as used on the MBA programme at Cranfield and, from observation at international business plan competitions, seems to be fairly universal.

Executive summary

This is the most important part of the plan and will form the heart of any presentation to the board, shareholders or prospective investors. Written last, this should be punchy, short – ideally one page but never more than two – and should enthuse any reader. Its primary purpose is to excite and inspire an audience to want to read the rest of the business plan.

The executive summary should start with a succinct table showing past performance in key areas and future objectives. This will give readers a clear

TABLE 12.2   Executive summary – history and projections

Last year	This year	Business area	Year 1	Year 2	Year 3 etc
		Sales turnover by product/service			
		1.			
		2. etc			
		Total sales			
		Gross profit%			
		Operating profit %			
		Total staff nos			
		Sales staff nos			
		Capital employed			
		Return on capital employed %			

view of the business's capacity to perform as well as the scale of the task ahead (Table 12.2).

Then the executive summary should continue with sections covering the following areas:

● what the primary products/services are and why they are better or different from what is around now;

● which markets/customer groups will most need what you plan to offer and why;

● how close you are to being ready to sell your product/service and what if anything remains to be done;

● why your organization has the skills and expertise to execute this strategy and if new or additional people are required, who they are or how you will recruit them;

● financial projections showing in summary the sales, profit, margins and cash position over the next three to five years;

● how the business will operate, sketching out the key steps, from buying in any raw materials through to selling, delivering and getting paid;

● what physical resources – equipment, premises – the plan calls for.

The contents – putting flesh on the bones

Unlike the executive summary, which is structured to reveal the essence of your business proposition, the plan itself should follow a logical sequence such as this:

- Vision: A vision's purpose is to stretch the organization's reach beyond its grasp. Generally, few people concerned with the company can now see how the vision is to be achieved, but all concerned agree that it would be great if it could be. Once your vision becomes reality it may be time for a new challenge, or perhaps even a new business.

- Mission: A mission statement explains concisely what you do, who you do it for and why you are better or different from others operating in your market. It should be narrow enough to give focus yet leave enough room for growth. Above all, it should be believable to all concerned.

- Objectives: These are the big picture numbers such as market share, profit, return on investment that are to be achieved by successfully executing the chosen strategy.

- Marketing: This section provides information on the product/service on offer, customers and the size of the market, competitors, proposed pricing, promotion and selling method.

- Operations: This area covers any processes such as manufacture, assembly, purchasing, stock holding, delivery/fulfilment and website.

- Financial projections: Detailed information on sales and cash flow for the period of the plan, showing how much money is needed, for what, by when and what would be the most appropriate source of those funds: long- or short-term borrowings, equity, factoring or leasing finance, for example.

- Premises: What space and equipment will be needed and how your home will accommodate the business while staying within the law.

- People: What skills and experience you have on board that will help run this business and implement the chosen strategy; what other people you will need and where you will find them.

- Administrative matters: Do you have any IP (intellectual property) on your product or service; what insurance will you need; what changes if any will be needed to the accounting and control and record systems.

- Milestone timetable: This should show the key actions you have still to take to be ready to achieve major objectives and the date these will be completed.

- Appendices: Use these for any bulky information such as market studies, competitors' leaflets, customer endorsements, technical data, patents, CVs and the like that you refer to in your business plan.

All these topics are covered in this book and by using the index and table of contents you can find your way to them quickly.

Using business planning software

There are a number of free software packages that will help you through the process of writing a business plan. The ones listed below include some useful resources, spreadsheets and tips that may speed up the process, but are not substitutes for finding out the basic facts about your market, customers and competitors:

- American Express (**http://home3.americanexpress.com/ smallbusiness/tool/biz_plan/index.asp**): American Express runs something it calls the Small Business Exchange Business Plan Workshop. This workshop will help you create a business plan to guide your business through the start-up or growth phase, or with a search for capital. Learning on its fictional plan, you will be ready to create one of your own.
- BizPlanit.Com (**www.bizplanit.com/free.html**) has free resources, including free business plan information, advice, articles, links and resources and a free monthly newsletter, the 'Virtual Business Plan', to pinpoint information.
- Bplans.com (**www.bplans.com**), created by Palo Alto Software, offers thousands of pages of free sample plans, planning tools and expert advice to help you start and run your business. Its site has 60 free sample business plans on it and its software package, Business Plan Pro, has these plans plus a further 140. The sample business plans are tailored for every type of business, from aircraft rental to wedding gowns.
- Royal Bank of Canada (**www.royalbank.com/sme/index.html**) has a wide range of useful help for entrepreneurs as well as its business plan writer package and three sample business plans.

What business are you really in?

This is the question posed by Harvard's Theodore Levitt in his quintessential *Harvard Business Review* article 'Marketing Myopia', published in 1960. In the article he argued that business strength and growth opportunities resided in customer relationships and not in products alone. So start and finish any strategic analysis with this question.

INDEX

Also available from **Kogan Page**

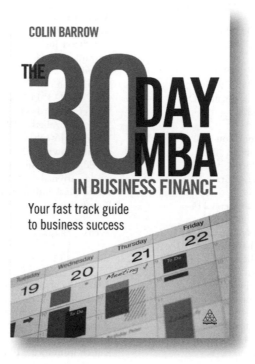

COLIN BARROW

THE **30** DAY MBA
IN BUSINESS FINANCE

Your fast track guide
to business success

ISBN: 978 0 7494 6215 4 Paperback 2011

Order online at **www.koganpage.com**

Find out more; visit **www.koganpage.com** and
sign up for offers and regular e-newsletters.

Kogan Page

Also available from **Kogan Page**

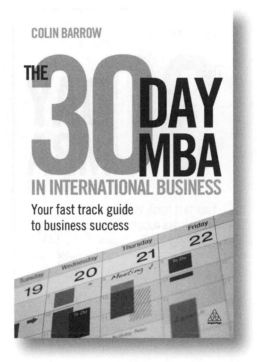

ISBN: 978 0 7494 6213 0 Paperback 2011

Order online at **www.koganpage.com**

Find out more; visit **www.koganpage.com** and
sign up for offers and regular e-newsletters.

Also available from **Kogan Page**

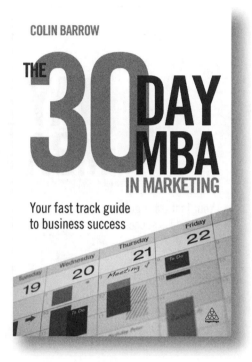

COLIN BARROW

THE **30**DAY **MBA**
IN MARKETING

Your fast track guide
to business success

ISBN: 978 0 7494 6217 8 Paperback 2011

Order online at **www.koganpage.com**

Find out more; visit **www.koganpage.com** and
sign up for offers and regular e-newsletters.

KoganPage

The sharpest minds need the finest advice. **Kogan Page** creates success.

www.koganpage.com

You are reading one of the thousands of books published by **Kogan Page**. As Europe's leading independent business book publishers **Kogan Page** has always sought to provide up-to-the-minute books that offer practical guidance at affordable prices.

KoganPage